IMAGES
of America

STUART

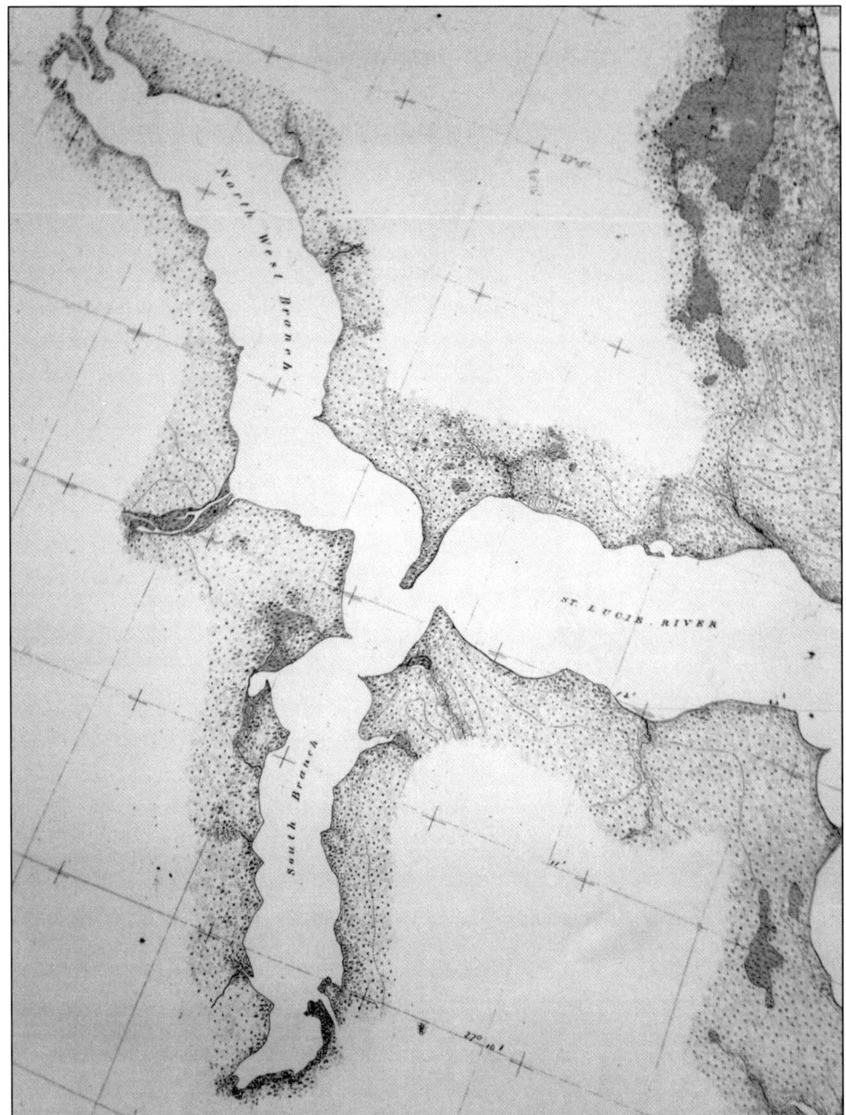

Easily seen in this 1883 geodetic survey are the waterways and land of the mainly uninhabited region that would within 12 years be known as Stuart. This area south and west of the Indian River was surveyed by E.L. Taney and B.A. Colonna. The St. Lucie River comes off from the Indian River to the east, with the Sewall's Point peninsula separating the two rivers. The St. Lucie then wraps around a peninsular area and branches into the North and South Forks. (Courtesy of US Coast and Geodetic Survey.)

On the Cover: The 1913 Henry Feroe Building featuring Frazier faux blocks located at Flagler and St. Lucie Avenues became the heart of Stuart when the town's post office moved in by 1915 next to the Stuart Drug Co. The building was right across from the railroad depot, so when the train stopped twice daily, the citizens gathered to greet the train, collect their mail, and make purchases from the sundae store. Seen around 1917 are, from left to right, five unidentified; Ivy LeRoy Ricou, son of Postmaster Ernest J. Ricou; and unidentified. (Courtesy of the Stuart Heritage Museum.)

IMAGES
of America

STUART

Alice L. Luckhardt

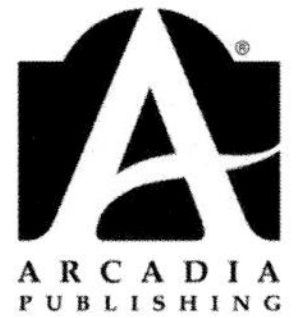

ISBN 978-1-4671-1643-5

Published by Arcadia Publishing
Charleston, South Carolina

Printed in the United States of America

Library of Congress Control Number: 2015957321

For all general information, please contact Arcadia Publishing:
Telephone 843-853-2070
Fax 843-853-0044
E-mail sales@arcadiapublishing.com
For customer service and orders:
Toll-Free 1-888-313-2665

Visit us on the Internet at www.arcadiapublishing.com

This book is dedicated to my husband, Greg, a native Stuart lad.

It is also dedicated to the pioneer families who took photographs and preserved them for future generations.

Contents

Acknowledgments

Special thanks are given to the following families who contributed their photograph collections: Thurlow, Coutant, Ricou, Taylor, Hartman, Kitching, Paradise, Ashley, Coventry, Lockwood, Wiley, Roebuck, Frazier, Murray, Penhale, Cuthbert, Huf, Rue, Luckhardt, Hipson, Laraway, Witham, Ruhnke, Clark, McPherson, Gaines, Lyons, Brock, Axwell, Mills, Powers, McNabb, Hall, and Strauss.

My gratitude also goes to the following organizations: Stuart Heritage Museum, Stuart Woman's Club, Florida Memory Project, Martin County Historical Society (MCHS), and the Elliott Museum for contributing photographs. The Stuart Heritage Museum, a local nonprofit museum, collects and preserves artifacts, memorabilia, photographs, and the history of Stuart and other communities in Martin County.

To Martin County's "History Lady," Sandra H. Thurlow, who has always been an inspiration and encouraged me in the pursuit of learning and preserving as much as possible about the area's history and its people, I am very appreciative and offer a personal thank-you.

Unless otherwise noted, all images are courtesy of the Stuart Heritage Museum (SHM).

Introduction

The town of Stuart, Florida, which is bordered by the St. Lucie River, has a short history. It did not start attracting settlers until the 1880s, with Hubert W. Bessey and his brother Willis from Ohio arriving along the banks of the St. Lucie in 1882 to what was known as the St. Lucie Colony. Being so impressed with the endearing waterways, they decided to settle there, camping out in a tent. Willie was not cut out for pioneer life and returned to Ohio, but Hubert loved it. He purchased just over 24 acres in what was the northern portion of Dade County in 1884, later adding 148 acres in 1890. Hubert Bessey built the first house along the river's shore, later known as Bessey's Point, and became the area's first resident. He felt he had found paradise.

The growing of pineapples was already a proved venture for settlers in Eden and Jensen just to the north, so Bessey planted pineapple slips and began building boats while the pineapple fields matured. With a rail system in the 1880s only to Titusville, 119 miles north, getting the pineapple crop to the train station was difficult. Bessey eventually took on the position of keeper of Gilbert's House of Refuge on nearby Hutchinson Island to support himself. He married Susan C. Corbin, a teacher from Tennessee, in February 1895, who he met at a dance in Eden. The couple moved back to Stuart by the beginning of the 20th century, living on the property Hubert had originally acquired in 1884. He was no longer the sole resident, as more people had started to discover the beauty that was Stuart. Bessey sold partials of his property as town lots to the newcomers in this growing community. Some of the other early pioneer families included the Schroeders, Stypmanns, Parks, Johns, McPhersons, Fraziers, Kruegers, and Walter Kitching.

Albert Krueger, a bachelor, first came to the area in 1887 based on the recommendation of friend Ed Gutsch, who had homesteaded land north of the river. Krueger located some available property south of the river that bordered a creek. He also set out pineapple slips to grow. He married in March 1893 to Anne Donaldson Kincaid Speirs, a niece to Capt. Benjamin Hogg of Waveland, north of the river.

Reuben and Margaret Frazier with their children came to the St. Lucie River area in August 1887 for Reuben's health. They loaded a barge with all their household possessions to make the trip south along the Indian River, settling near property owned by Hubert Bessey. Reuben worked hard clearing much of the land with his bare hands to start his pineapple production and applied for his homesteaded 160 acres by April 1894.

Benjamin Parks with his wife and children from North Carolina learned of the mild winters farther south, so he made a trip down Florida's east coast and chose the region along the St. Lucie River for his future home by October 1891. He immediately became a pineapple and fruit tree farmer on 80 acres he purchased. Benjamin's son George established a commercial store in front of the train depot by 1901.

The Stypmann brothers—Otto, Albert, and Ernest—were from Germany. Ernest came to the Titusville and Sebastian areas of Florida in the late 1870s to early 1880s. He first homesteaded land in Sebastian and married Frances Palmer Hunter in 1884. Encouraged by Ernest, Otto came from New York in July 1882 down the Indian River to the St. Lucie River, where he purchased 131 acres and later, an additional 146 acres. Ernest, having already seen this pristine region, purchased about 33 acres for $1.25 an acre right along the St. Lucie River. To build their homes, lumber from Titusville was brought in by steamboat. Albert and his wife, Jane, also traveled to the St. Lucie River area, raised pineapples until 1888, and returned to New York.

Morris R. Johns came to the area in 1890 to establish a pineapple plantation on land owned by another individual, O.K. Wood of Cocoa. Johns was so successful that this bachelor purchased 160 acres of land nearby for his own pineapples and promptly married Augusta Mae Parks, daughter of Benjamin Parks, in January 1893.

Robert and Marcia McPherson came to the area from Nebraska in 1891 with their children to improve the health of one of their sons. They later purchased 40 acres from Otto Stypmann, built their home, and began pineapple production.

Originally from England, Walter Kitching had purchased property, sight unseen, in 1883 along the St. Lucie River. By May 1892, he had his brother Broster start planting pineapples, and then, by mid-1894, operate a boardinghouse, small store, and post office in a 20-by-30-foot building. Walter captained his schooner along the Indian River supplying settlers with necessary goods. With a large home built on his property by 1895, he and his bride, Emma, settled permanently in the community. Kitching gave up his trade boat in 1896 to build, in 1897, a general merchandise store across from the train depot, which had been moved south of the river by 1895. He encouraged family members, such as nephew Stanley Kitching, to come to Stuart.

From Germany, Curt Emil Schroeder, a nephew of the Stypmanns, arrived in Potsdam in May 1893. He loved his new home and worked the land growing pineapples and vegetables, along with commercial fishing. Curt married Mary Emily Kitching, sister of Walter Kitching, on June 9, 1899. It was primarily bachelors who first came to the area for a new start on the frontier, and any females who came to teach or visit relatives soon found many male suitors.

When Henry Flagler brought the railroad south, it crossed the St. Lucie River over a wooden railroad bridge that Flagler had constructed, arriving in Potsdam (Stuart) by May 1894, where only about 10 families permanently resided.

With mainly German settlers, the name Potsdam, after a town in Germany, was selected for the post office and train station in 1894. As conductors approached Potsdam, they would shout "Dam Pots" to inform passengers of the next stop, which was quite upsetting to the ladies on board. A relative of Homer "Jack" Stuart, who lived by the station, suggested that his Scots name would be a less offensive replacement. It was agreed, and in 1895, the village became known as Stuart, officially recognized by the US Post Office.

Besides growing the prickly pineapple fruit, the residents also fished, caught green turtles, and built boats while waiting for the crops to grow. People had to be self-reliant, clearing the land, trading with the native Indians, and building their homes. Yet, it was truly a pioneer life as most of the settlers originated from the more advanced and cultured Northern states or from the British Isles and Germany.

Fishing was becoming a very popular sport at the turn of the 20th century, especially for northern visitors. It was not uncommon for an angler to catch a 300-pound tarpon in the river. Wildlife was plentiful, and even panthers or wildcats ventured quite close to the homes.

Sailing and boating were pleasurable activities, but also necessities before bridges were built across the St. Lucie in 1918 and Indian River in 1925, providing an improved method of transportation. Unpaved, sandy or muddy roads made travel in a buggy difficult.

Slowly, the wilderness areas were giving way to a populated town. In the 1910s, there was more development, and people were eager to settle along the St. Lucie. Homes, churches, and buildings were being constructed, and new businesses were started. A concrete auto bridge over the St. Lucie River opened in 1918, and a wooden bridge was opened in 1919 to nearby Palm City.

With more arrivals, there were homes, bungalows, and even massive estates built in Stuart. The primary builder was Sam Matthews, who was the contractor for the Bank of Stuart, Feroe Building, Kimberly Apartments, Woodmen Hall, St. Lucie Hotel, Sunrise Apartments, and many others.

Stuart really started growing, which was evident in the daily publishing of a newspaper in April 1913. By May 1914, the community incorporated as the city of Stuart. The decades that followed gave rise to a sense of community that made everyone glad they selected Stuart by the St. Lucie River.

One

The Allure of Paradise

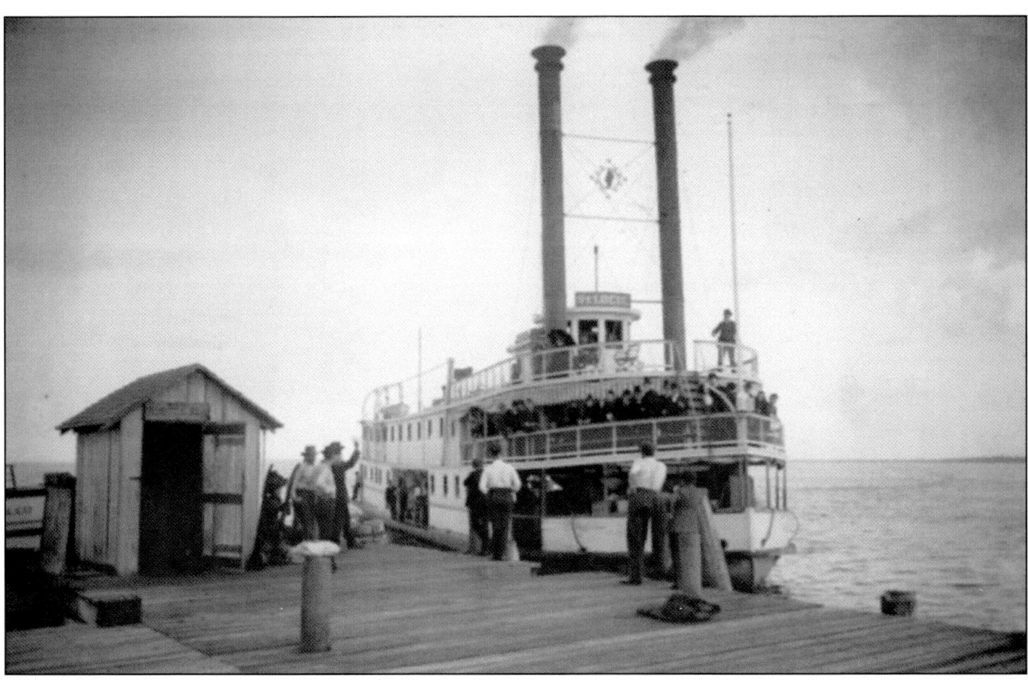

Steamboats like the *St. Lucie* were the only method of travel in the 1880s and into the beginning of the 1890s for the early settlers in the region bordered by the Indian and St. Lucie Rivers. The railroad only went as far south as Titusville, so people, along with their possessions, had to pay passage on the steamers to come farther south into the wilderness. (Courtesy of Florida Memory Project.)

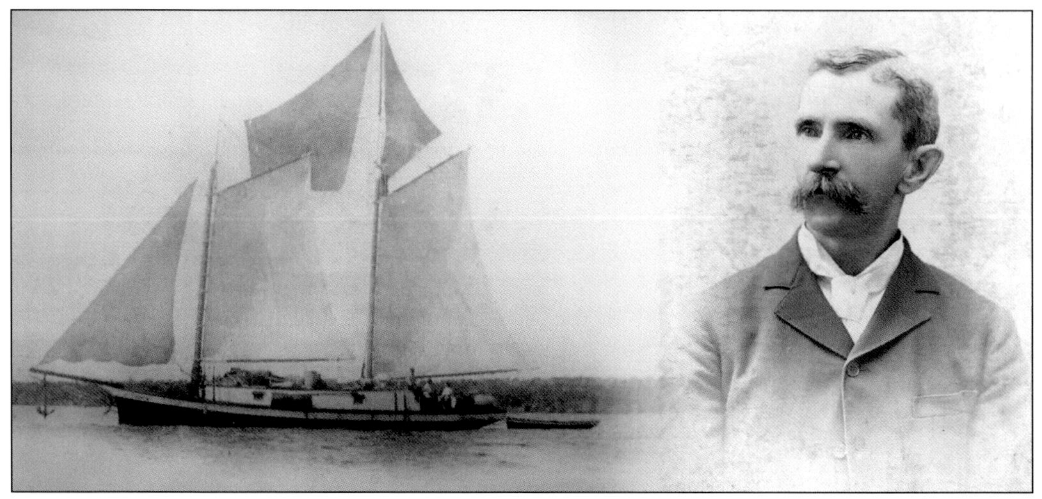

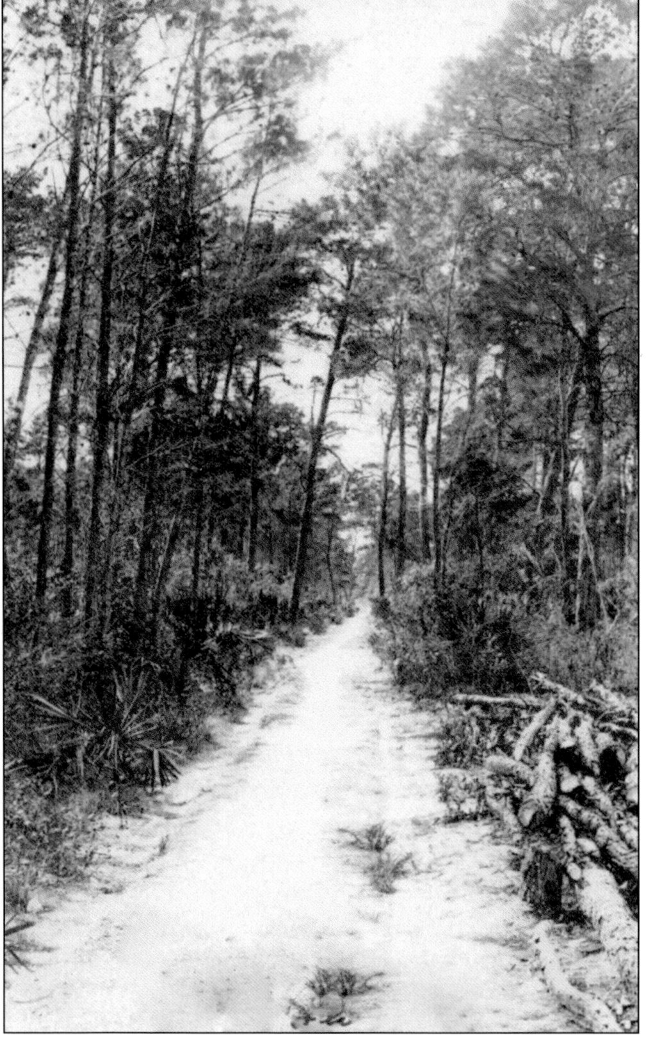

In 1887, Walter Kitching (pictured), with Col. Samuel F. Travis of Cocoa, used the one-masted sloop *Wave* to travel the Indian River providing necessary supplies to settlers. This was so successful that a second sloop, the *Sparkle*, was put into service. Next, Travis and Kitching built a 60-by-20-foot two-masted schooner, named *Merchant* (pictured), with a capacity of 36 tons. Kitching became the chief trading grocery supplier along Florida's east coast down to Miami. (Courtesy of Jo Marie Paradise.)

With luck, there might be a path like this to travel with a wagon, but it was highly unlikely. From the 1880s into the early 20th century, the area of Stuart could be reached only by boats on the Indian and St. Lucie Rivers. That is the reason most homes and businesses were close to the shorelines. Years later, this particular path eventually became US Highway 1. (Courtesy of Jo Marie Paradise.)

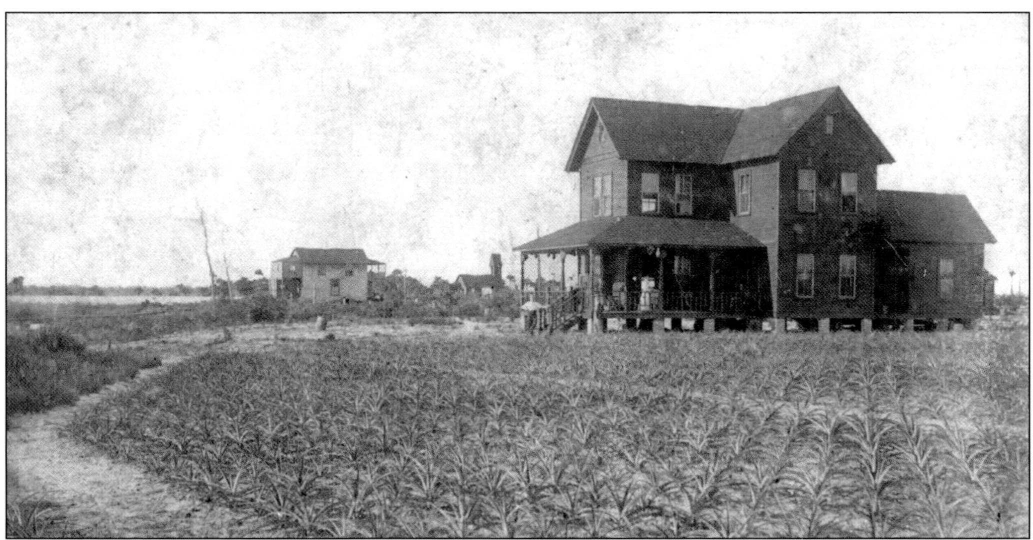

The home of Walter Kitching, the grocer on the supply schooner *Merchant*, was located in Potsdam, renamed Stuart in 1895. He had married Emma Jane Michael on February 23, 1894, in Wabasso, Florida. By the fall of 1894, the home Walter had constructed on his 16 acres of Stuart property was finished, and he and Emma moved in. Egyptian Queen pineapples had already been produced since 1892 by Broster Kitching, Walter's brother. Broster also ran a boardinghouse, store, and post office, seen in the background. (Courtesy of Jo Marie Paradise.)

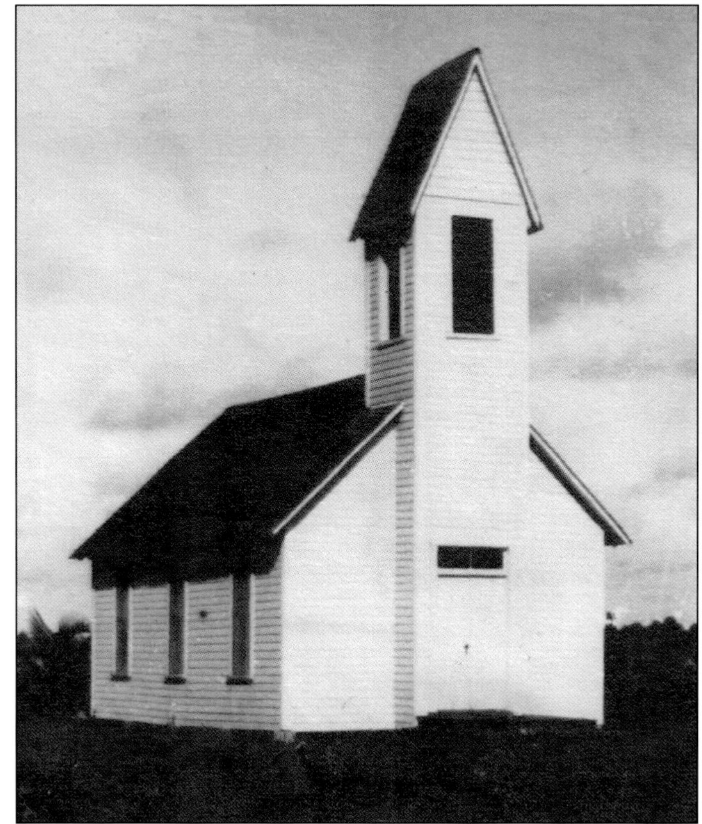

In Potsdam, a lot was provided by Walter and Emma Kitching for the First Methodist Episcopal Church, with its dedication in June 1895. It also served as a community church for other denominations to use until their own churches were constructed. A tall steeple was a special feature, intentionally placed so any train passengers seeing it would know that Stuart was a civilized town, with a church. The First Methodist Episcopal Church used the building until 1907, when a larger church was built a few blocks away. (Courtesy of Jo Marie Paradise.)

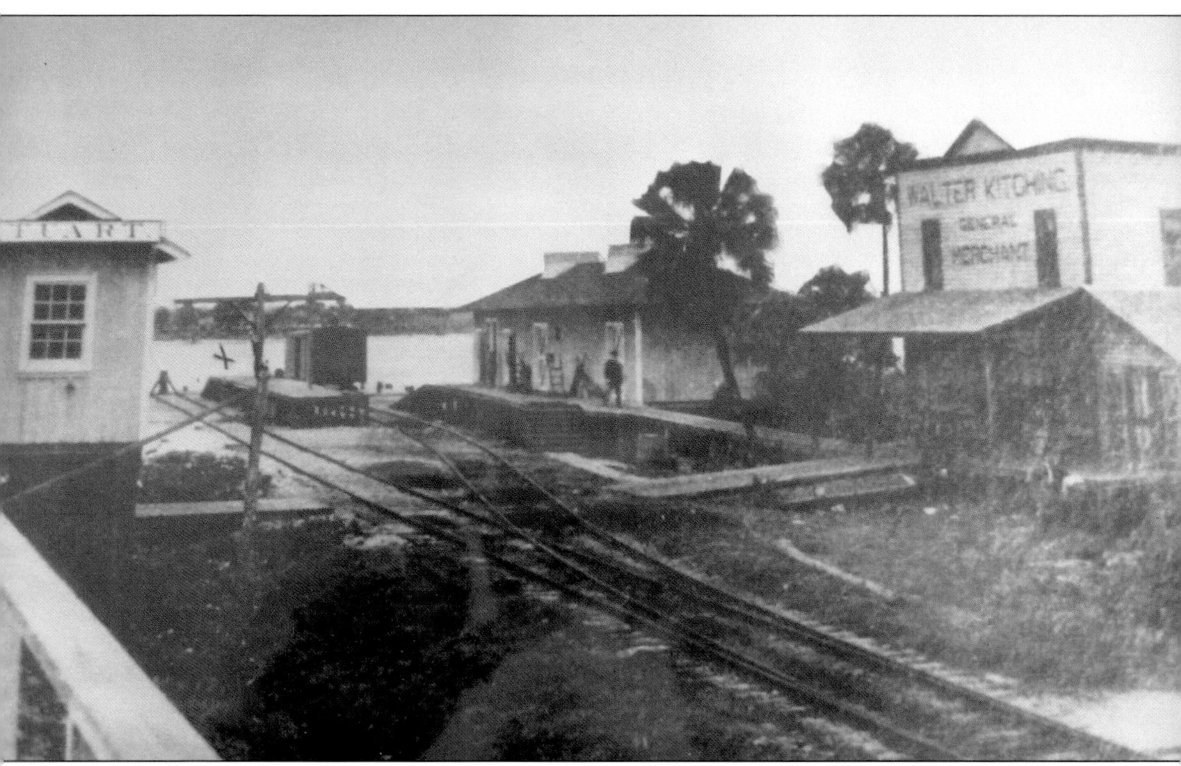

Walter Kitching had turned his schooner *Merchant* over to his wife's nephew by late 1896. Henry Flagler's Florida East Coast (FEC) Railway had come through in 1894, with the Potsdam depot built north of the St. Lucie River. Following controversy over the name Potsdam, changed by mid-1895 to Stuart, Walter Kitching wanted Stuart's train depot moved to the south side of the river, which Flagler agreed to. Kitching then built a general merchandise store in early 1897, directly across the street from the newly relocated FEC depot. (Courtesy of Jo Marie Paradise.)

Two

Pineapples, River, and Railroad

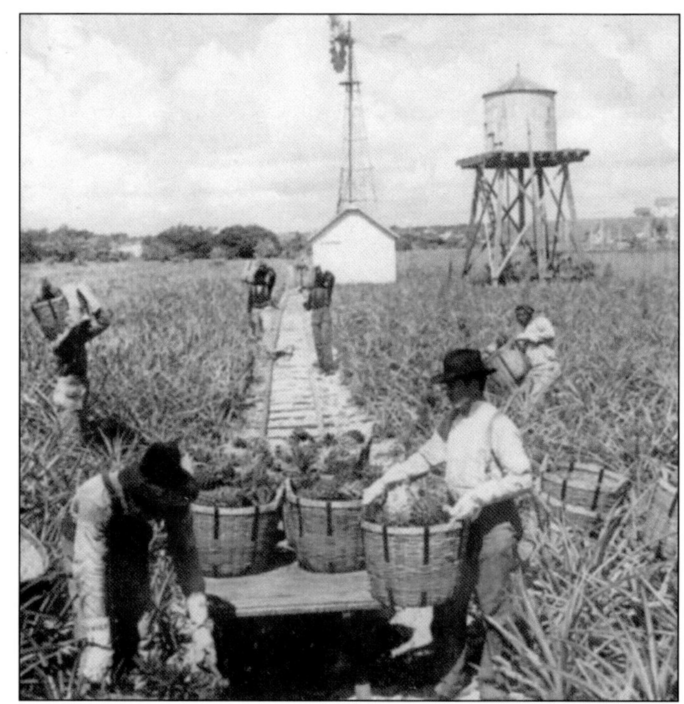

The massive production of commercial pineapples, or what were referred to as "pines," had begun in the Eden and Jensen area in 1880. As new settlers came to the shores along the St. Lucie, they also planted lucrative pineapple slips. Vast fields everywhere were put into production by Stuart's early settlers, such as Hubert W. Bessey and Otto Stypmann in 1882, Albert Krueger and Reuben Frazier in 1887, and Morris R. Johns in 1890. The fields were similar to this one in Jensen. (Courtesy of Florida Memory Project.)

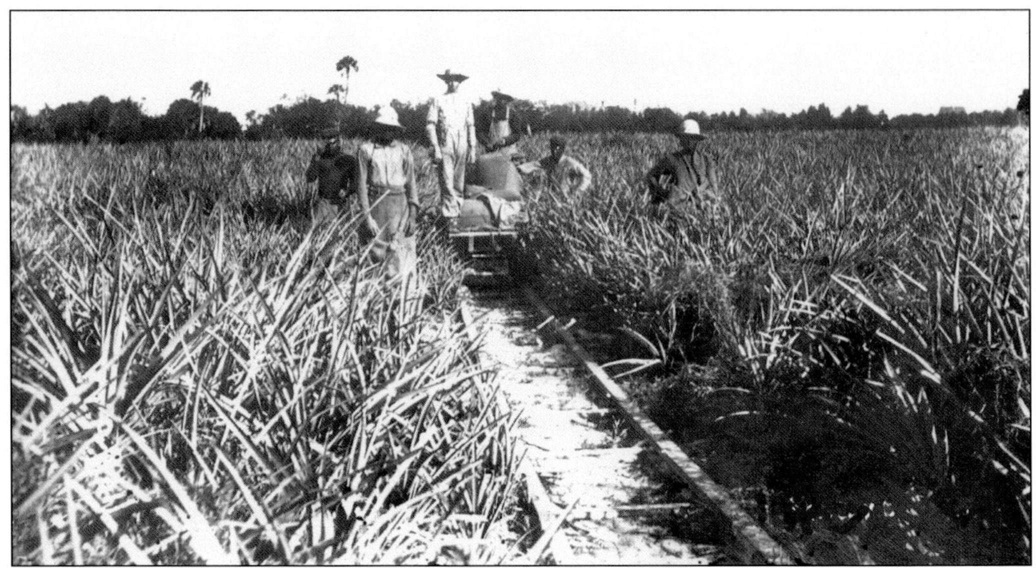

Land for pineapple production was purchased from the US government or worked for a homestead patent for land ownership. With acres in production, a tram on tracks carried the harvested pineapples to a warehouse for storage. Pineapples were packed in barrels or boxes and then moved in wagons to the steamboats to be transported to the southern terminus of the railroad in Titusville. No pineapple canning or preserving was done in those early years of the 1880s and 1890s.

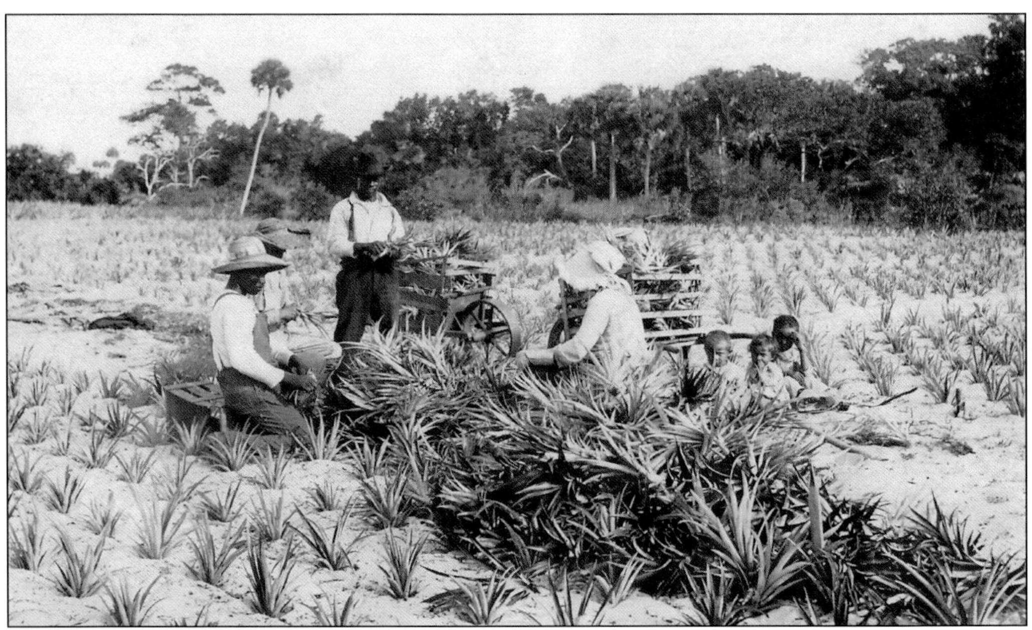

After harvest of one section in the spring, the planting of the pineapple slips began again, with pineapples ready within 18 months. Since the fruit had already been grown for years in their homeland, many of the laborers for the fields were originally from the Bahamas. Some of the early families included the McHardys, Greens, Moores, Mackeys, and Christies. In 1900, there were only about 15 African Americans along with those of Bahamian heritage in Stuart.

In the heart of downtown Stuart, pineapple fields were everywhere. This c. 1906 photograph, taken near the town's community church and the train depot, shows a small boy carrying pineapples. (Courtesy of the McFarlan Collection, Stuart Heritage Museum.)

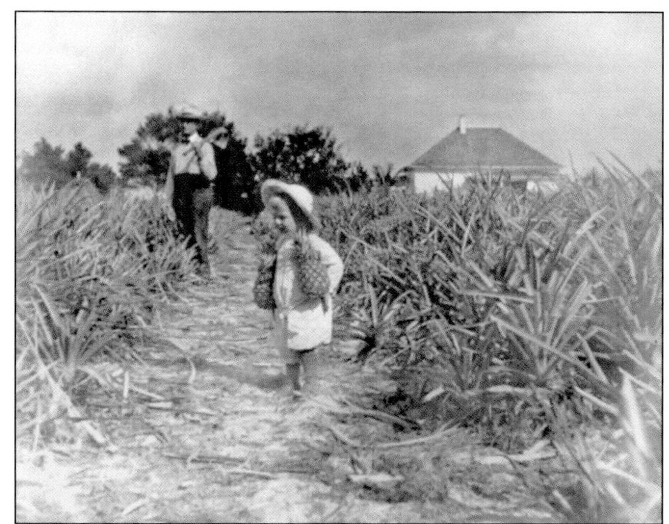

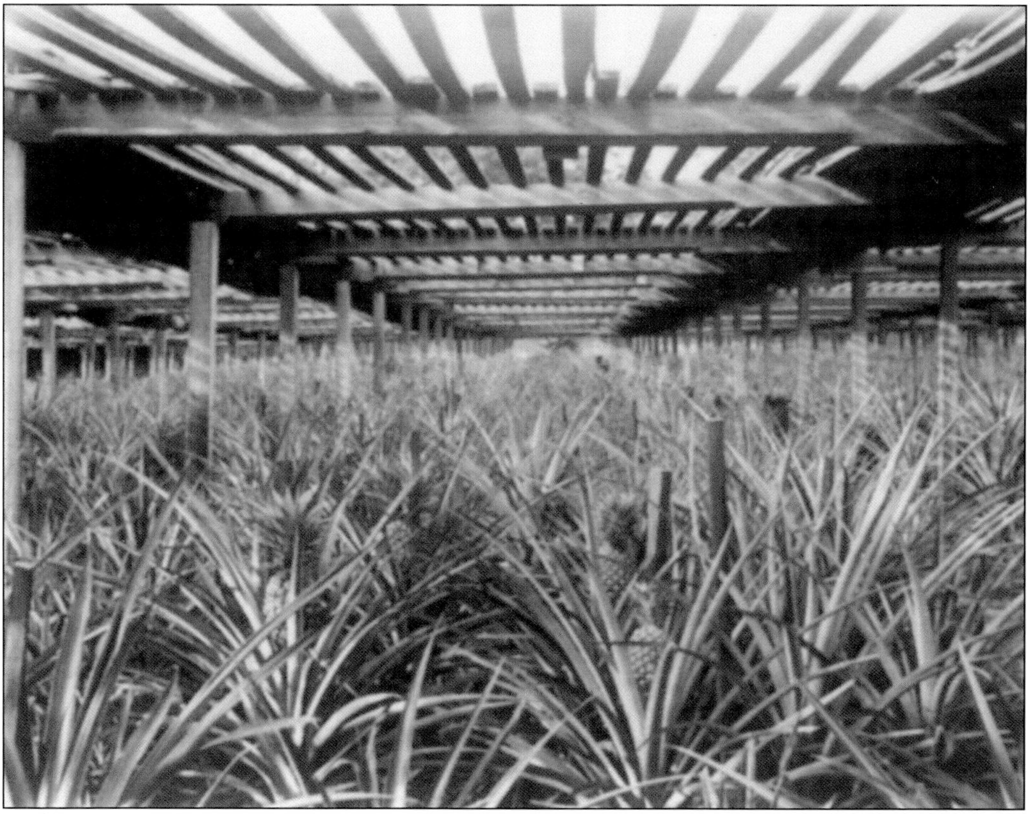

Disastrous freezes on December 28, 1894, and February 14, 1895, resulted in 95 percent of the pineapple crops in Stuart being destroyed. Morris Johns of Stuart had erected the first pineapple shed in the summer of 1895 to protect the sensitive pines. These sheds, constructed of slats positioned in a north-south direction, provided a period of direct light on the plants each day as the sun proceeded across the sky from east to west. In Stuart, by the end of 1899, there were more than 600 acres under pineapple sheds to shelter the fields from frost and freezing temperatures. (Courtesy of Florida Memory Project.)

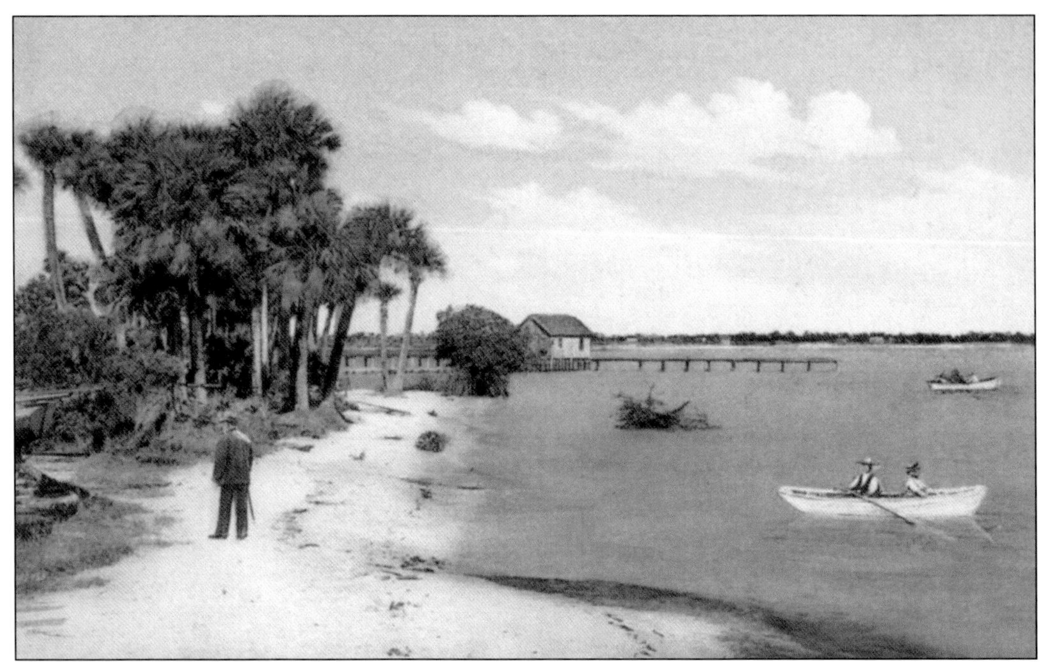

The majestic St. Lucie River has always been the heart of Stuart, with the river encircling the land with its North and South Forks. To travel from one side of the river to the other, boats of all shapes and sizes were used. The river supplied a multitude of fish as a food source for the settlers. Recreation included a pleasant boat trip on the river or swimming near the shore.

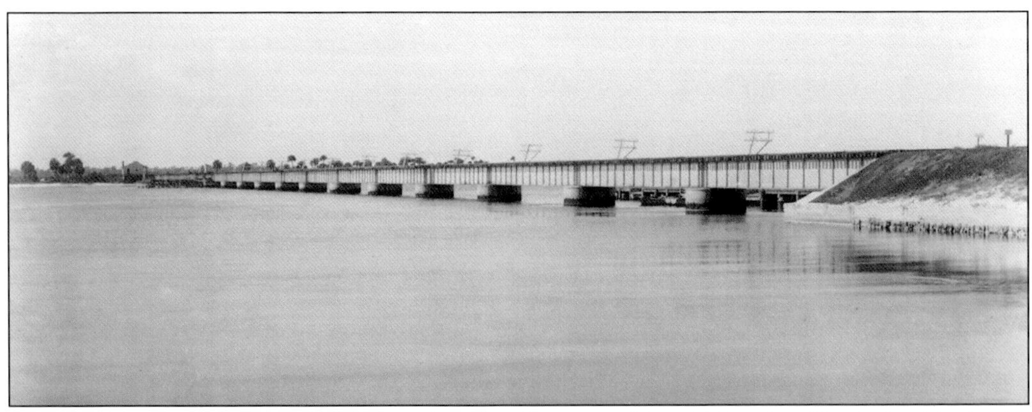

With the coming of Henry Flagler's railroad to Stuart in May 1894, after Flagler had built the railroad bridge to cross the St. Lucie River, it proved to be a major boon to the small community of just 10 families. With encouragement from Walter Kitching that the train cross the river there rather than through the Sewall's Point peninsula, the transport of goods and products in and out of Stuart greatly improved. (Courtesy of Martha Penhale Cuthbert.)

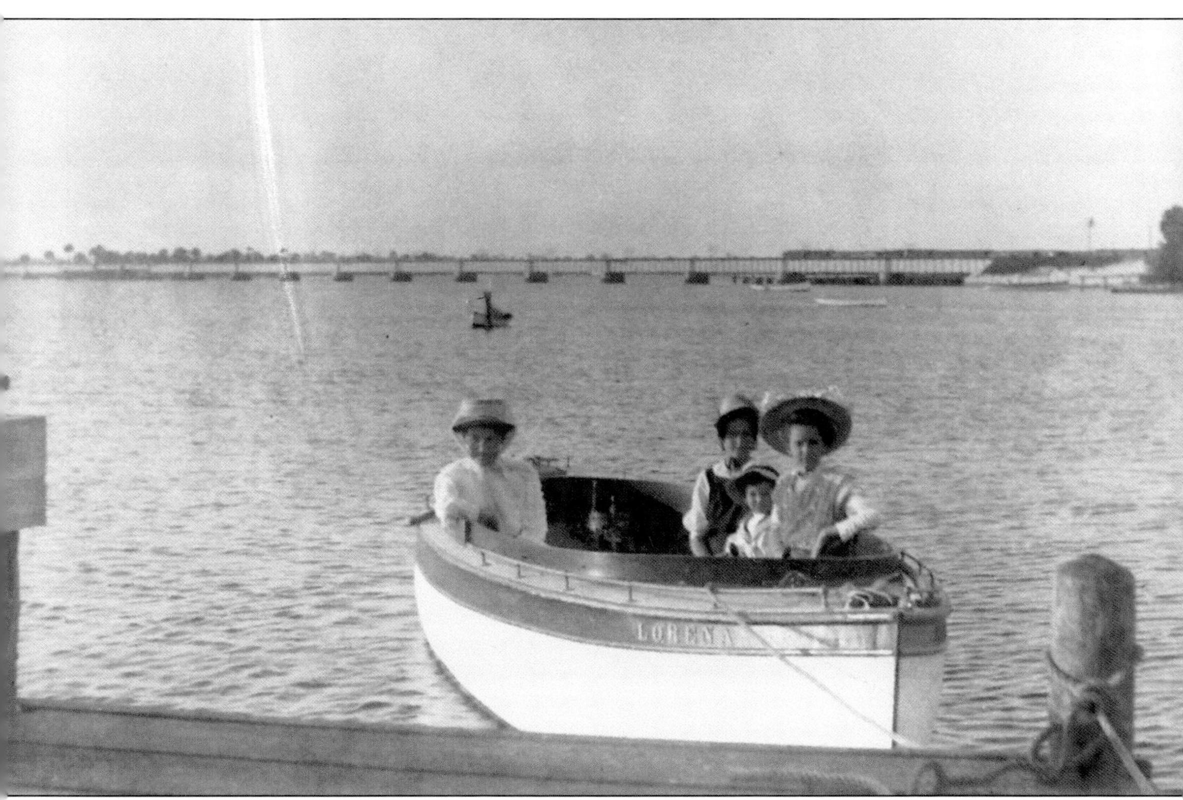

With the St. Lucie River as a vital part of life for all residents and visitors to Stuart, the use of boats was essential, as illustrated in this 1905 photograph. Boatbuilders were always in demand for construction of all types of vessels. Since roads were practically nonexistent during the 1880s and into the early years of the 1900s, the river was the highway of social, commercial, and recreational life. Also important was the railroad system, with the train bridge crossing the St. Lucie River in the background.

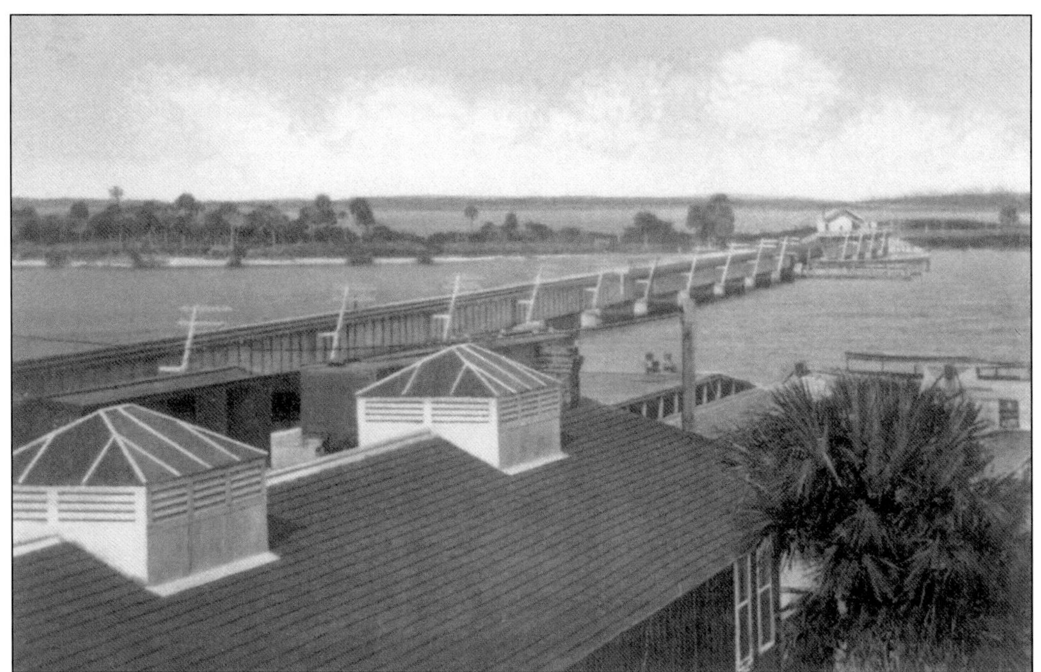

The 1894 railroad bridge across the St. Lucie River was always a welcome sight for Stuart residents. Now some goods like cheese and canned meats, as well as passengers, could be transported much easier, along with the pineapples. The mail and newspapers could arrive in two days instead of seven days. Getting dental or medical care was quicker when traveling by train to West Palm Beach or Titusville.

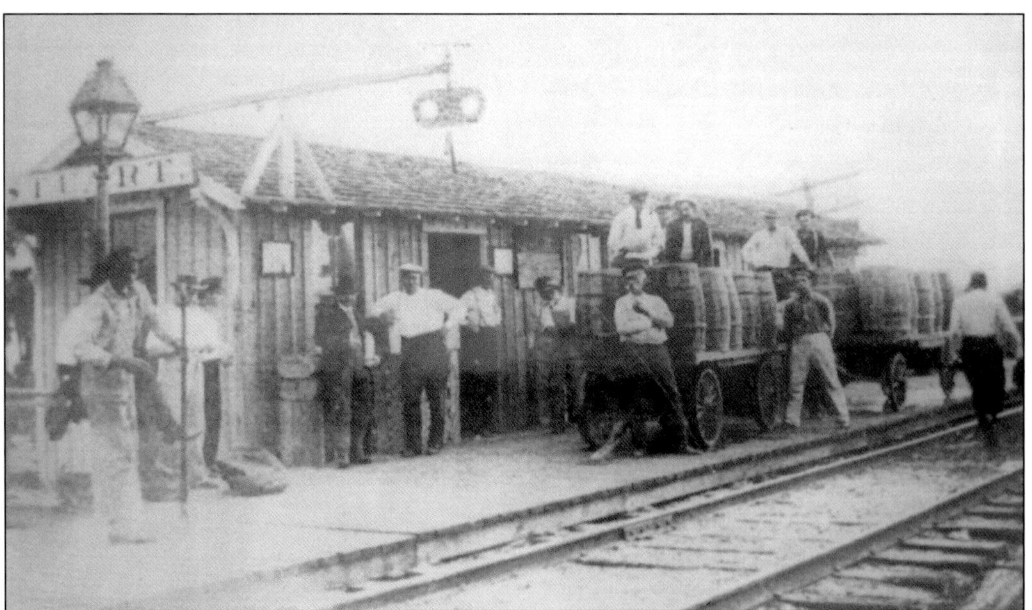

The Stuart train depot in the late 1890s on the south side of the St. Lucie River was the hub of the town. Barrels of local produce and pineapples could always be seen awaiting the arrival of the daily train. (Courtesy of Jo Marie Paradise.)

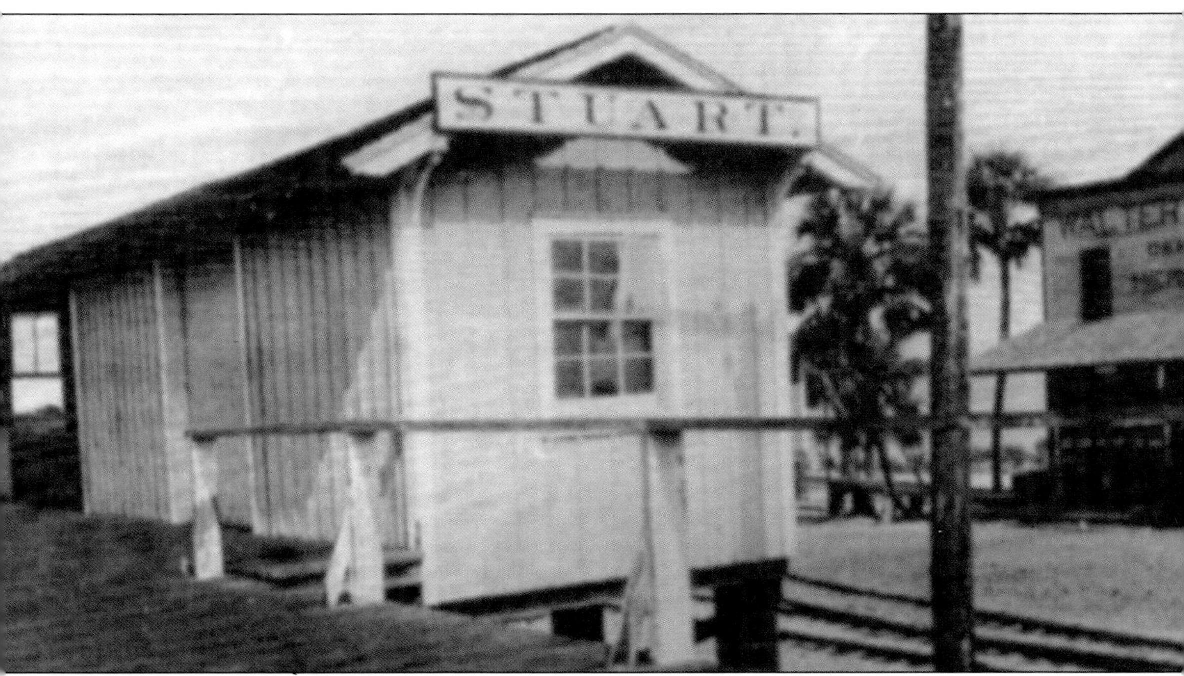

With Walter Kitching's earlier purchase of 16 acres in 1883 right in that vicinity, he offered Flagler the necessary land and right-of-way for the tracks to be built south of the river. Through negotiations between Flagler's railroad executives and Walter Kitching, his general merchandise store of 1897 faced the Stuart train depot.

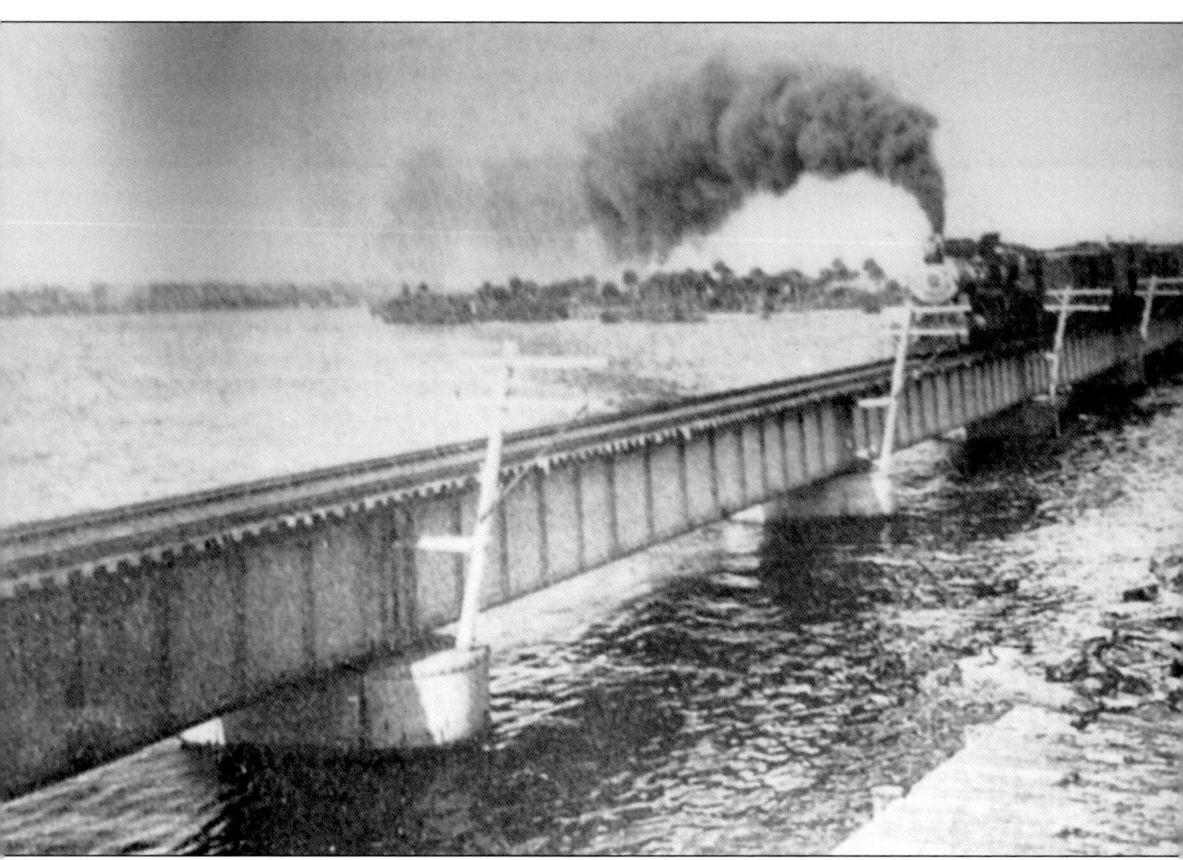

With the FEC train crossing the St. Lucie River daily and traveling through Stuart, expansion of commerce paralleling the tracks occurred gradually. The dawn of the 20th century witnessed more people settling in Stuart to start their own farms and businesses or simply visiting during the winter to enjoy the mild weather. The railroad ensured Stuart's expansion. By 1905, a new concrete-and-steel railroad bridge was built to replace the 1894 wooden bridge. (Courtesy of Sandra and Tom Thurlow.)

Three

The Dawn of the 20th Century

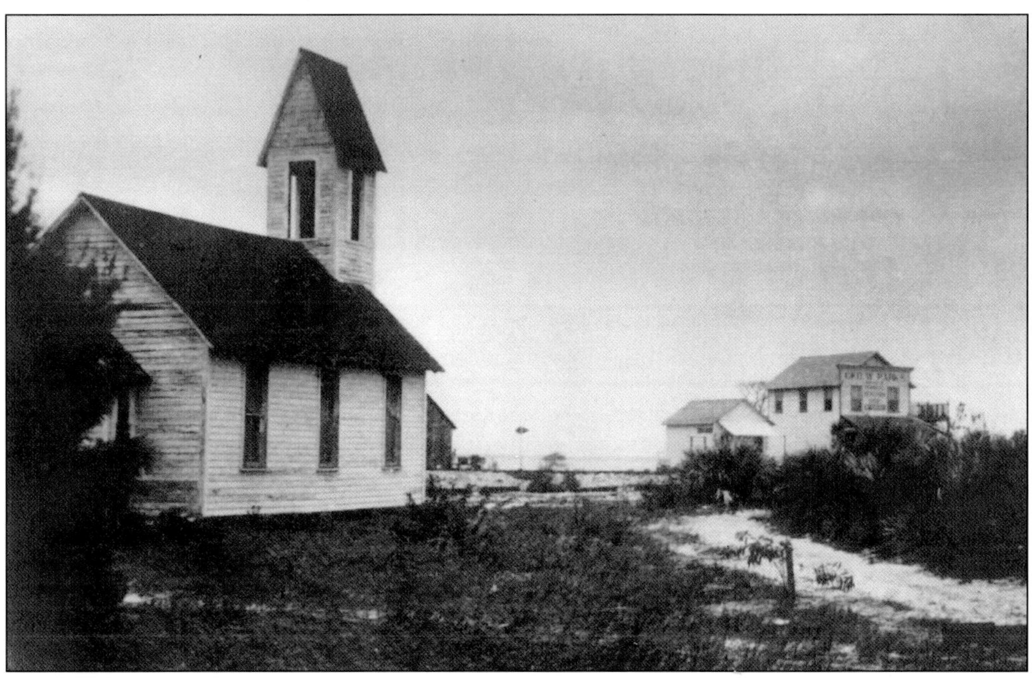

The 1895 First Methodist Episcopal Church (left) was a community church. The two stores across the railroad tracks were the George W. Parks General Merchandise, built in 1901, and the smaller drink stand, started in 1902 by Stanley Kitching. Walter Kitching, Stanley's uncle, had a larger store (just out of frame to the left), which was opposite the early train depot. In just three years, Stanley had a larger two-story building on the site, with a drugstore, tackle shop, and the Southern Express office. (Courtesy of Jo Marie Paradise.)

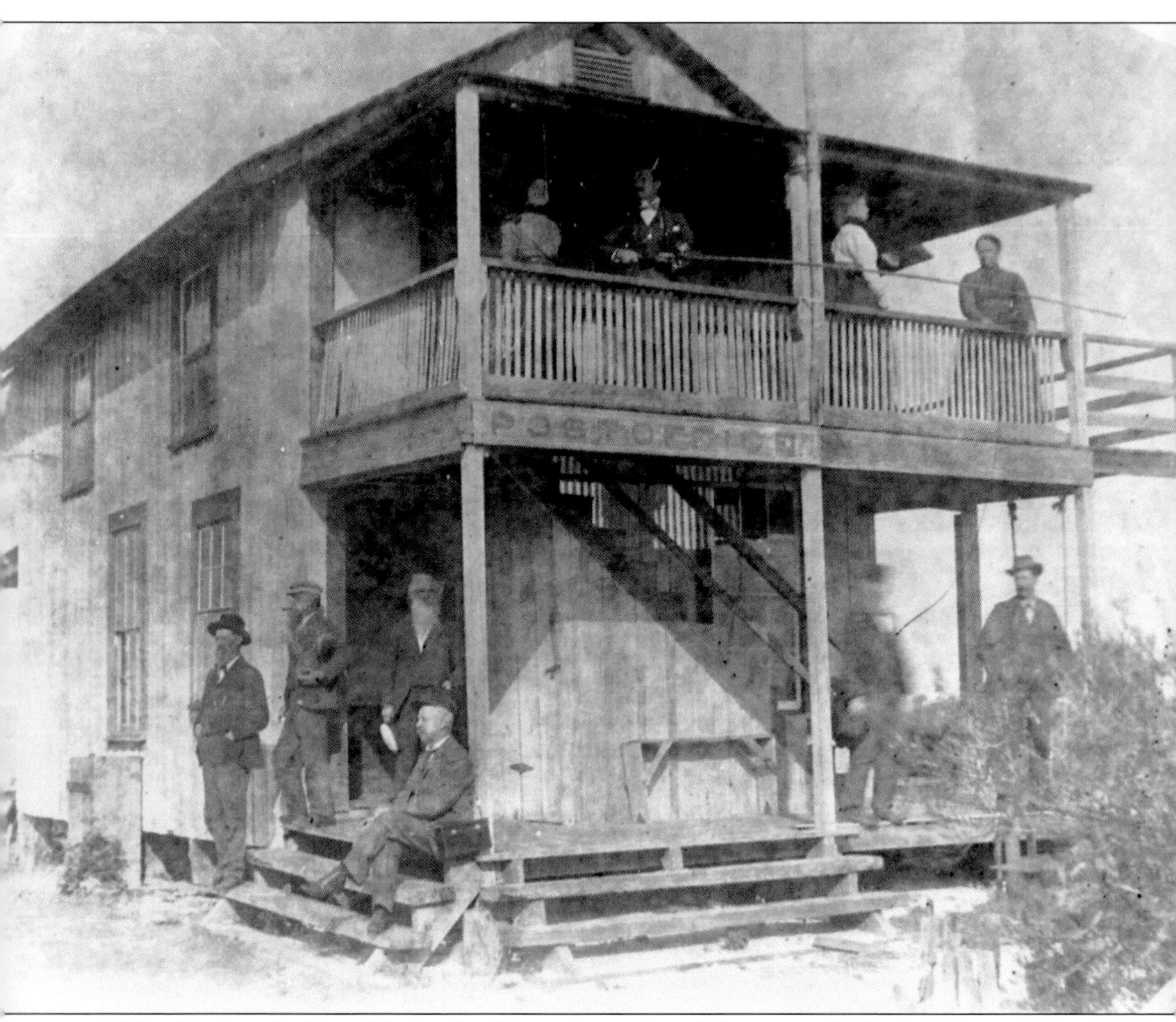

Walter Kitching had his older brother Broster come from Sebastian to Walter's property along the St. Lucie River by 1892 to start planting pineapples. A two-story building was constructed nearby to be a general store, and the upstairs operated as a boardinghouse known as the Stuart House. By 1894, the Potsdam Post Office was moved from Otto Stypmann's home to the same building, and Broster was named official postmaster in June 1895 for the Stuart Post Office. (Courtesy of the McFarlan Collection, Stuart Heritage Museum.)

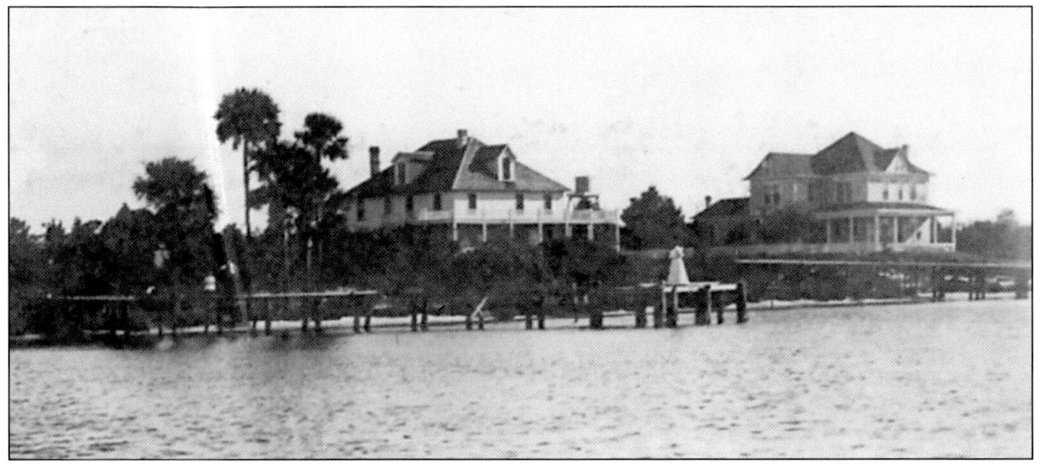

The Danforth Hotel, on the left, began with the 1892 Danforth floating hotel, a 125-foot sternwheeler boat built by John S. Danforth. It was used by paying guests on fishing and hunting excursions along the Florida coast. After some damage to the boat, Danforth converted it to the Danforth Hunters Camp on land. This was so successful that Danforth purchased property from Walter Kitching on the banks of the St. Lucie River to build an impressive hotel, the Danforth House, which opened for the season of 1900–1901. To the right is the George Perkins home. (Courtesy of Doug Witham.)

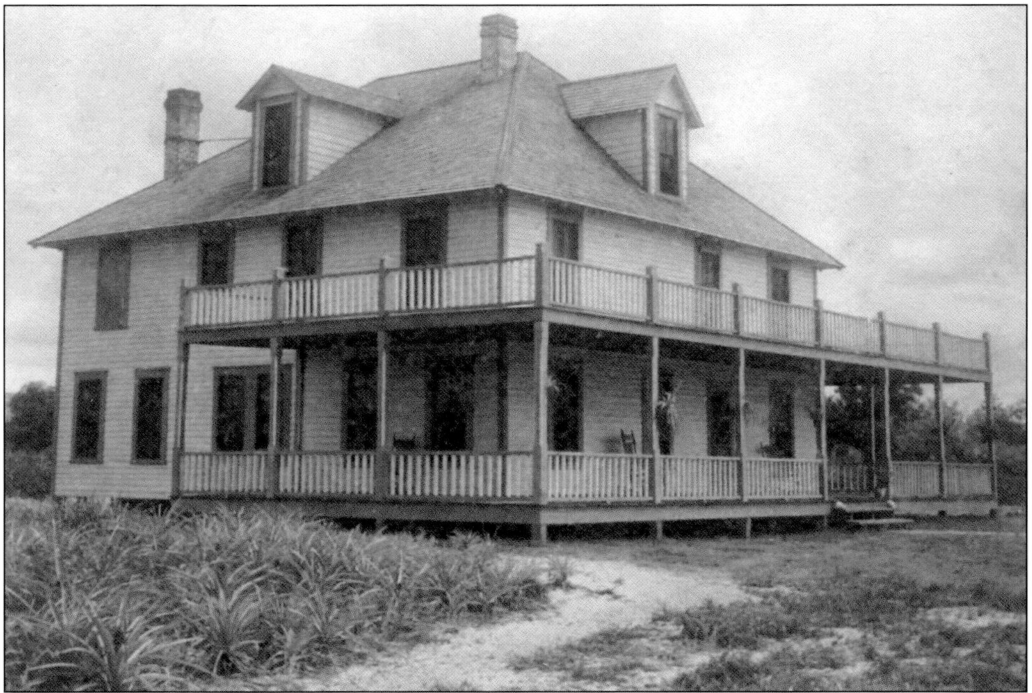

After the death of John Danforth's wife in 1901, Hubert and Susan Bessey moved into the Danforth just to have it occupied. By the fall season of 1901, the Besseys had numerous requests for accommodations, so the couple became hotel managers, eventually purchasing the property from John Danforth. Many dignitaries, such as former president Grover Cleveland, stayed there. Hubert died in 1918, and Susan closed the Danforth Hotel in June 1920. The structure was torn down by late 1921, with some of the material used to build Susan a new home.

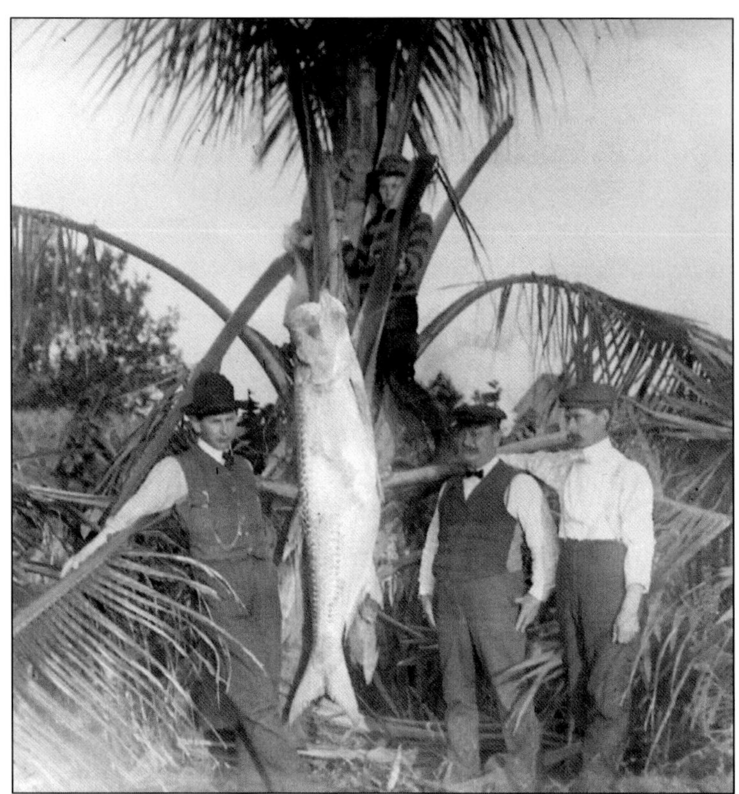

An early winter visitor to Stuart was Louis Cass McFarlan, a Pennsylvania merchant, along with his cousins Bill and Robert McFarlan, who loved fishing. They were informed that the best place to fish was the village of Stuart. So intrigued by the prospect of great fishing grounds, they came to Stuart immediately in 1895. The fishermen on the left and right may be cousins Bill and Robert. Louis C. McFarlan is second from the right. His son Billy McFarlan is possibly the boy in the palm tree. (Courtesy of the McFarlan Collection, Stuart Heritage Museum.)

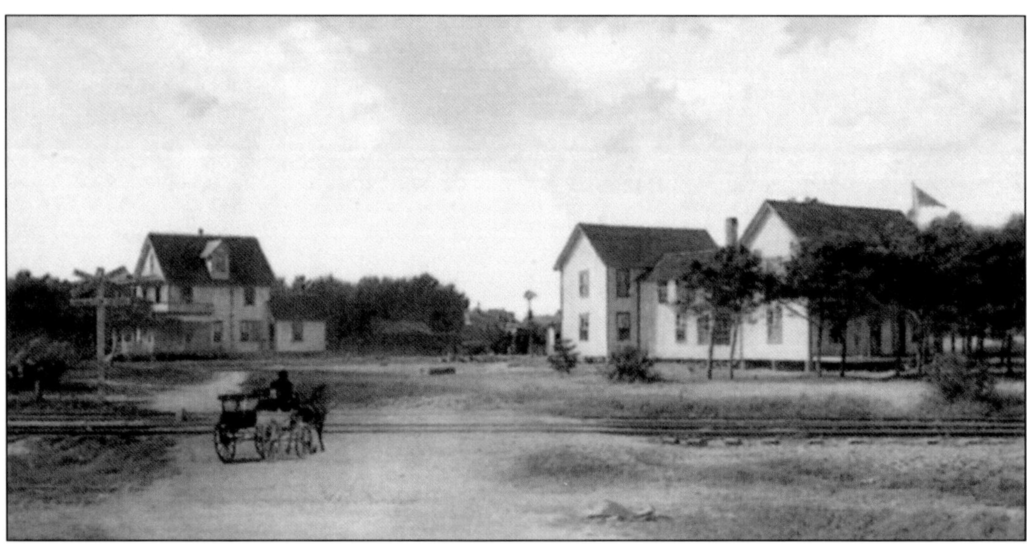

The opening of the 20th century saw more permanent residents, those willing to build substantial homes here. Robert and Marcia McPherson had a second home built in 1904 (at left), located near the Stuart House-Hotel (at right), which had been the earlier Broster Kitching's boardinghouse and store. The McPherson house was built by Stuart's extraordinary contractor Sam Matthews. (Courtesy of Doug Witham.)

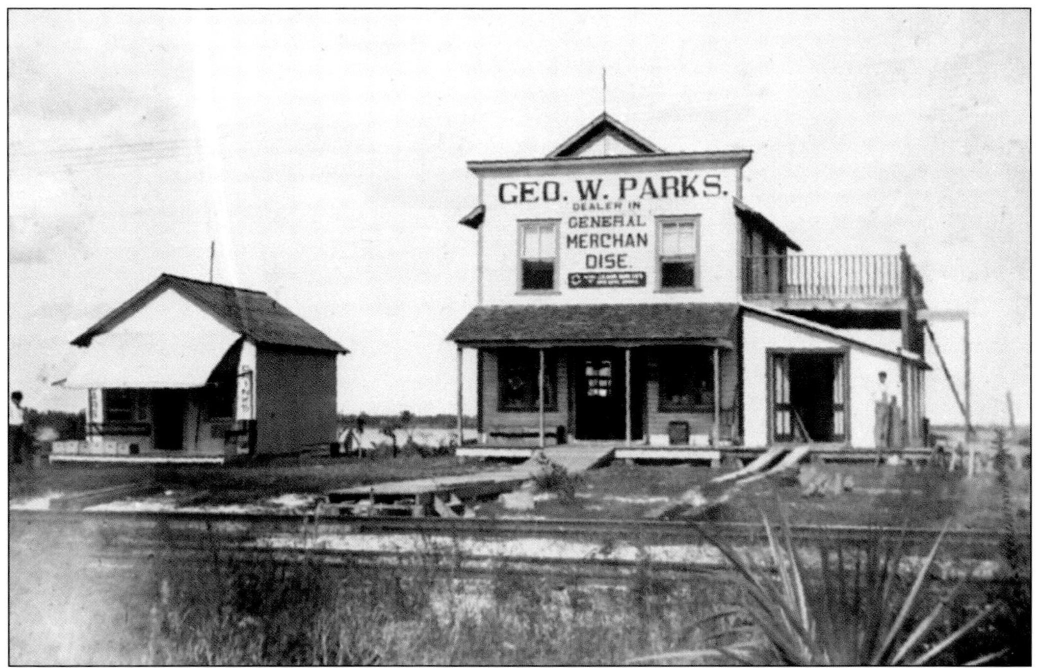

In 1901, George W. Parks opened his general merchandise store facing the railroad tracks. By November 20, 1901, he married Julia Taylor, and their home was the apartment above the general merchandise store. They raised two children, daughter Anita, born in 1905, and son George Jr., born in 1907. The store has a wood-frame vernacular style with a false front and a gabled tin roof. It still stands between the St. Lucie River and the railroad tracks. The smaller building to the left was the drink stand operated by Stanley Kitching in 1902. (Courtesy of Sandra and Tom Thurlow.)

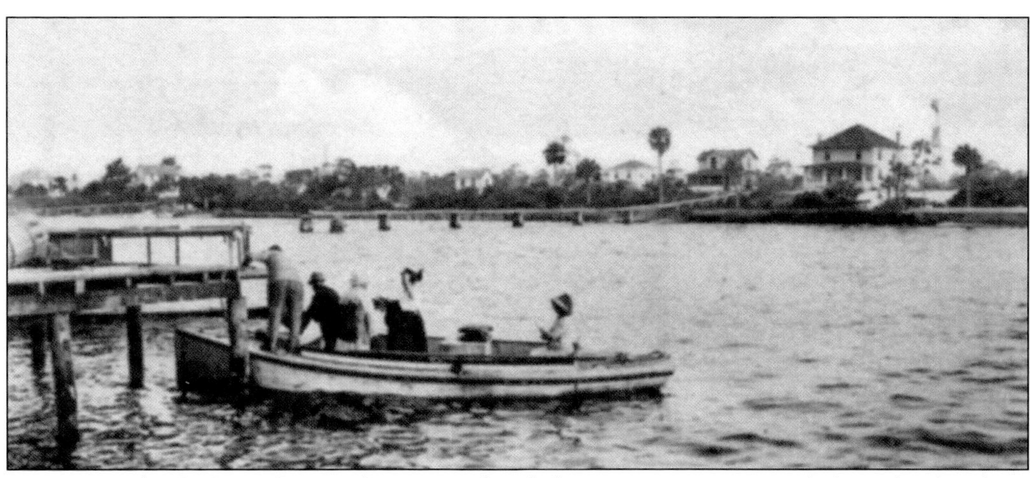

Boating on the St. Lucie River, where several early homes were constructed along the shoreline, was a pleasant day's activity in the early 1900s. Maj. Richard Houston Dudley, from Tennessee, a former Confederate officer, had a home built in 1908 along the river and owned a motor boat with a speedy six-horsepower motor by 1910. (Courtesy of Doug Witham.)

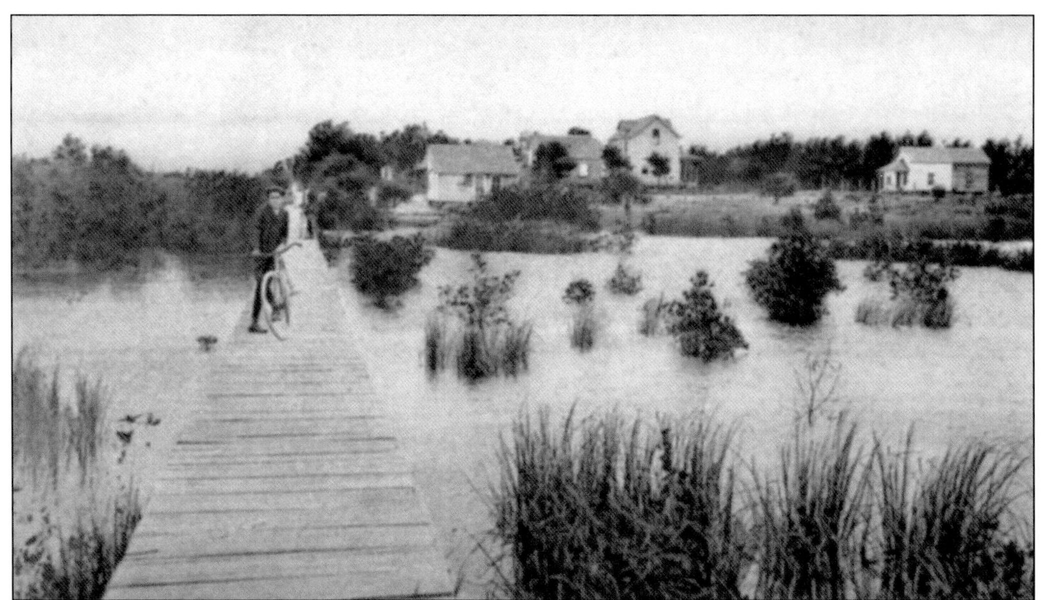

In about 1906, this was a typical scene in Stuart, with a foot and bicycle bridge across the Frazier Creek. In the 1920s, this path would become US 1, with a concrete auto bridge across the creek. The boy pictured is Charles Lee Beville, about age 14. These houses were owned by Judge John Ballard Adams, Robert L. Beville, and Felix A. Gibson, all located at the corner of Albany Avenue and Fourth Street. (Courtesy of Doug Witham.)

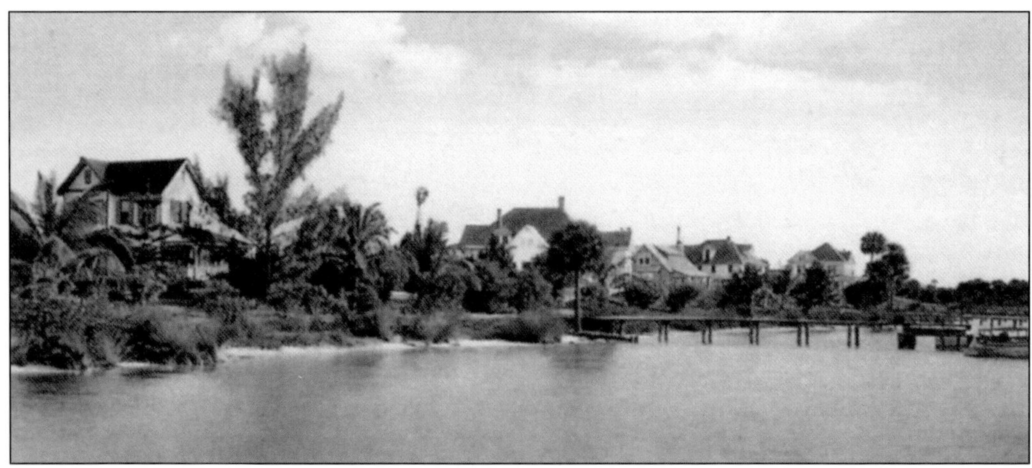

Here is a string of residences with a fabulous view of the St. Lucie River in 1909. Identified homes are those of Walter Kitching, John C. Hancock, and Dick and Blanche DeVault. The Kitching and Hancock houses are still standing, and owned by the families' descendants. (Courtesy of Doug Witham.)

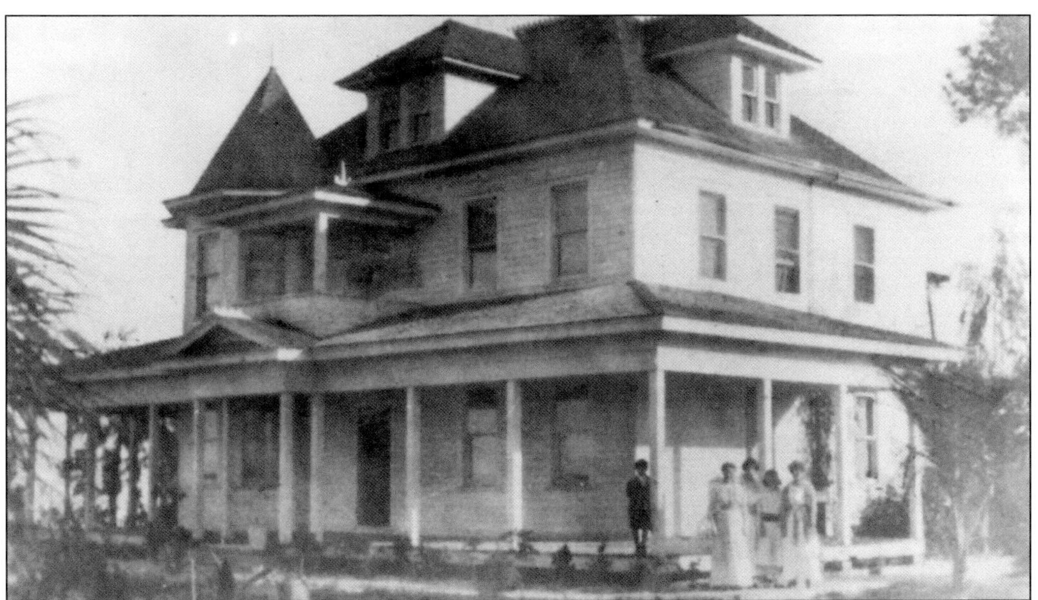

This is the 1908 home of Stuart pioneer Curt Emil Schroeder, who came in May 1893. He married Mary Emily Kitching, sister of Walter Kitching, on June 9, 1899. Their house on Osceola Street near the St. Lucie River was built by contractors J.A.Y. Speirs and Sam Matthews. The Schroeder children were Helena, Curt Jr., and Broster Joseph Schroeder, all of whom grew up in this house. Some of the Schroeder family members are seen standing in front of the home.

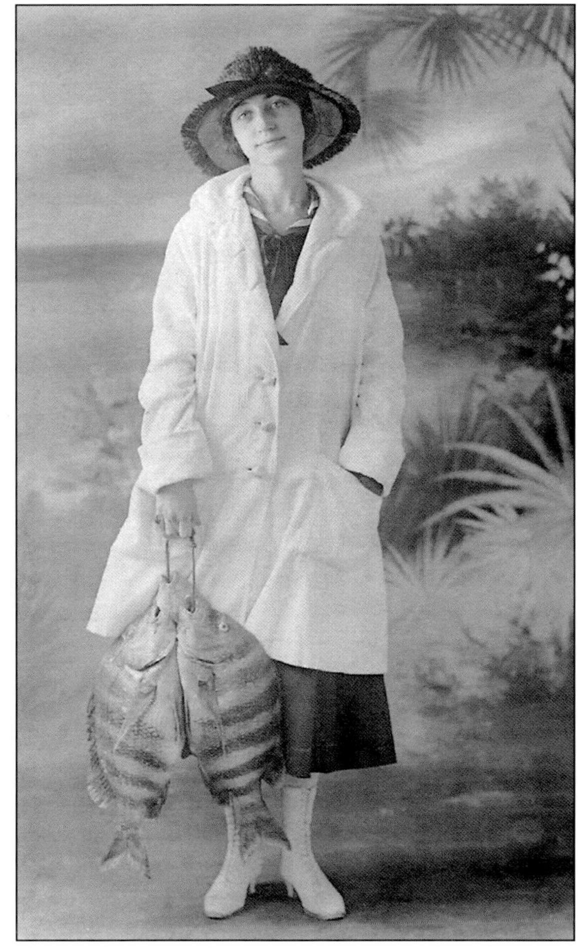

Pictured here with a backdrop of tropical vegetation and a nice haul of fresh fish in her hand is Irene Gaines, who surely made her friends and family back north jealous that she was in paradise. Irene's father, Henry N. Gaines, came from Kansas around 1909 to see what type of land opportunities were available in the Stuart area. Irene later married Robert Lawton McPherson, who was born November 13, 1899, in Stuart. (Courtesy of Frank Clark.)

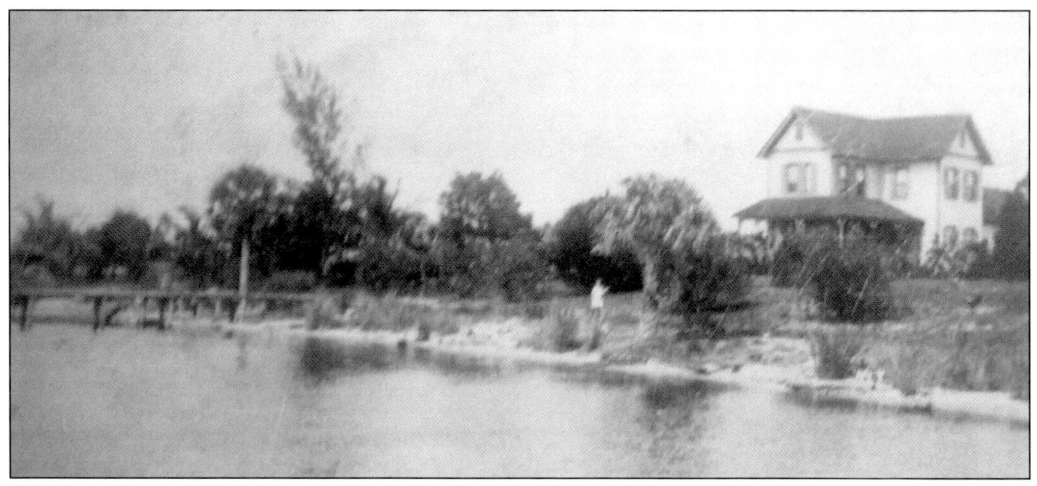

Emma and Walter Kitching had a daughter, Sarah Josephine Kitching, born March 10, 1895, in the family residence. Modern improvement to the house included Stuart's first windmill, erected around 1902, and the first indoor bathroom. During the early 1900s, several river-border parcels belonging to Kitching were sold to John Danforth, Charles Woodward, John C. Hancock, Thomas E. Matthews, and Maj. Richard Dudley for homes to be constructed on the sites. (Courtesy of Jo Marie Paradise.)

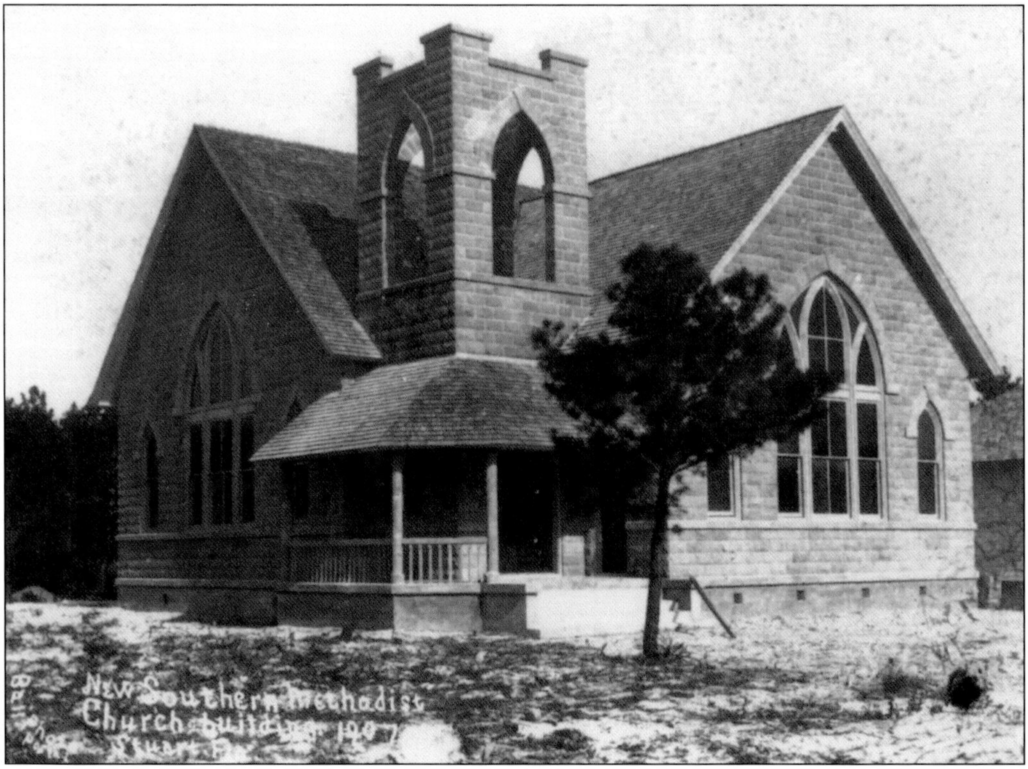

When the First Methodist Episcopal Church (Southern Methodist Church) needed to expand due to increased membership, a new block church was constructed at the corner of Avenue D (Albany Avenue) and Second Street in 1907. The congregation moved from the 1895 wooden church building that faced the railroad tracks to the new church. (Courtesy of MCHS, Elliott Museum.)

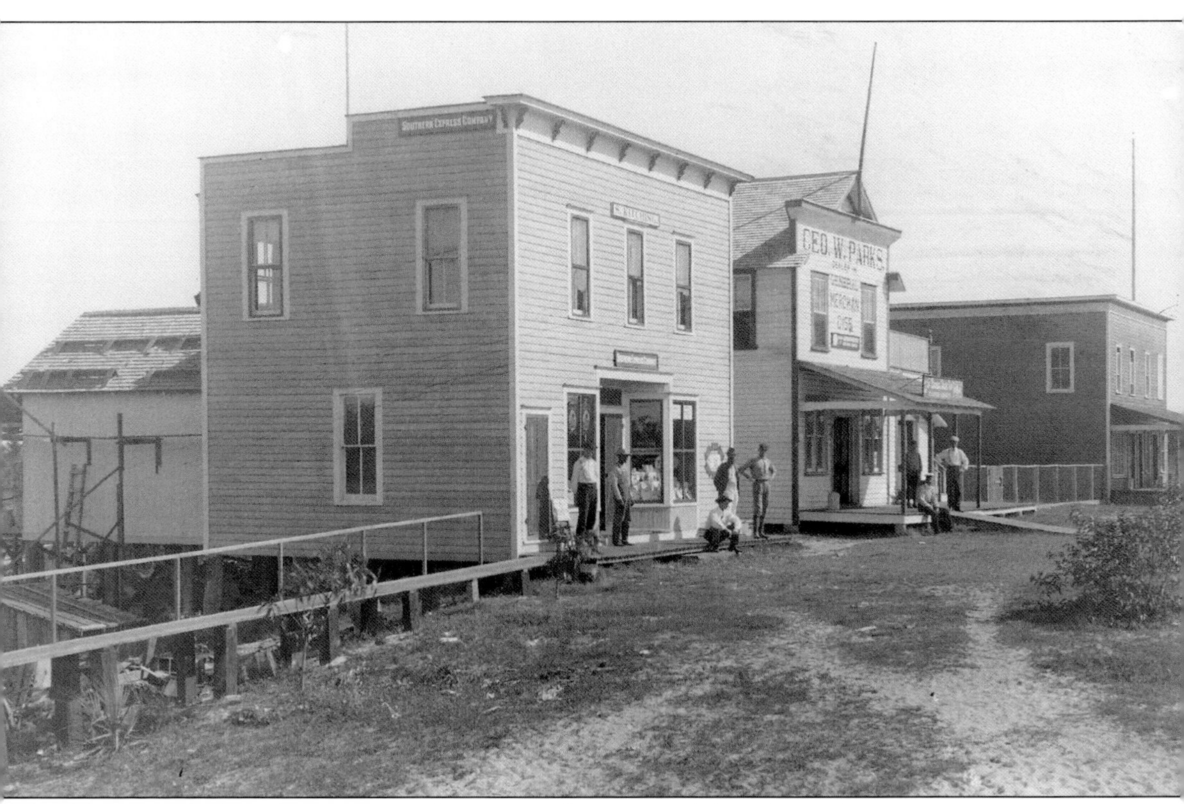

Stores, homes, boardinghouses, and the post office were side by side in what was considered the downtown commercial district, between the St. Lucie River and the railroad tracks in the early 20th century. From left to right are the new 1905 Stanley Kitching drugstore, tackle shop, and the Southern Express office; the 1901 George W. Parks general merchandise store; and the new 1905 Broster Kitching boardinghouse containing the Stuart Post Office, with Kitching's home behind the boardinghouse. Set back and between Parks's store and the boardinghouse was the 1903 home of Noah Parks, older brother of George.

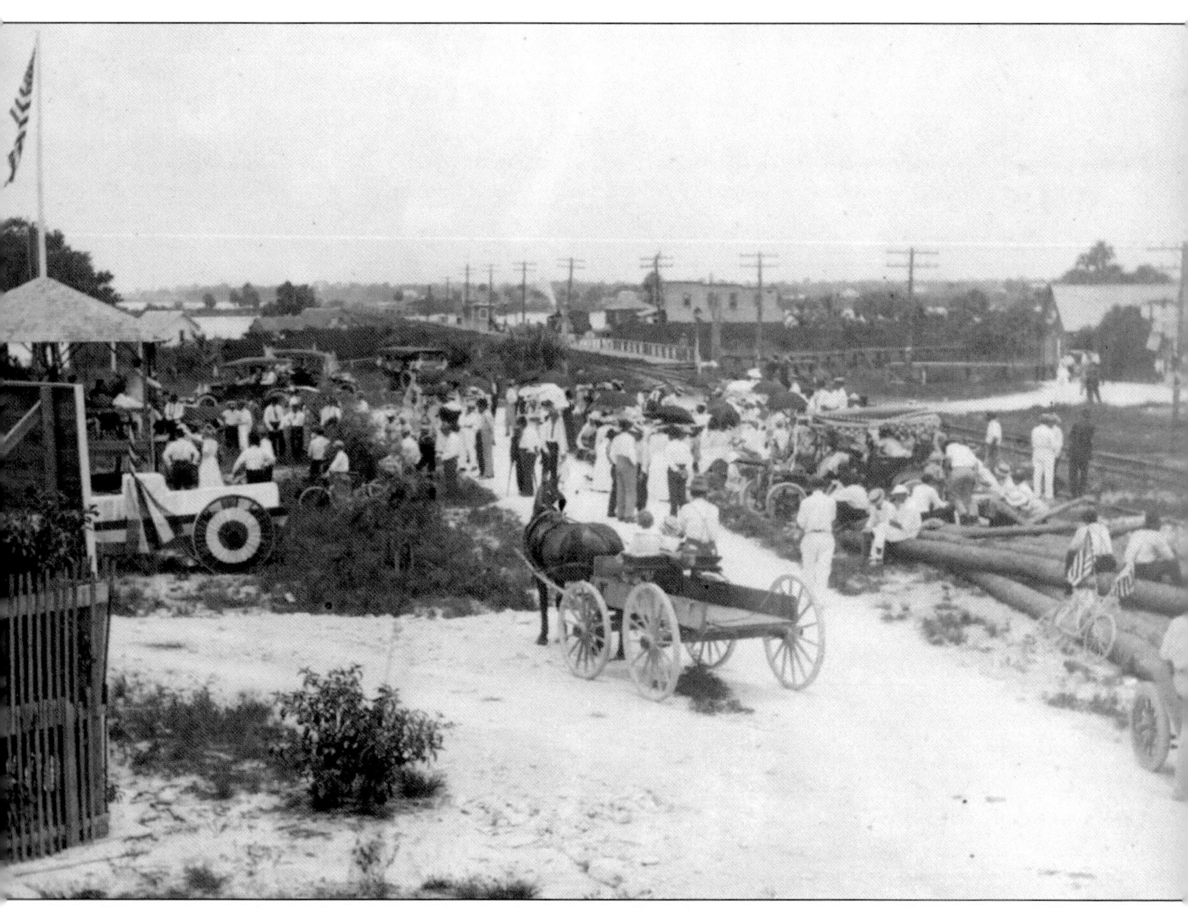

Moving into the 20th century, Stuart became a close-knit community, and the townsfolk took advantage of every opportunity for a get-together, especially celebrations. Parades were very popular, but here, they are displaying their patriotic US flags and gathered near the bandstand for a local musical performance. Everything was near the heart of town, which included the essential railroad tracks and the ever-beautiful St. Lucie River. (Courtesy of Dave Murray.)

Four

Growth and Development in the 1910s

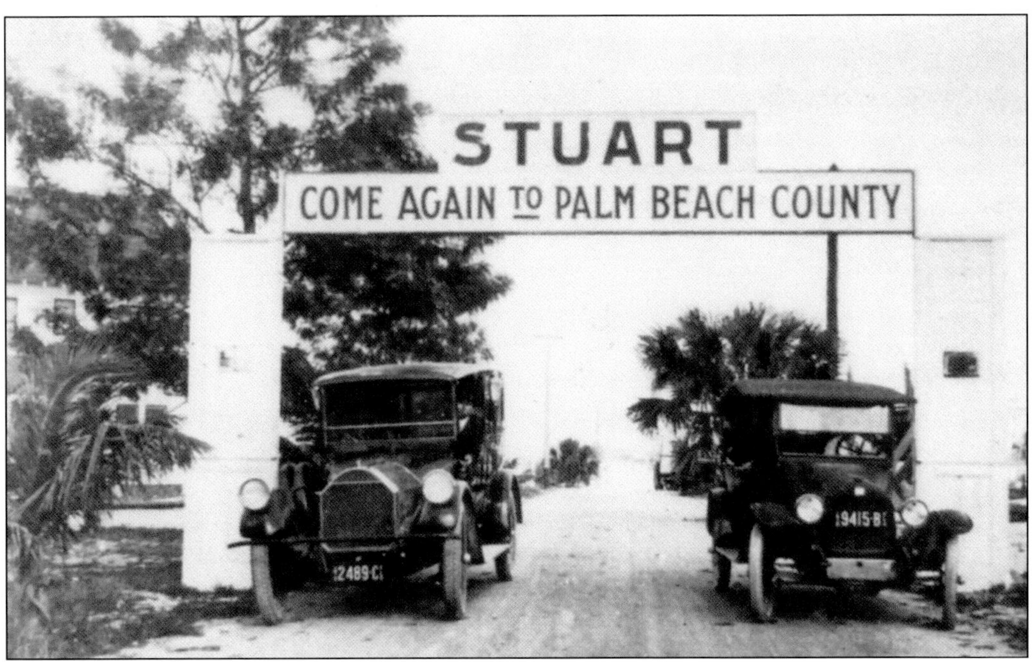

Here is the welcome sign for all those arriving in Stuart in the 1910s. It was located near the Stuart House-Hotel, which was to the left of the gateway and close to the train station. Beginning in 1909, the St. Lucie River was the northern boundary of the newly created Palm Beach County. North of the river was St. Lucie County. (Courtesy of the Sandra and Tom Thurlow.)

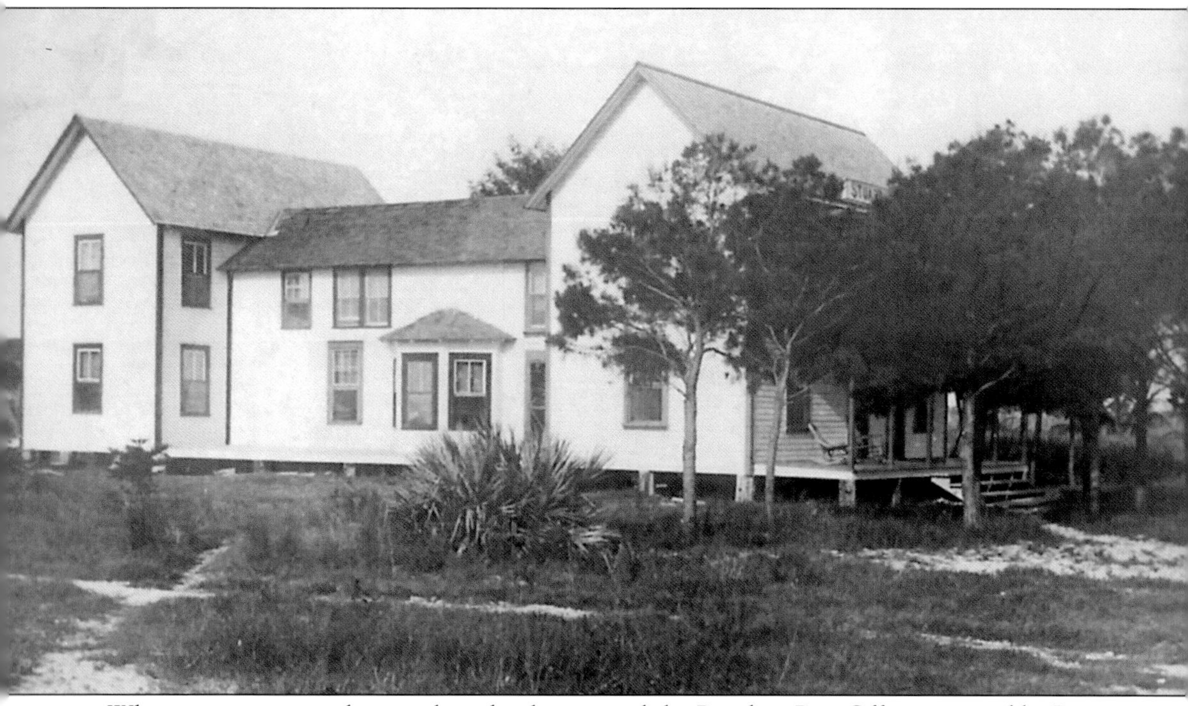

What once was a simple store, boardinghouse, and the Potsdam Post Office operated by Broster Kitching in the mid-1890s was now, in the 1910s, a first-class hotel, the Stuart House-Hotel. There were two additions placed onto the original wooden structure, one in the center and one to the far left. The new owners were Charles and Edith Kitching Glass. In 1916, there were grander expansions made to the hotel due to its popularity as a destination for both visitors and locals. (Courtesy of Doug Witham.)

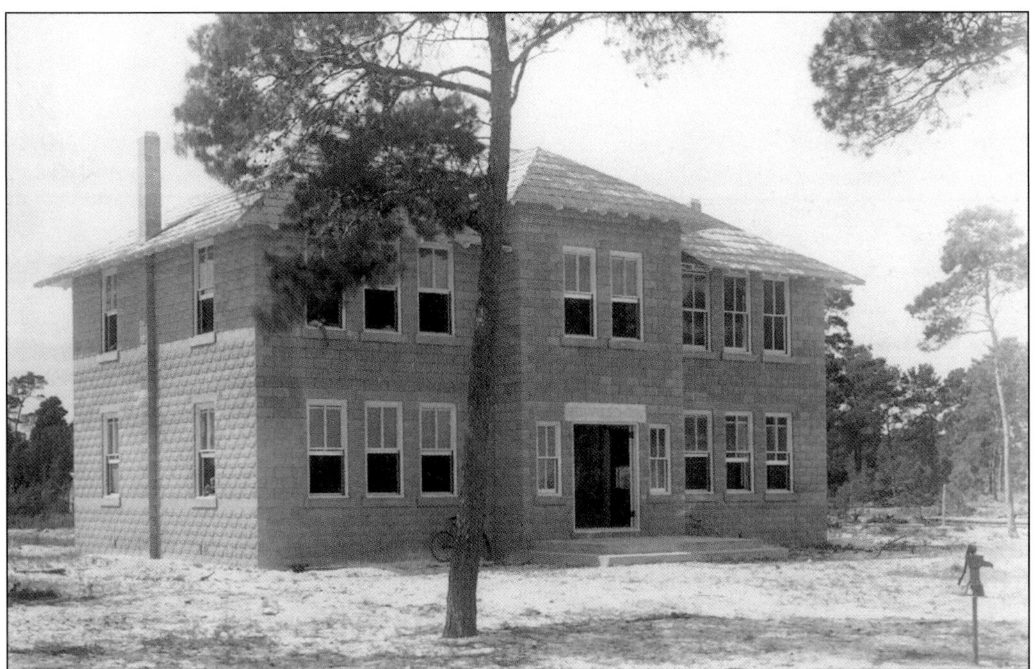

With population growth, Stuart also had more children who needed schooling. The inadequate two-room school, situated close to Osceola Street, was replaced by a two-story, four-room concrete-block building, featuring Frank Frazier faux blocks all around the outside. It was located on Fourth Street (East Ocean Boulevard) and opened in May 1909 with a capacity of about 120 students. Many residents commented that the school was "way out of town in the woods." (Courtesy of Martha Penhale Cuthbert.)

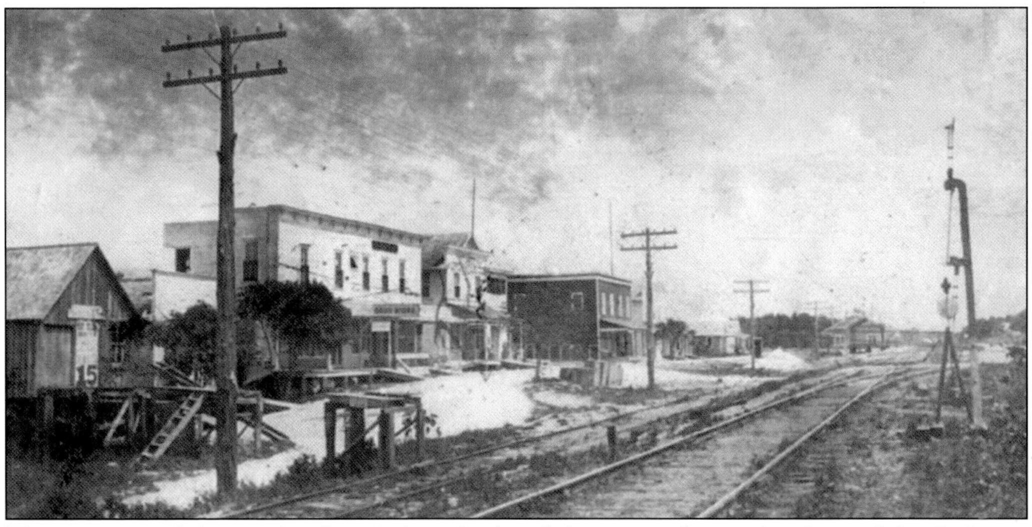

The commercial district developed along Railroad Avenue and near the shore of the St. Lucie River. The simple, frontier-style structures each represented a steady expansion of the community over the last couple of years. Visible at far right, close to the tracks, a new passenger train depot had been constructed by March 1913, sparked by the monetary donations from local businessmen Charles C. Chillingworth, Stanley Kitching, and Henry C. Feroe. (Courtesy of Karen Hartman Malfregeot.)

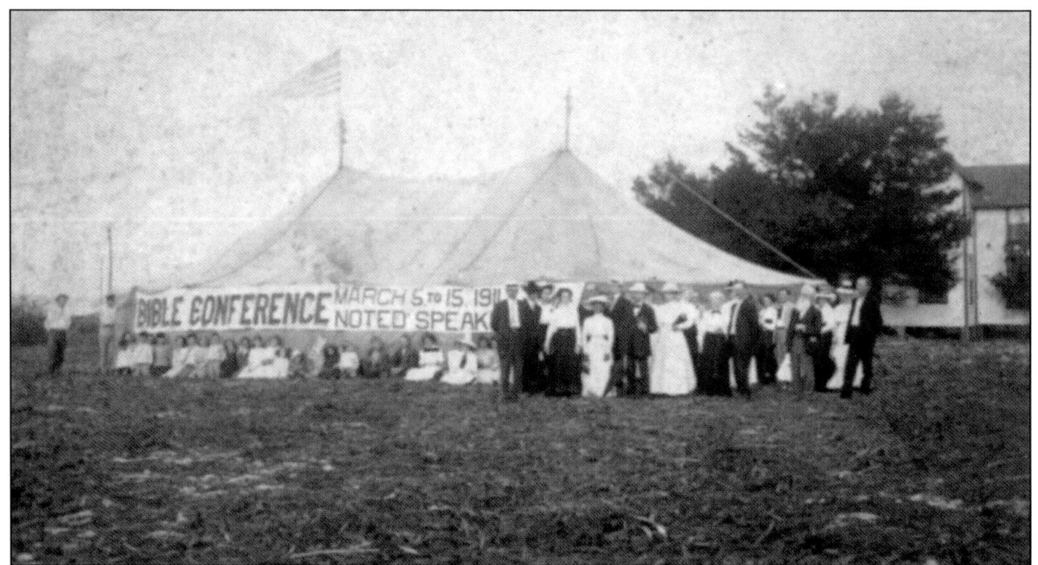

A Bible conference was held for a couple years in Stuart on the grounds near the Stuart House-Hotel (right). Local resident Rev. Neil McQuarrie founded the "Gospel Navy" at Stuart in 1909 to provide gospel services to people in remote locations. Those attending this 1911 conference are, from left to right, Mr. Schwartz, Dr. Charles E. Roberts, Mattie B. Roberts (no hat), Rev. Harry H. and Mary Louisa Jones, Susan Kitching, Rev. Neil McQuarrie, Broster Kitching (beard), two unidentified, and James R. Pomeroy. (Courtesy of Charles and Mattie Roberts, SHM.)

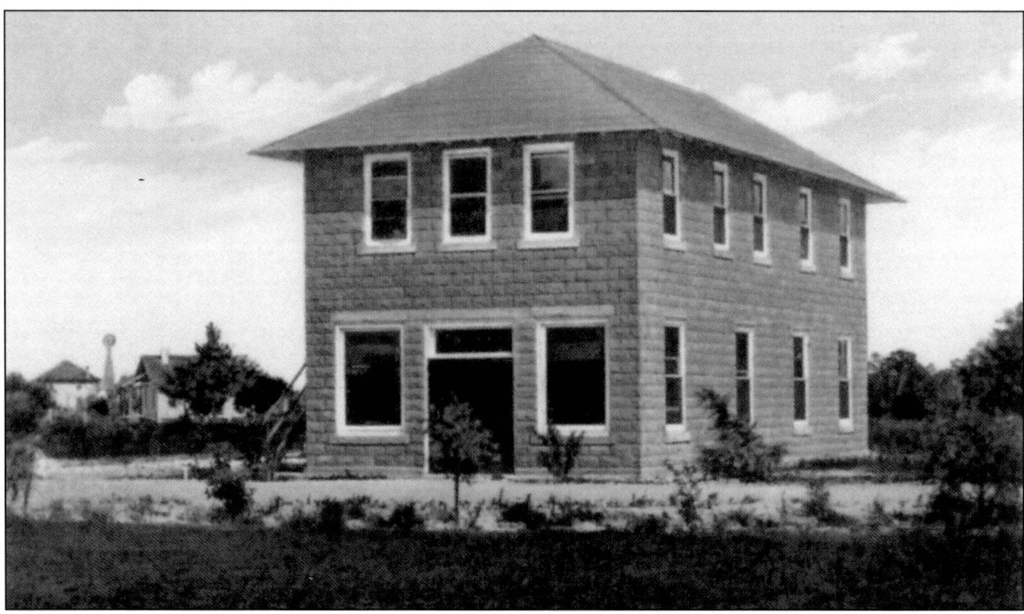

Henry C. Feroe saw the need for a bank to be established, so he donated land in 1912 at the corner of St. Lucie and Osceola Avenues. Walter Kitching was the Bank of Stuart's president, and other founding members included Charles C. Chillingworth, Edward A. Fuge, George W. Parks, Stanley Kitching, and Henry C. Feroe, all prominent businessmen. This first bank opened November 1, 1912, with capital stock totaling $15,000. By January 1913, it had 126 depositors. (Courtesy of Doug Witham.)

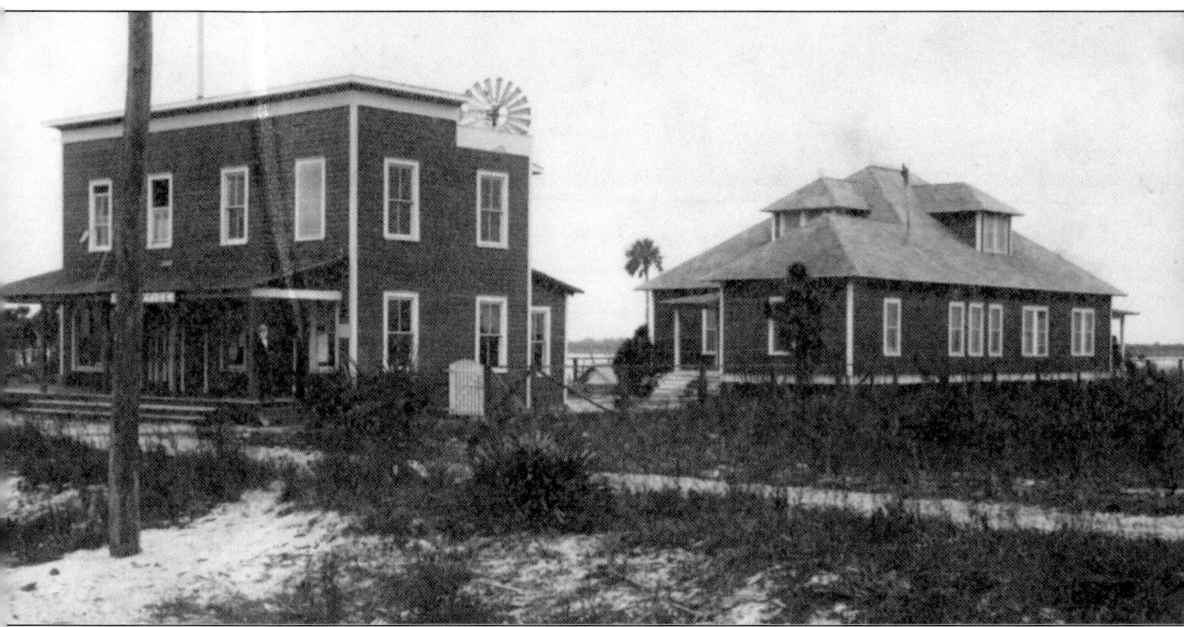

Situated between the railroad tracks and the St. Lucie River was the business building (left) and behind it, the home of Broster Kitching (right). His sister Susan Kitching also lived in the house with her brother. Constructed for brothers Walter and Broster, the front two-story wooden building served as Susan Kitching's Necessity Shop, a telegraph office, the Stuart Post Office between about 1905 and 1913, and a boardinghouse upstairs. Broster remained postmaster until his retirement in mid-1913. (Courtesy of Sandra and Tom Thurlow.)

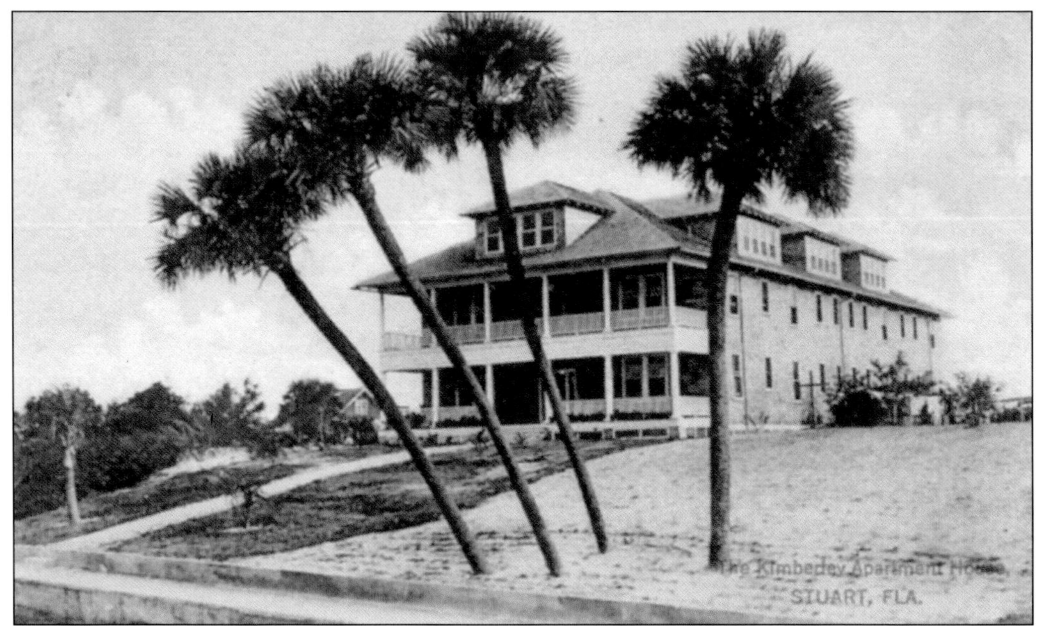

On original homesteaded land of Otto Stypmann, Charles Porter acquired the former pineapple acreage in 1909. Elmer and Mary Kimberly of Pennsylvania purchased several lots in the Porter Addition in 1913. They hired contractor Sam Matthews at a cost of $17,000 to build a modern, two-story, 21-room apartment building with third-level dormers on Cherokee Avenue (Seminole Street) overlooking the St. Lucie River. (Courtesy of Doug Witham.)

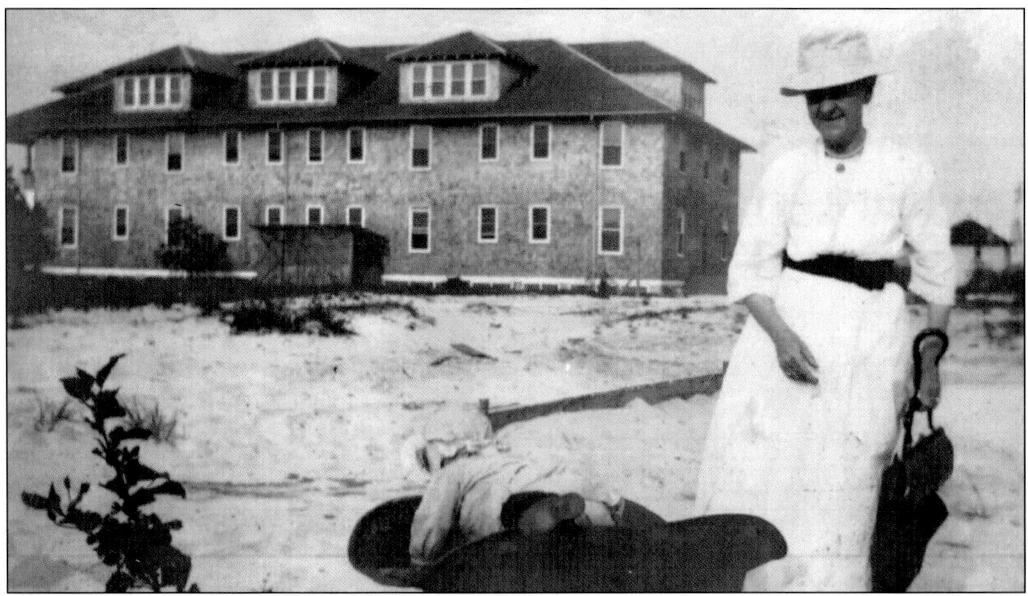

The Kimberly Apartments were the elite of housing, popular with the winter residents. Each apartment featured utilities, gas, running water, a furnished 12-by-18-foot living room, a fully equipped kitchenette, and a bedroom supplied with linens. A special feature added by contractor Sam Matthews was a hidden bed that was accessible by pulling out the drawers of what appeared to be a chest of drawers. The woman and child pictured here are unidentified. (Courtesy of the Edith Coventry Collection, Elliott Museum.)

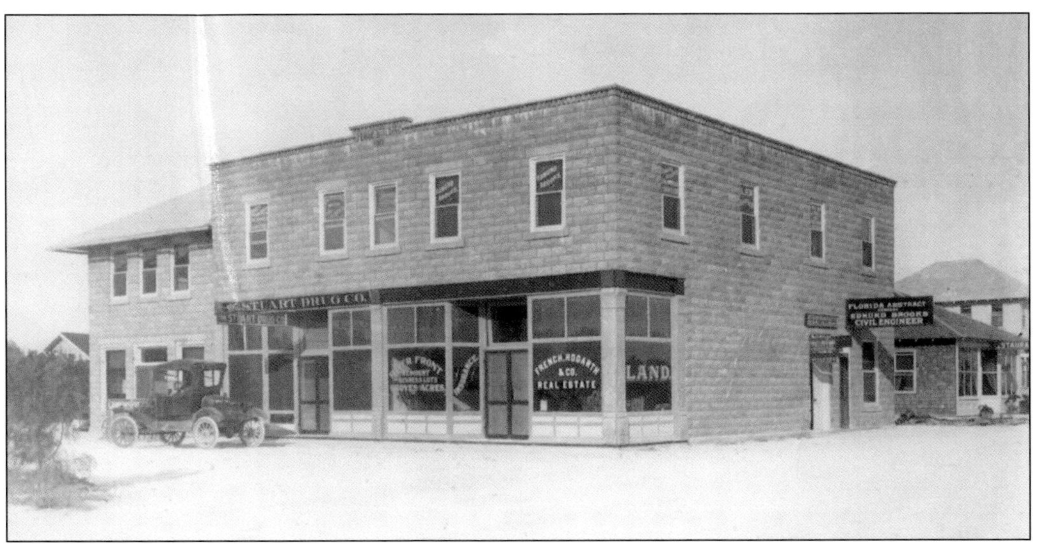

In 1913, Henry C. Feroe had built a business building next to the new Bank of Stuart. The two-story, concrete-and-Dade-County-pine building featured faux-stone concrete blocks on the outside, a specialty of local manufacturer Frank Frazier. The inscriptions "Feroe Building" and "1913" were placed near the top of the structure. Two of the earliest tenants were Stuart Drug Co. and French-Hogarth real estate/insurance firm. Other businesses rented several of the upstairs offices.

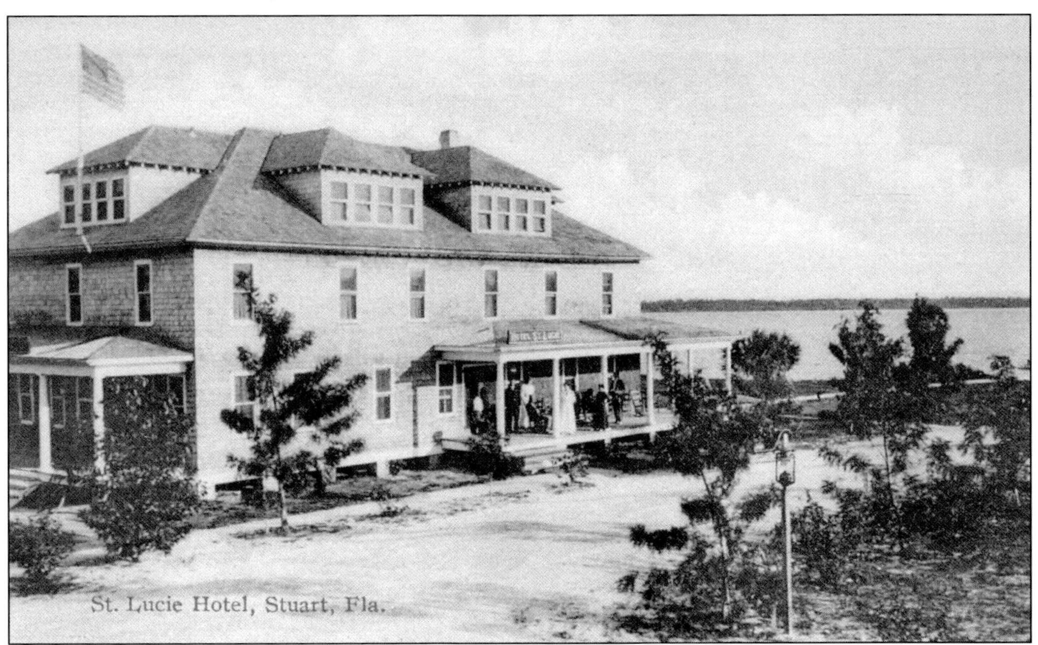

The Hotel St. Lucie (St. Lucie Hotel) was built in early 1913 for Henry C. Feroe by local contractor Sam Matthews and was located across from the Bank of Stuart. It featured 25 modernly furnished rooms, a dining room, and many amenities for visitors. Being so close to the St. Lucie River and the commercial district of Stuart was a bonus. (Courtesy of Sandra and Tom Thurlow.)

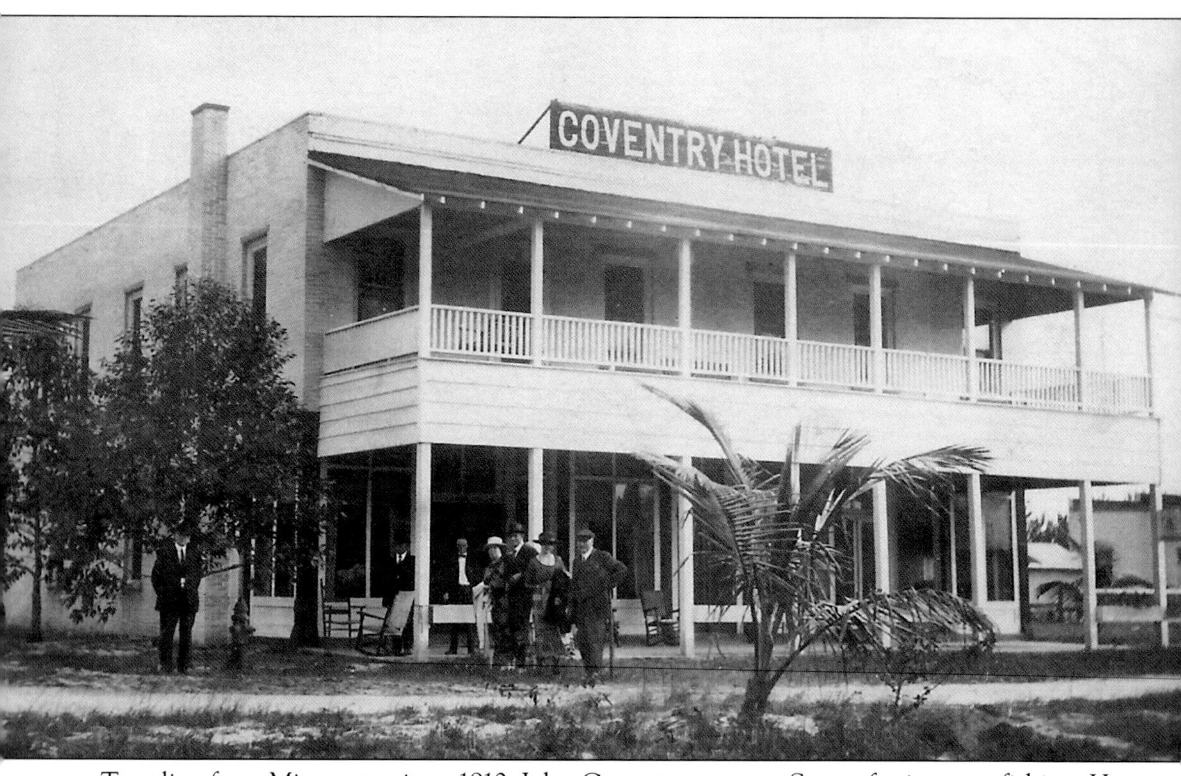

Traveling from Minnesota since 1910, John Coventry came to Stuart for its great fishing. He constructed the Coventry Hotel in 1914 to accommodate other fishing fans. The two-story brick building had the lower level for shops and the upper for rental hotel rooms. One of the largest structures at the time, it measured 50 by 45 feet, costing over $5,000. From left to right are three unidentified men, and then Coventry family members Charlotte, Frank, Edith, and John. Just behind the hotel to the right was the first Lyric Theatre, built by John Hancock in 1914. (Courtesy of Doug Witham.)

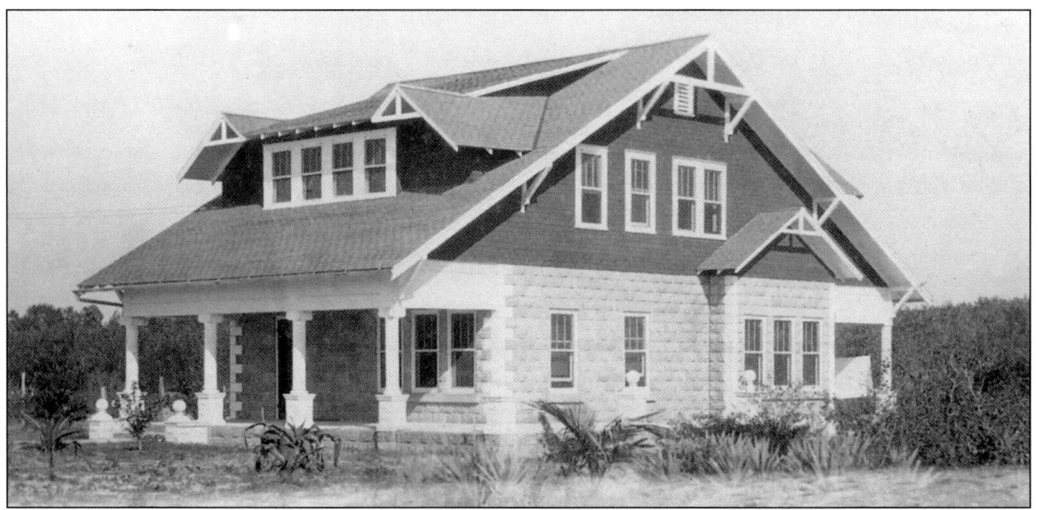

Frank J. Frazier, who had been manufacturing a very steady and attractive faux block used in the exterior construction of several buildings in Stuart, built a home for his widow mother, Margaret Frazier, in 1914. The Frazier family had arrived at the wilderness area along the St. Lucie River in 1887 and homesteaded 160 acres. Margaret's new second home located in Frazier Crescent, south of Frazier Creek, still faces Avenue E (US 1) today. (Courtesy of Dave Murray.)

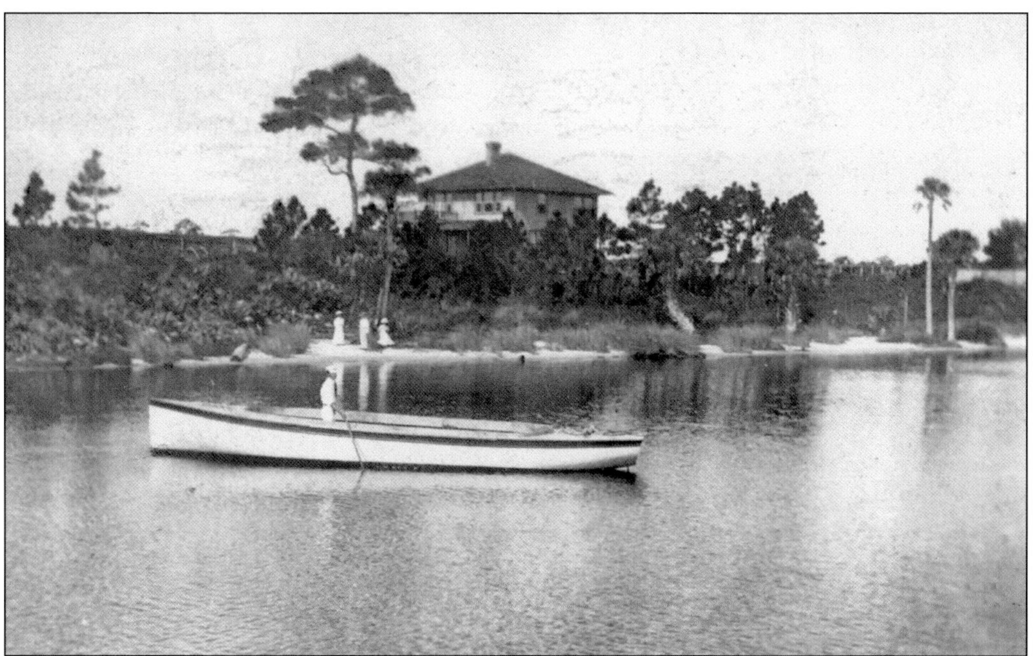

Lisle D. Tucker married Georgia Capron in 1901 in New York. She suffered from tuberculosis, and Lisle felt she would be better in a warmer climate. They came to Stuart, where Lisle was a fruit farmer by 1906, and he had a fine two-story home named Las Piñas built along the St. Lucie, which faced north. Standing on the shore are, from left to right, Georgia, her father Eliab W. Capron, and her sister Jessie. Lisle is in his boat *Dione*. Georgia Tucker died October 30, 1909. Lisle remained a few years in Stuart until he went to serve in the military during World War I. (Courtesy of Sandra and Tom Thurlow.)

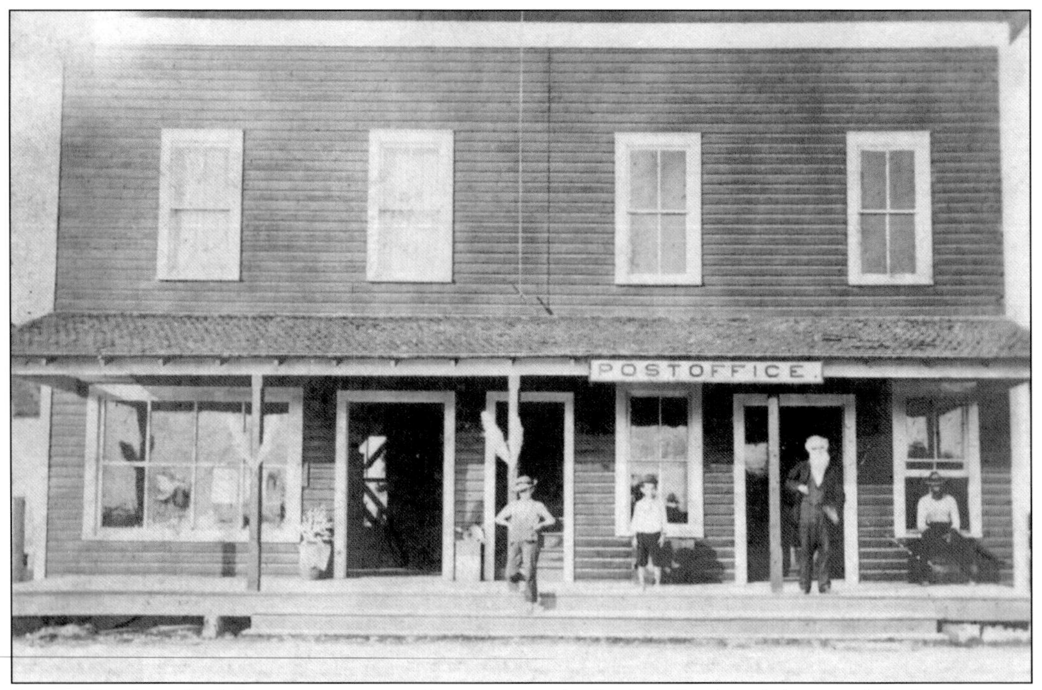

Broster Kitching had this two-story wooden structure built along Railroad Avenue (Flagler Avenue) about 1905 to serve as his sister Susan Kitching's Necessity Shop, as well as to house the town telegraph office, a boardinghouse, and a post office. Broster was postmaster. The elderly man with the beard standing to the right was Broster Kitching. (Courtesy of Jo Marie Paradise.)

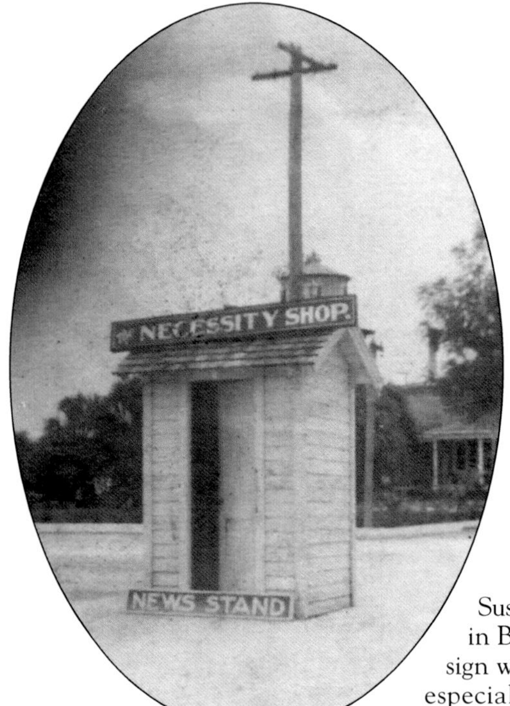

Susan Kitching's Necessity Shop was actually located in Broster Kitching's post office building. The shop's sign was often removed and placed in other locations, especially at Halloween, by the local young people. (Courtesy of MCHS, Elliott Museum.)

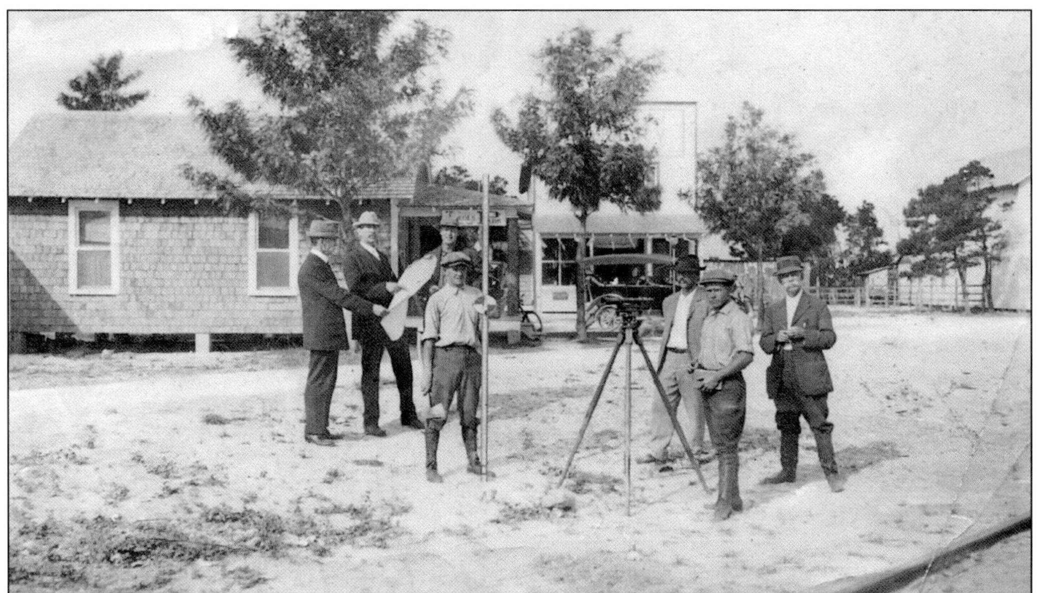

In 1914, Stuart's leaders, including Mayor McDonald, are surveying the area that would become A1A (Dixie Highway) parallel to the railroad tracks. With a new road on the other side of the tracks, the plan was to promote new businesses on that side. The surveyors are, from left to right, unidentified, Jackson B. McDonald with survey paper, and five unidentified. The sign on the building at left reads "Lincoln Park." Bentel's Bakery in the background at right was an early business in that area, with its new location there in March 1907 at Avenue C (Akron Avenue) and Second Street. (Courtesy of Karen Hartman Malfregeot.)

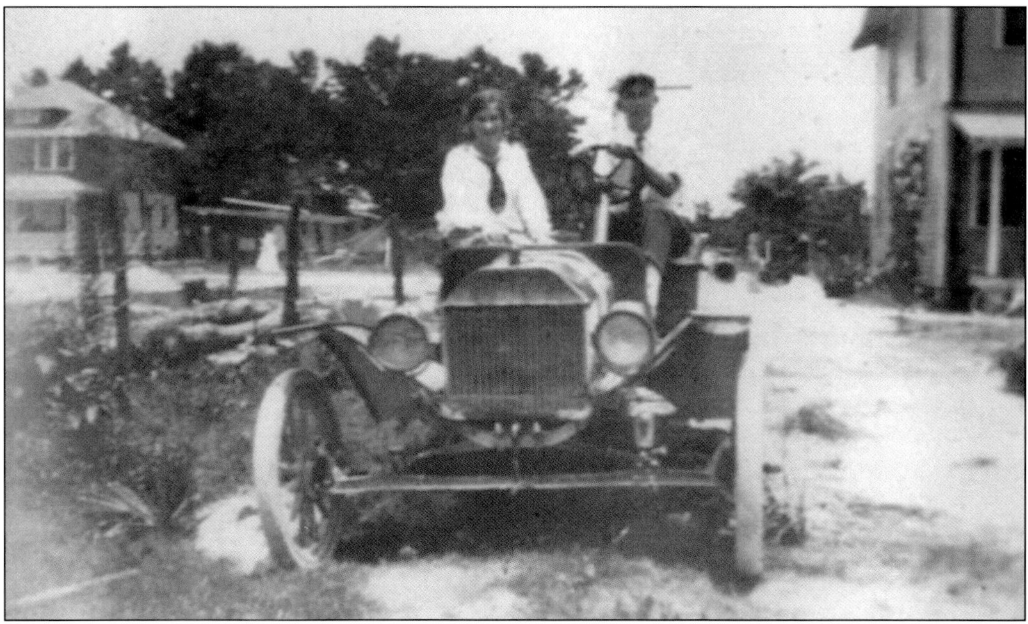

With the growth of businesses and homes in Stuart, more of the new motorized vehicles made an appearance. Roads were still dirt or occasionally crushed oyster shells as a roadbed, making a smooth ride difficult. In the Ford car, nicknamed "Henry," was Mary McDonald with a friend going for a casual ride in 1916. (Courtesy of Karen Hartman Malfregeot.)

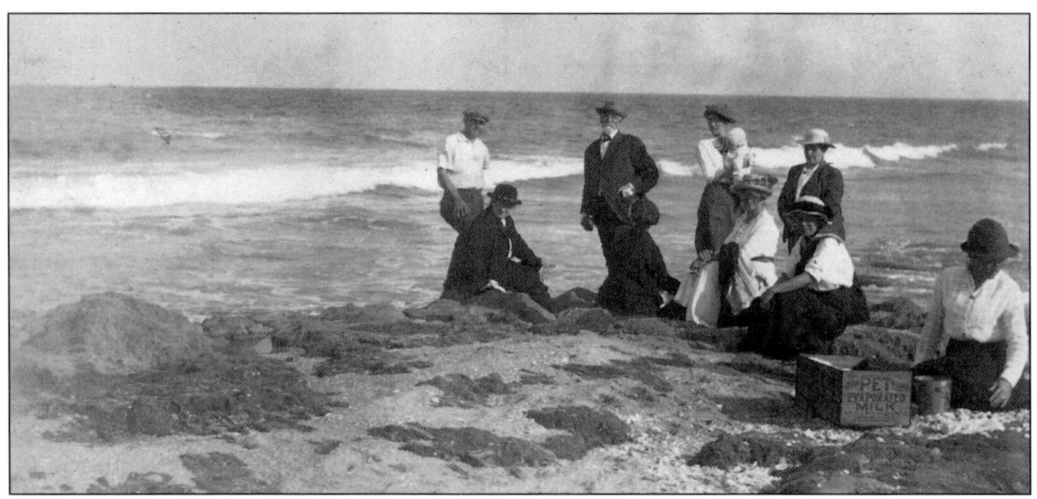

Besides the St. Lucie and Indian Rivers, recreation included a trip to the beach on nearby Hutchinson Island. Young and old alike enjoyed the occasional trip out to the shore of the Atlantic Ocean, where a picnic could be enjoyed. On this occasion in February 1916, it was a beach picnic in honor of a Mrs. Yost. (Courtesy of Karen Hartman Malfregeot.)

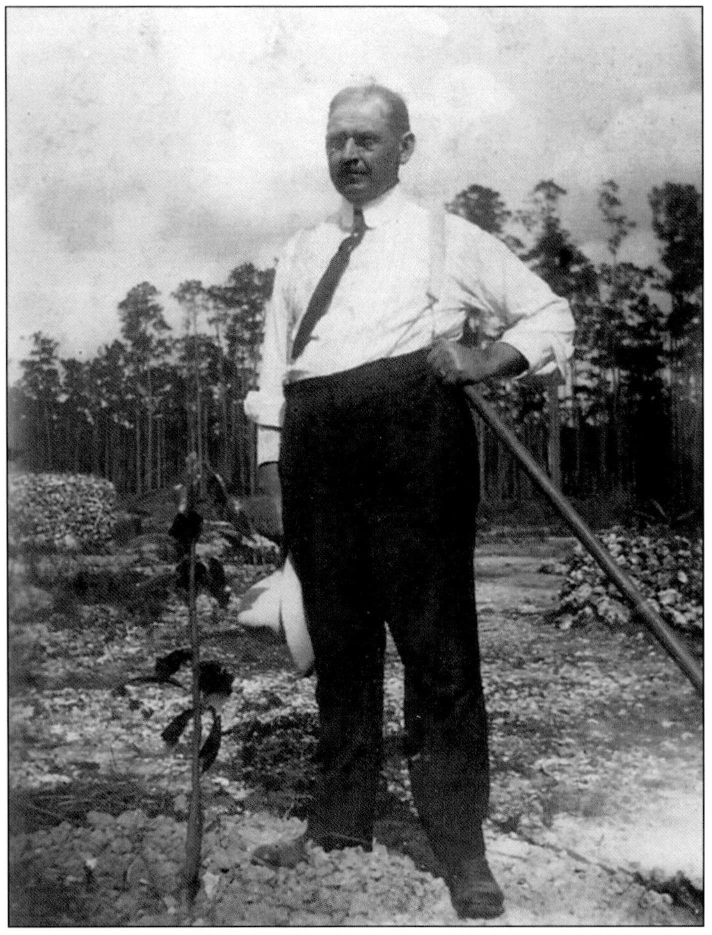

Many newcomers staked out acreage outside the town, in what was known as Tropical Farms, along the South Fork of the St. Lucie River. Henry N. Gaines left Kansas in the early 20th century, where he had been a teacher and then a newspaper owner. He saw the possibilities of agriculture in the Stuart area and developed Tropical Fruit Farms, producing grapefruit and orange orchards and then a large dairy and poultry ranch. Gaines is pictured with his first citrus tree planting in 1913. (Courtesy of Frank Clark.)

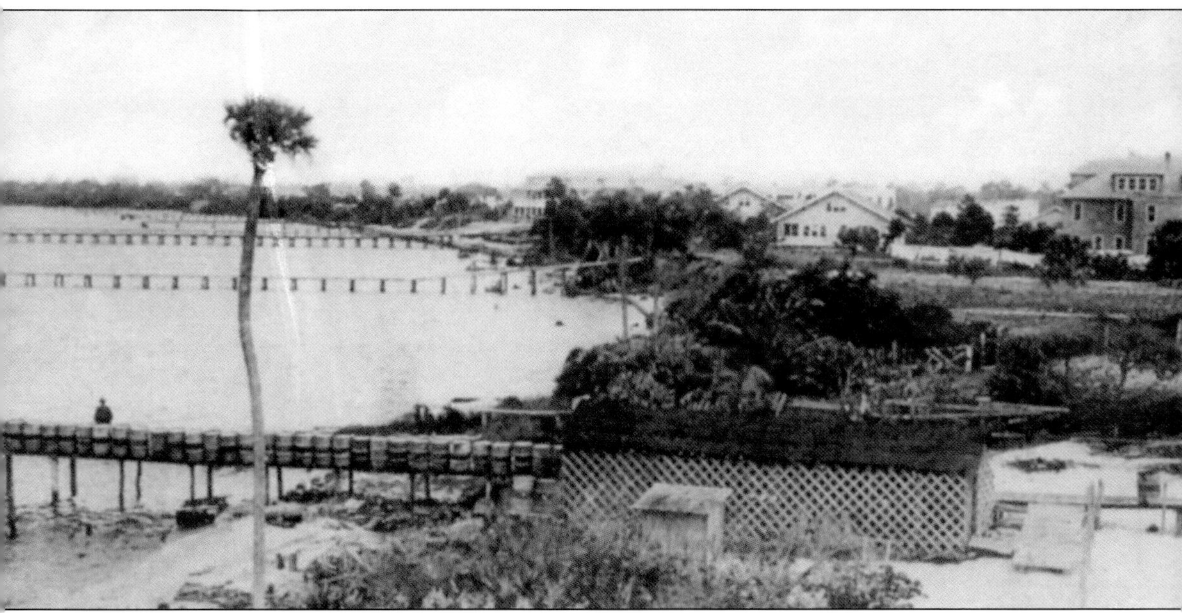

This is a wonderful view of Stuart along the north side facing the St. Lucie River in 1914. Numerous docks jut out into the river, with businesses, hotels, apartments, and homes on or near the shoreline. Most notable was the new St. Lucie Hotel on the far right and the Kimberly Apartments with third-floor dormers at center. The oil drums on the dock were for sale at the nearby George Parks Store. (Courtesy of Doug Witham.)

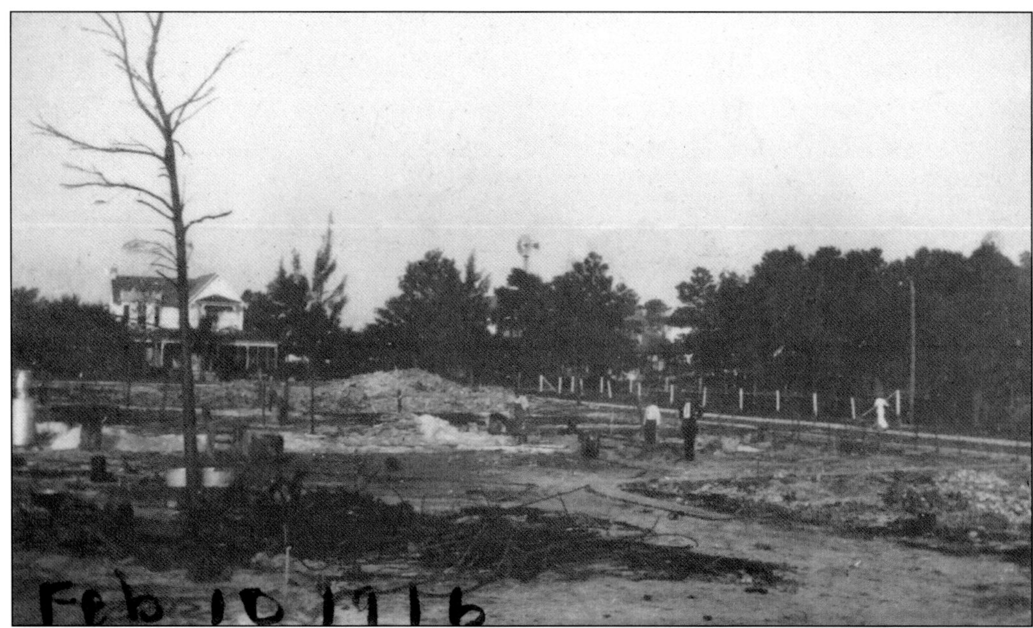

It was a day of celebration and tragedy on New Year's Day 1916. Most Stuart citizens had gone to Palm City across the St. Lucie River for a holiday picnic sponsored by the Palm Beach County Land Company. When a plume of black smoke was seen by the people in Palm City, a cry was heard: "Stuart is burning down!" Every able-bodied person immediately returned to help put out the fire. Businesses, homes, shops, and even the 1907 Methodist church were destroyed. Pictured here on February 10, 1916, people were still surveying the destruction. (Courtesy of McDonald and Thurlow families.)

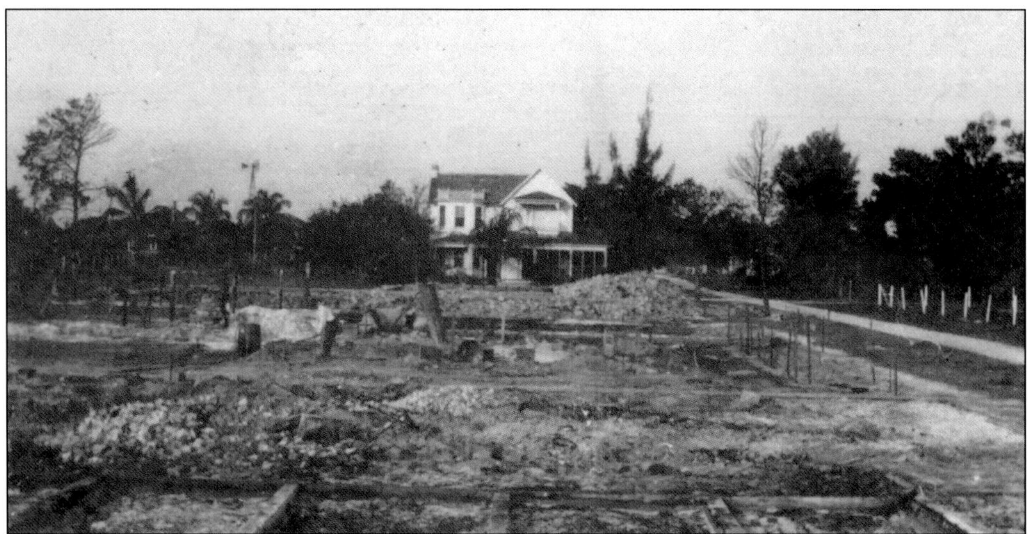

The January 1, 1916, fire scorched nearly everything in its path. Everyone was astonished after all the flames were put out that the George Thomas house, located at the far end of the block at the corner of Avenue D and First Street, was undamaged. True, neighbors were hurling water using hand buckets to help prevent any flying embers igniting the building. This 1904 two-story wood-frame home built by Thomas was lived in by the family for decades until the death of his daughter Pauline Thomas Edenfield in 2002. (Courtesy of McDonald and Thurlow families.)

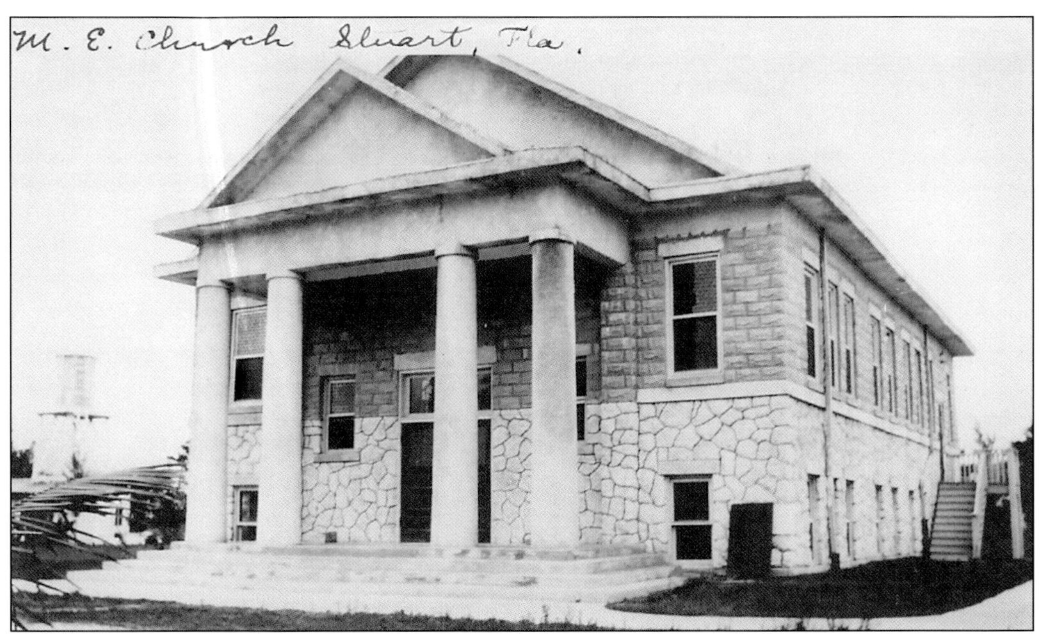

The Methodist church ruined in the January 1916 fire was rebuilt within a few months at a cost of approximately $15,000, on the site of the former church. It remained the congregation's sanctuary for decades. (Courtesy of Karen Hartman Malfregeot.)

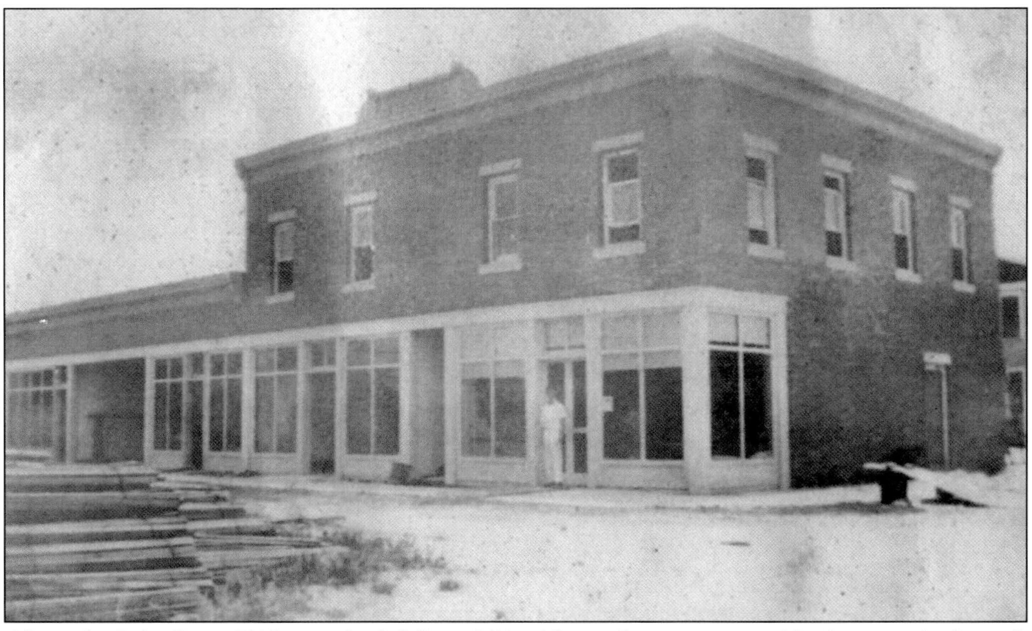

Also rebuilt by June 1916 was the McDonald building, this time using block instead of wood. Standing in the doorway of the new building is Jackson B. McDonald. As expressed in the 1916 *Stuart Messenger* newspaper, "The fire will only temporarily retard the growth of Stuart, for our people are made of the material that allows nothing to discourage them in Stuart's future. Stuart Will Win." (Courtesy of Karen Hartman Malfregeot.)

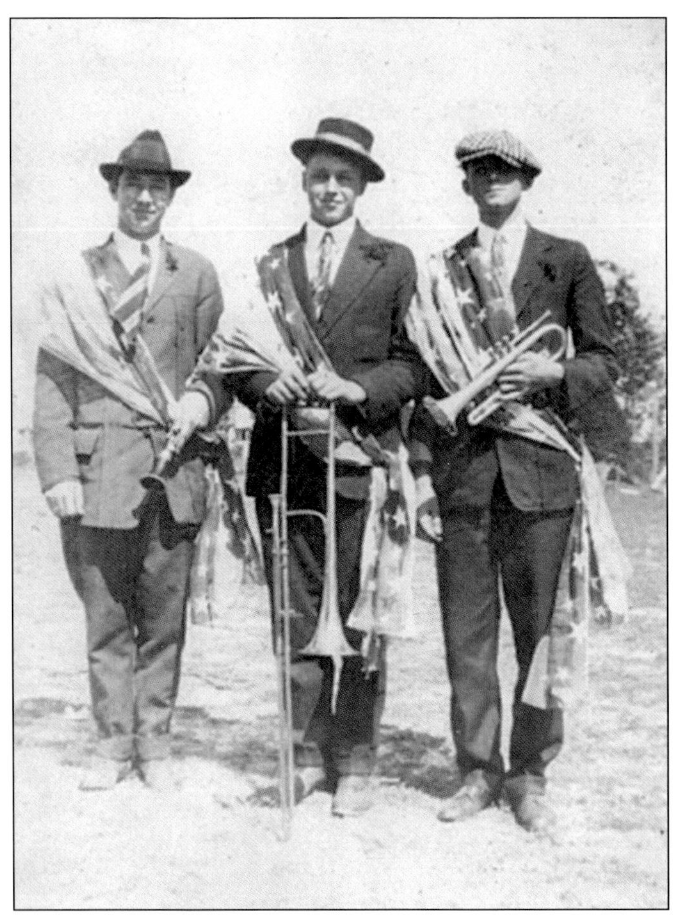

These three young Stuart fellows were part of the new flagpole and flag-raising ceremony on February 22, 1916, in front of the schoolhouse. Patriotic in dress with musical instruments in hand are, from left to right, Jack McDonald, age 16; Darrel Smith, age 16; and Leeson Hogarth, age 15. (Courtesy of Karen Hartman Malfregeot.)

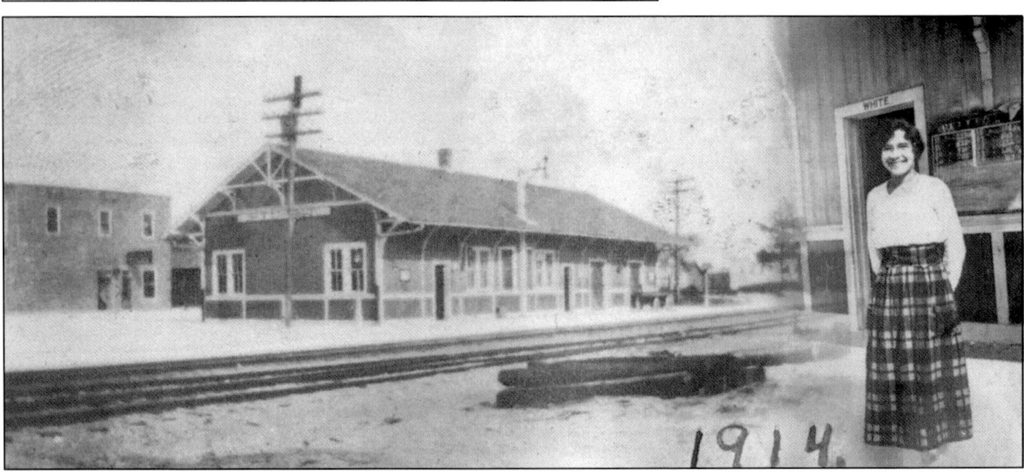

Mary Elizabeth McDonald, daughter of Jackson B. and Elizabeth McDonald, was born in 1902 in Oklahoma, coming to Stuart with her family in November 1912. Mary thrived along the St. Lucie River, making many friends. As with everyone in town, they loved to wait for the train's arrival. Note the schedule posted behind Mary. The 1913 Feroe Block business building to the left was across Railroad Avenue and the depot. Mary graduated from the local school in 1919, and in June 1922, she married Ralph W. Hartman. (Courtesy of Karen Hartman Malfregeot.)

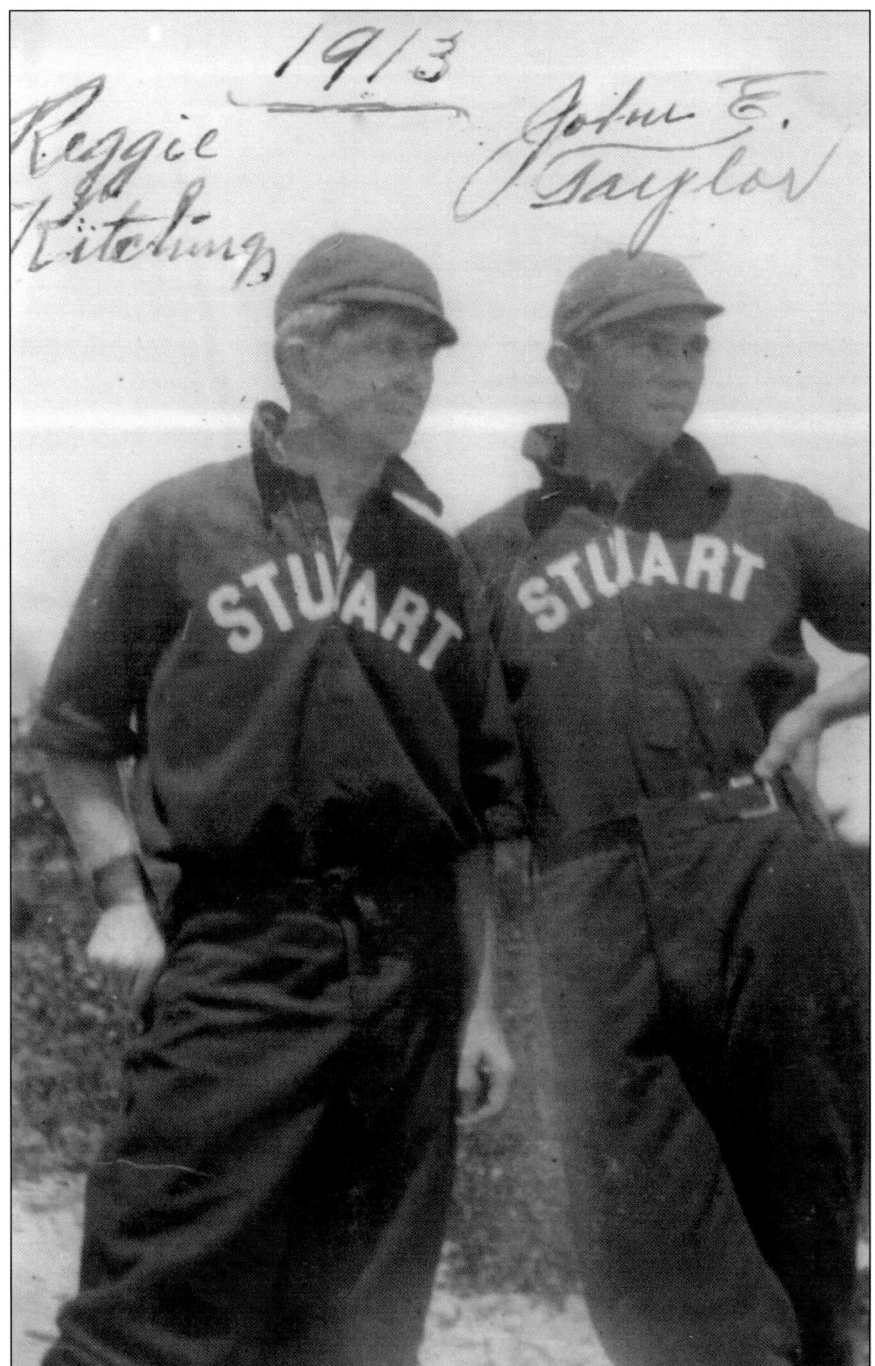

Sports of all types had been popular early on in Stuart. Recreational baseball in the Stuart, Palm City, Hobe Sound, and Jensen Beach areas has been a favorite activity since the early 1900s, with such teams as the Stuart Sailfishers, Palm City Swamp Angels, Acme Baseball Club, and several formed from church groups or civic organizations. Pictured in 1913 playing for Stuart are Reggie Kitching and John E. Taylor, both young businessmen in the community. (Courtesy of Jo Marie Paradise.)

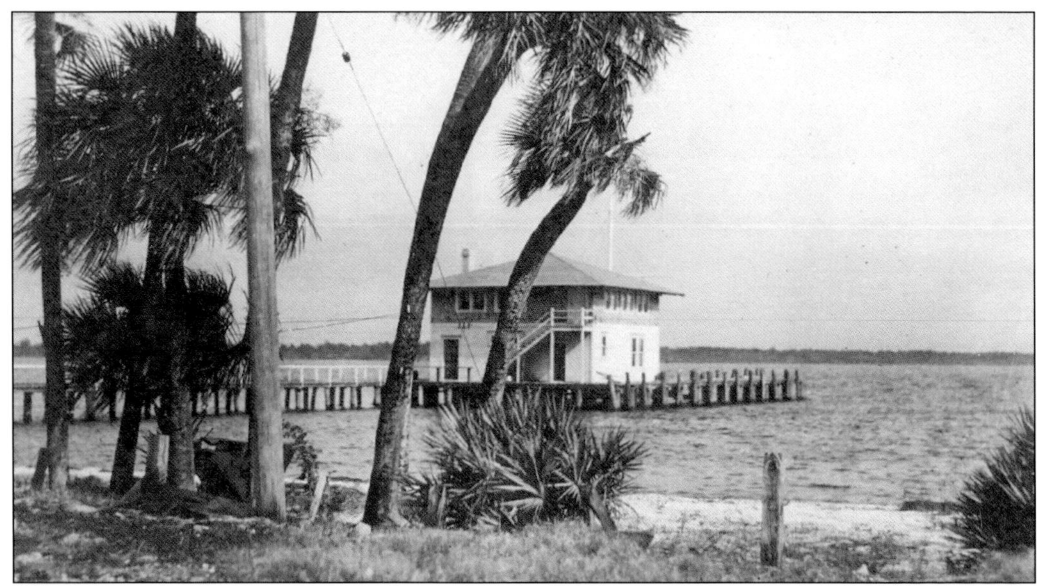

With Stuart's population at approximately 1,000 in December 1916, many of the local citizens wanted a special recreational facility. Six leading businessmen, headed by Stanley Kitching, came up with plans for an offshore two-story wooden club building to be accessible from land by a wharf. It was named the St. Lucie River Yacht Club and was completed along with a 250-foot dock into the river by January 1918.

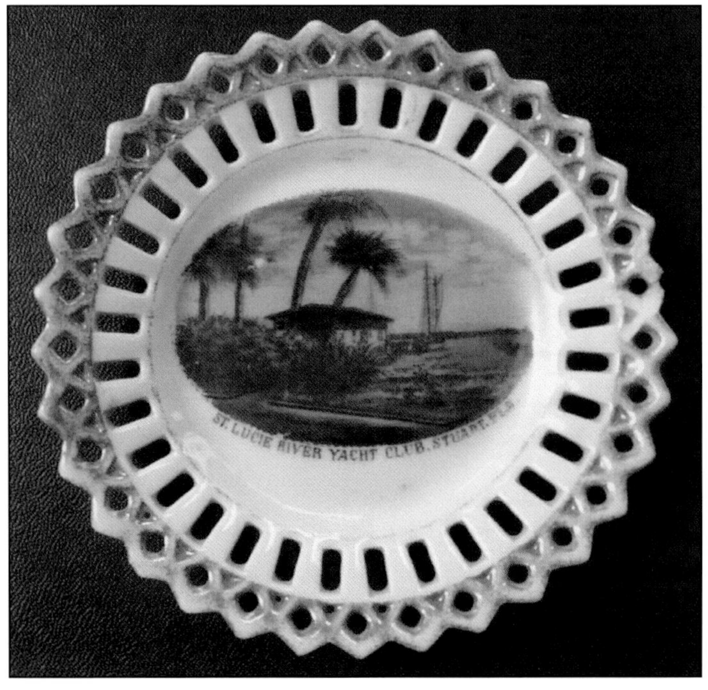

Here is a promotional plate of the St. Lucie River Yacht Club by merchant Stanley Kitching, who used his own funds to promote Stuart. He also had local scenic postcards produced by German printers. (Courtesy of Sandra and Tom Thurlow.)

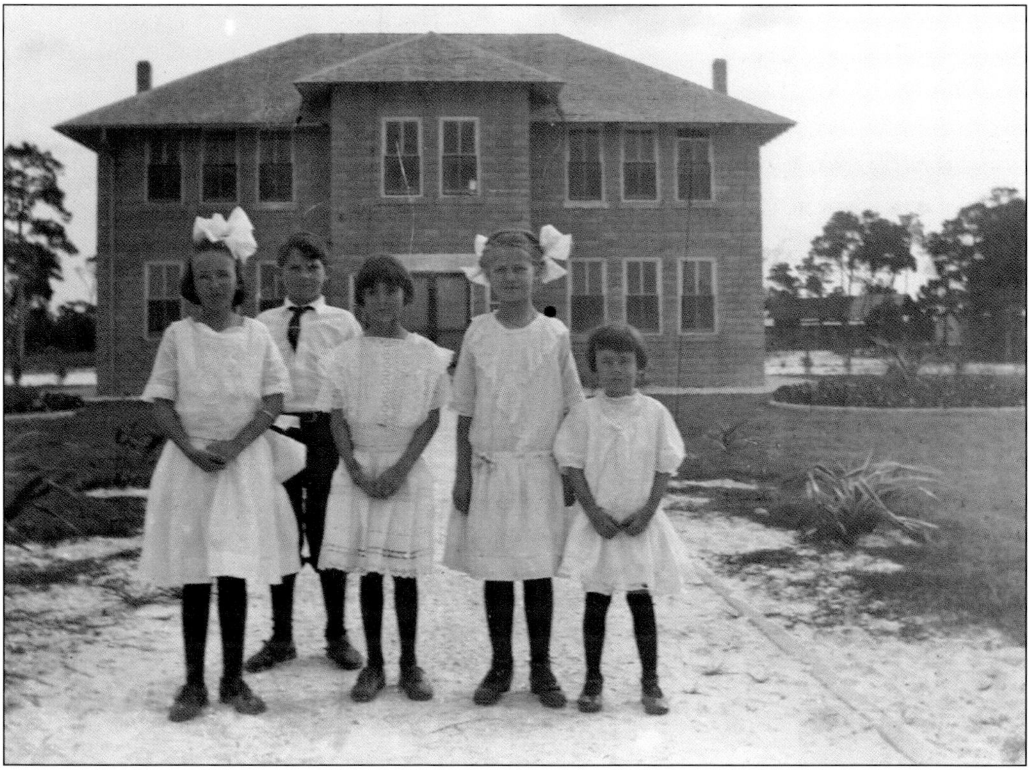

The further growth of population in Stuart quickly filled to capacity the Stuart School, which opened in 1909. The building served all grade levels. Five students pose in front in 1912; Clara E. White is in the center. (Courtesy of Garnett Rushing Early and Stephen Dutcher; Thurlow Collection.)

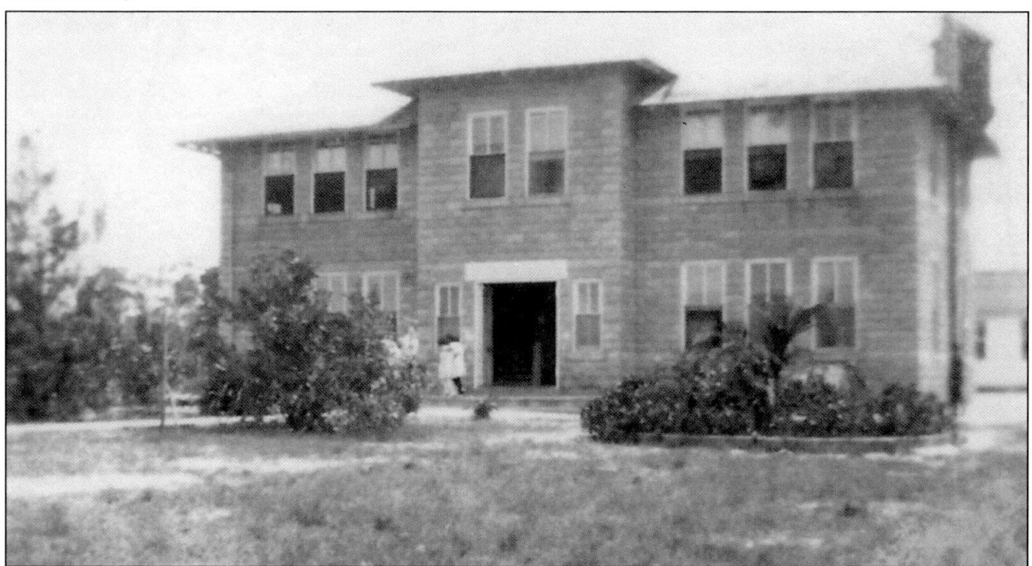

When a proposed 1914 bond issue for a new school did not materialize, a small wood-framed building was erected behind the school to provide additional classroom space (visible at right). A larger school became necessary as enrollment increased over the next few years.

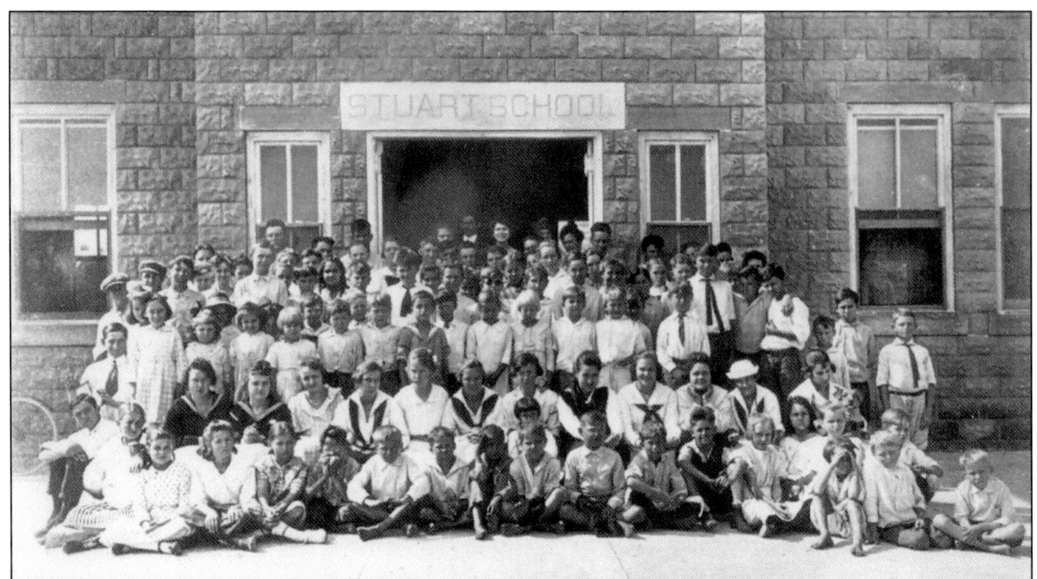

With all classes assembled, nearly 100 students are seen in front of the school in the mid-1910s. The first high school graduation took place in 1916 with just two students, Ethel Madsen and Merle Smith. The class of 1917 had one graduate, Loris B. Eurit. (Courtesy of the Edith Coventry Collection, Elliott Museum.)

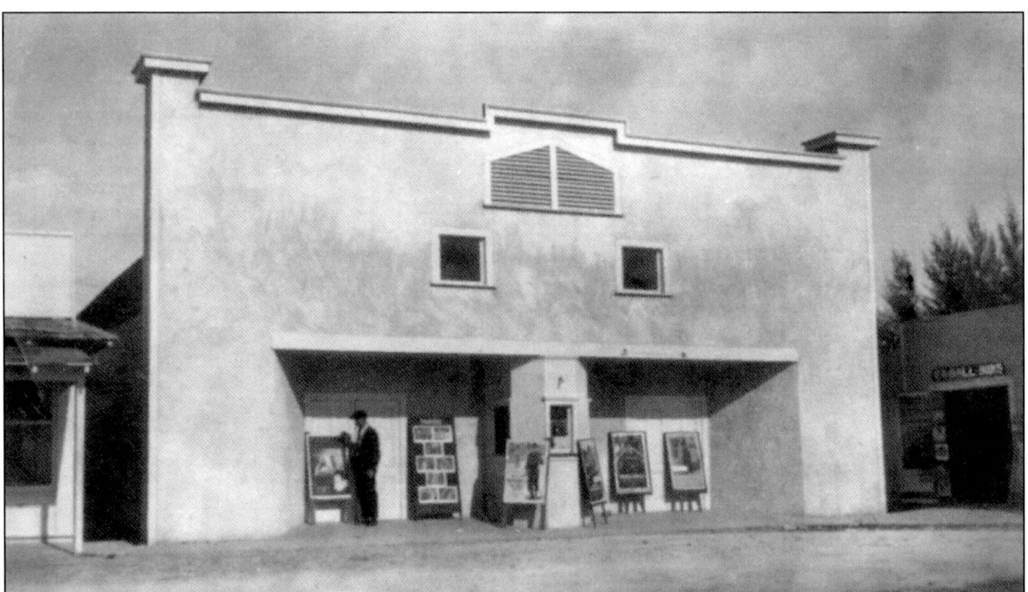

John C. Hancock established the first theater, named the Lyric, in Stuart in June 1914 and located it along Osceola Street, near the Coventry Hotel. Even with its 200-seat capacity, it soon proved to be inadequate. By early 1917, Hancock had architect's plans ready, with Sam Matthews being the contractor for a second, larger Lyric Theatre (pictured) on a site facing the railroad tracks along Railroad Avenue (Flagler Avenue). It opened in 1918. (Courtesy of MCHS, Elliott Museum.)

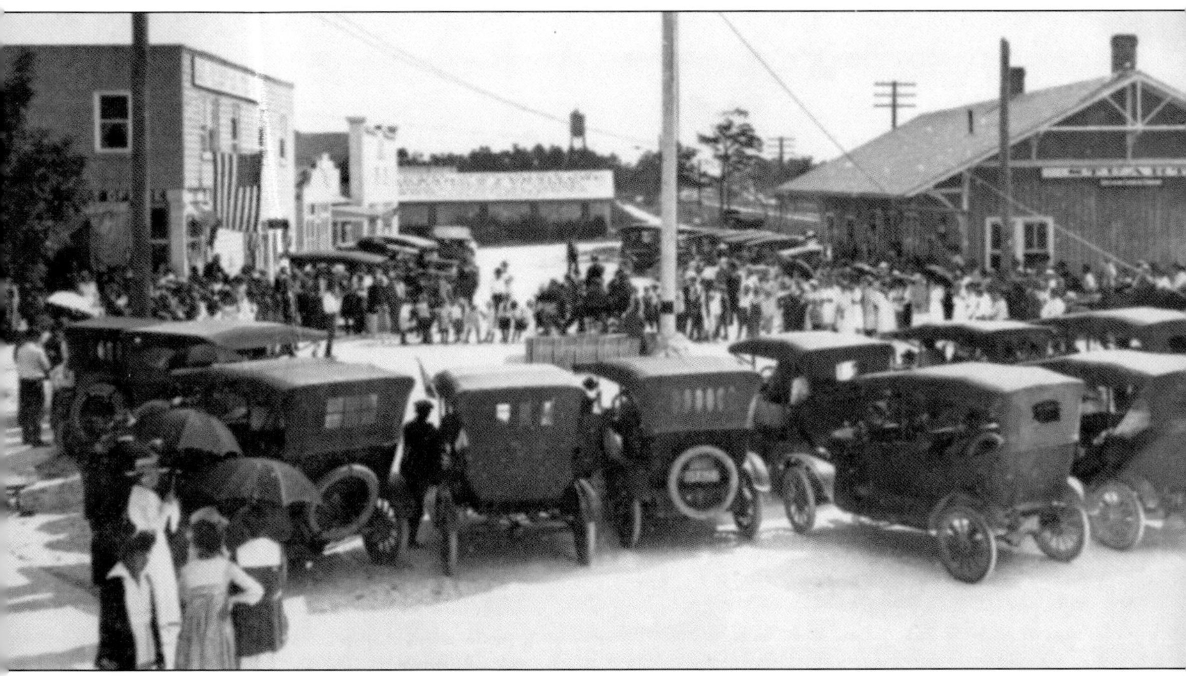

The center of Stuart expanded along the railroad tracks during the 1910s. At the heart was the intersection of Railroad and St. Lucie Avenues, near the passenger train depot. Placed at the intersection in early 1918 was a large cypress flagpole, which had many citizens turn out for its dedication. It was set 10 feet in the ground in concrete. (Courtesy of the Edith Coventry Collection, Elliott Museum.)

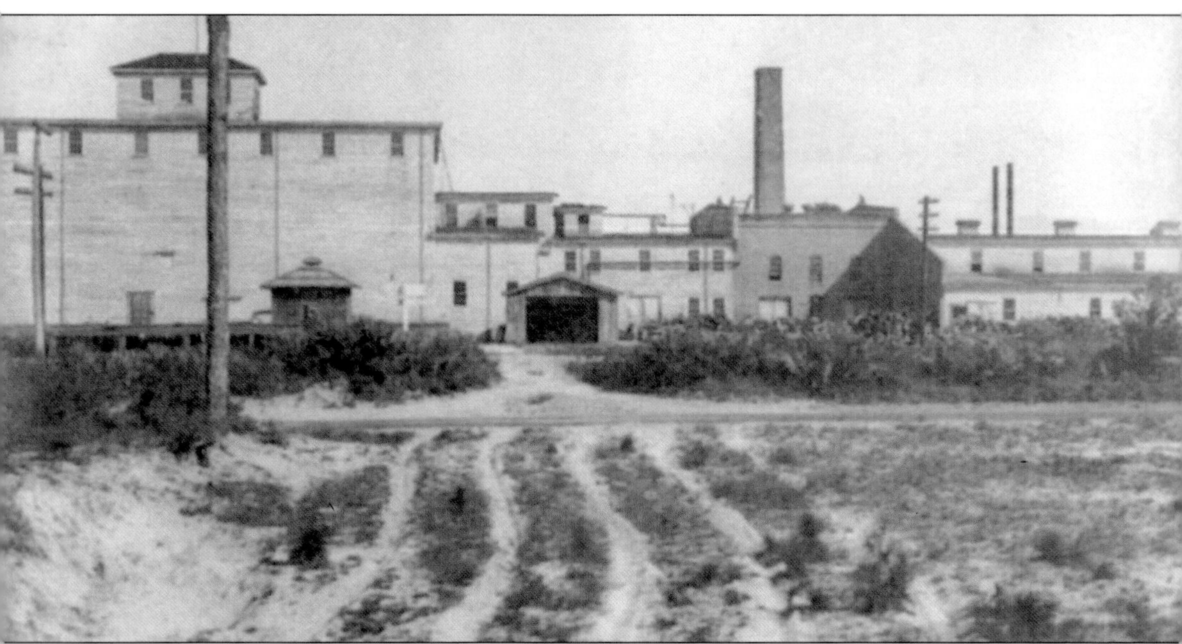

This massive structure built in 1913 north of the St. Lucie River was designed by Magnus J. Palson, a manufacturer of ice plants and fish freezing machinery. It was owned by Capt. R.H. Hammond and other investors, and was named the Florida Freezer and Fertilizer Company. Hammond was not experienced enough in such a major business, causing its failure just before his death. Harry Dutton bought out the factory in early 1917. It had a 200-horsepower engine with machinery for ice making, packing fish, and producing fertilizer from fish remains. Renamed Tropical Produce Company, it was in operation to the end of 1917, but closed down soon after. (Courtesy of Ted Huf.)

A new Walter Kitching Company store was built in February 1914; it was a two-story, frame-and-stucco structure on the corner of West First Street and Avenue E (US 1). During that year, Kitching sold the new store to his son-in-law John E. Taylor for $10,000, with a down payment of $100 and payments to Kitching of as little as a dollar whenever Taylor could manage it. (Courtesy of Jo Marie Paradise.)

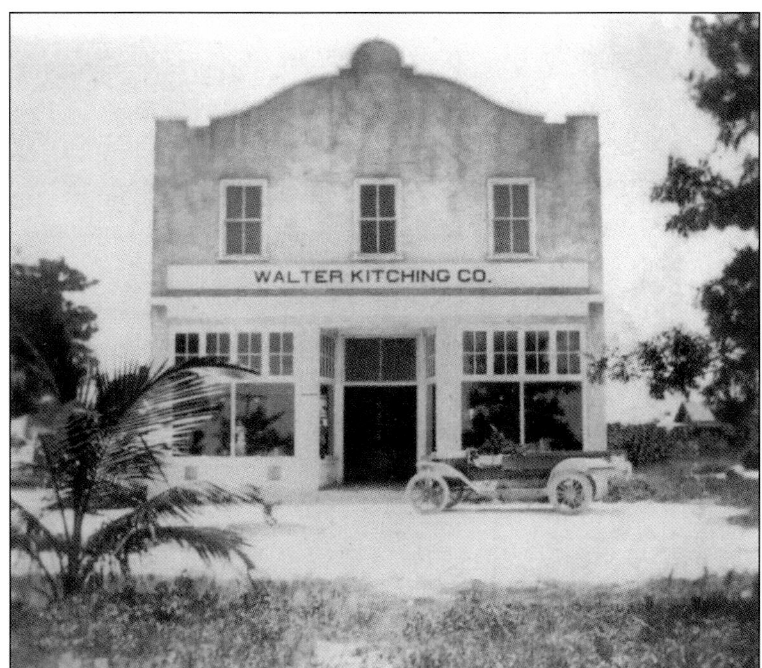

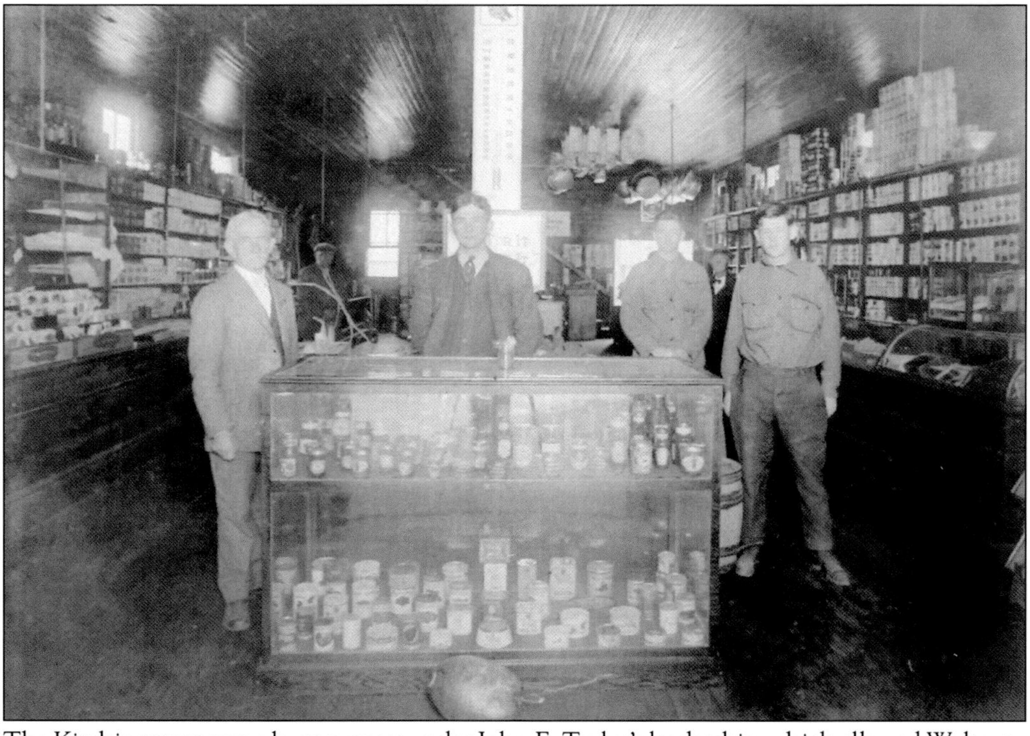

The Kitching store was a huge success under John E. Taylor's leadership, which allowed Walter to retire in 1917. Working in the store in February 1917 are, from left to right, Walter Kitching, John E. Taylor, Loris Eurit, and Jack H. McDonald. The building was sold by Taylor in early 1923 to Raulerson Grocery Company. During an August 1928 hurricane, the store's roof and the front of the building were blown off and water damaged the structure. (Courtesy of Jo Marie Paradise.)

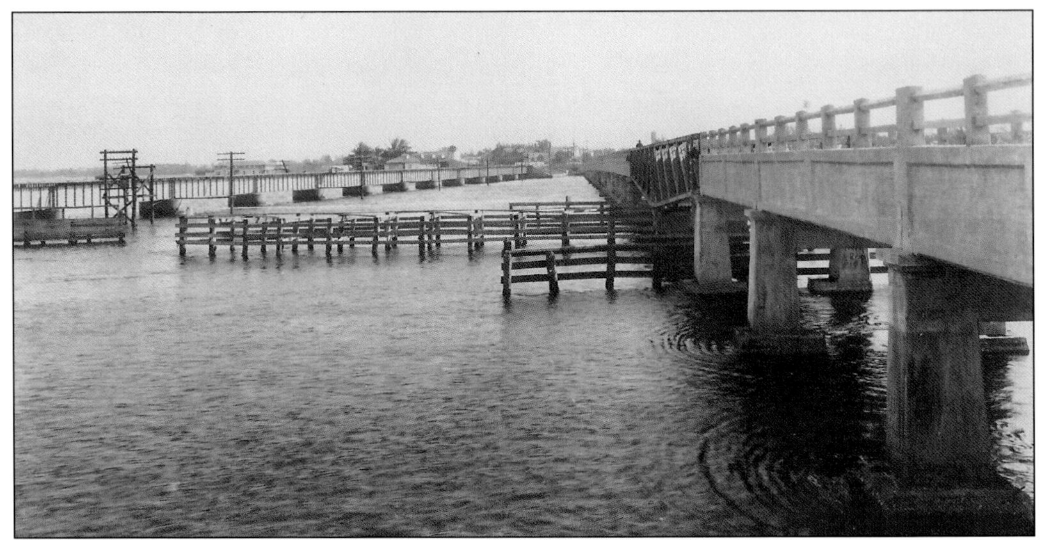

The view into Stuart was splendid across the St. Lucie River, whether traveling by train over the railroad bridge to the left or by car over the new steel-and-concrete bridge to the right. The grand opening on Monday, February 11, 1918, of the auto bridge marked the last missing link for the Dixie Highway running from Jacksonville to the southern tip of Florida, making the slow-moving ferry no longer needed.

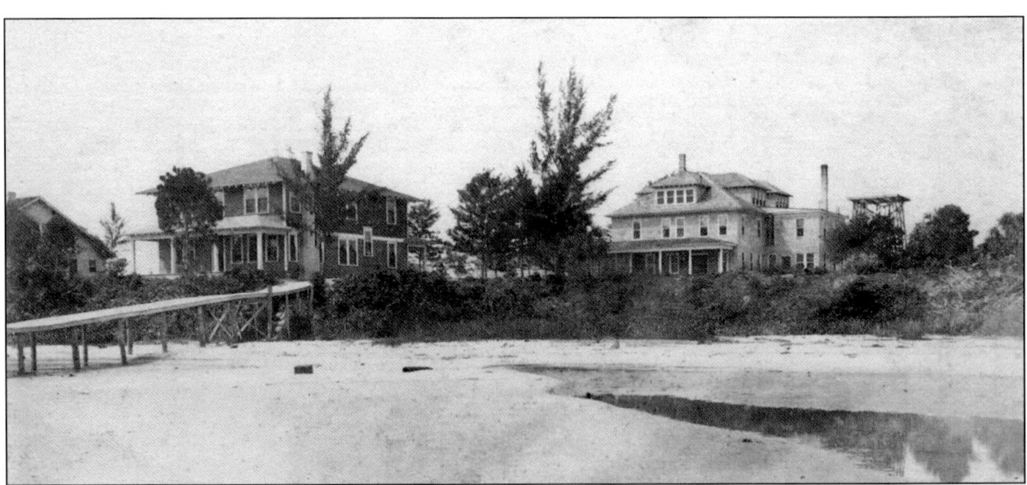

The grand 1913 St. Lucie Hotel (right) soon proved inadequate to accommodate the increasing number of tourists. By early 1916, this situation was remedied with the construction by brothers William and Lew Louis of an annex (left) adjacent to the hotel, along the St. Lucie River and at the end of St. Lucie Avenue. With electricity introduced in 1917, the hotel and its annex were very popular local social gathering places.

Five

Stuart's Roaring Twenties

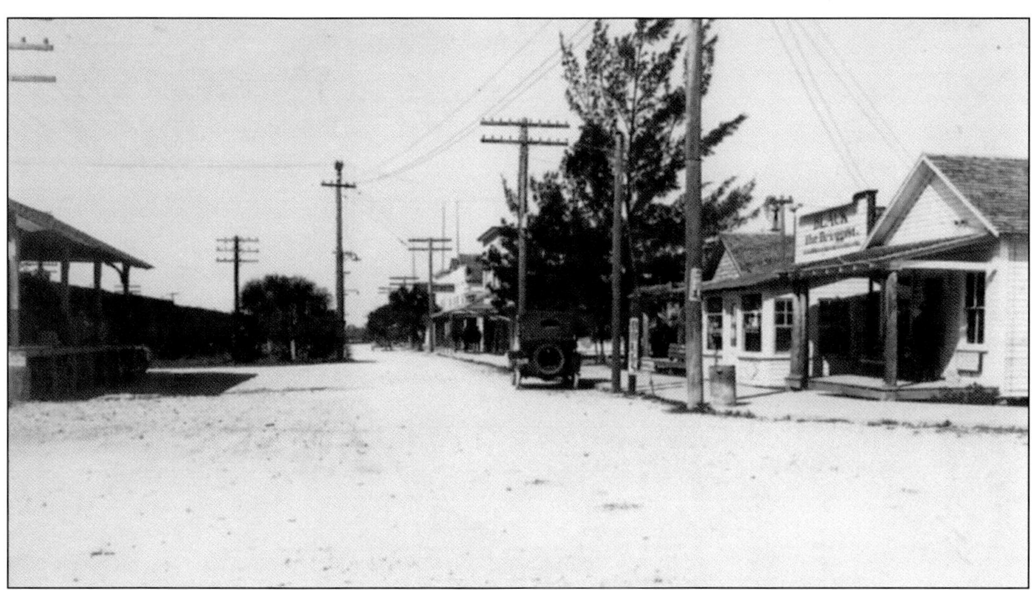

This view of the Stuart commercial district in 1921 shows the train and its platform to the left, Railroad Avenue in the center, and shops paralleling the roadway at right. On the corner, near St. Lucie Avenue, was Black's Drugstore, owned and operated by Samuel and Essie G. Black. (Courtesy of Doug Witham.)

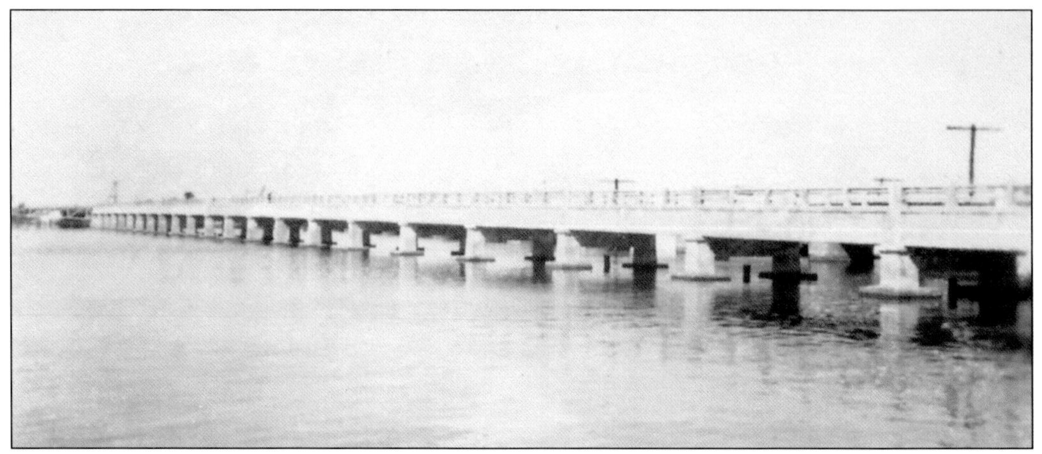

The new concrete-and-steel auto drawbridge proved to be a great asset to the development of Stuart at the beginning of the 1920s. America was beginning to become a motoring nation, and many people came south to Florida along the Dixie Highway. Another new bridge had been completed in February 1919 that crossed the South Fork of the St. Lucie River, making travel to and from neighboring Palm City much easier.

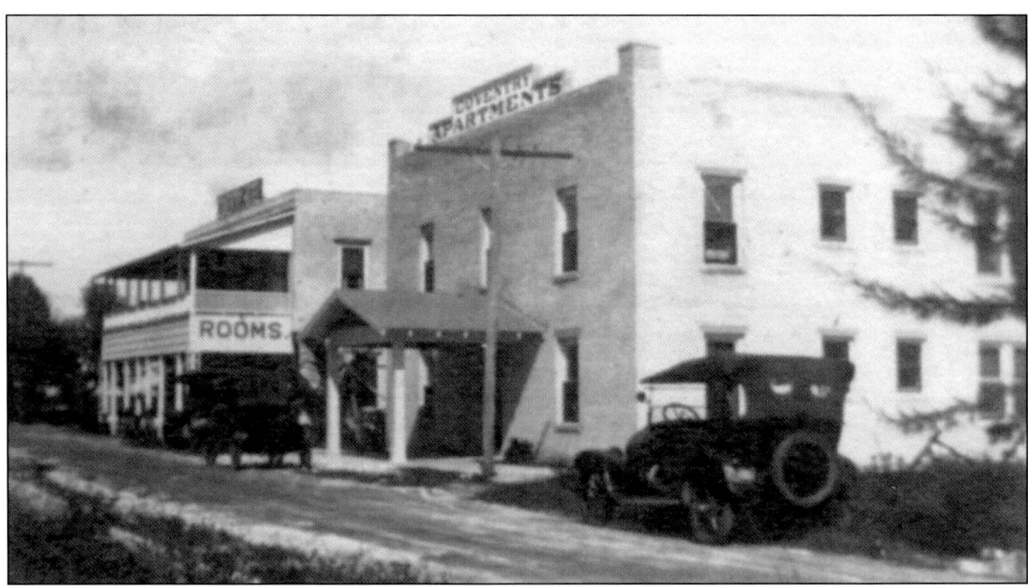

Stuart expansion included newer residences for the winter visitors as well as those coming permanently to live in Stuart. John Coventry, who owned the 1914 Coventry Hotel, had a two-story apartment house, Coventry Apartments, built in 1922 adjacent to his hotel to serve those needing year-round accommodations.

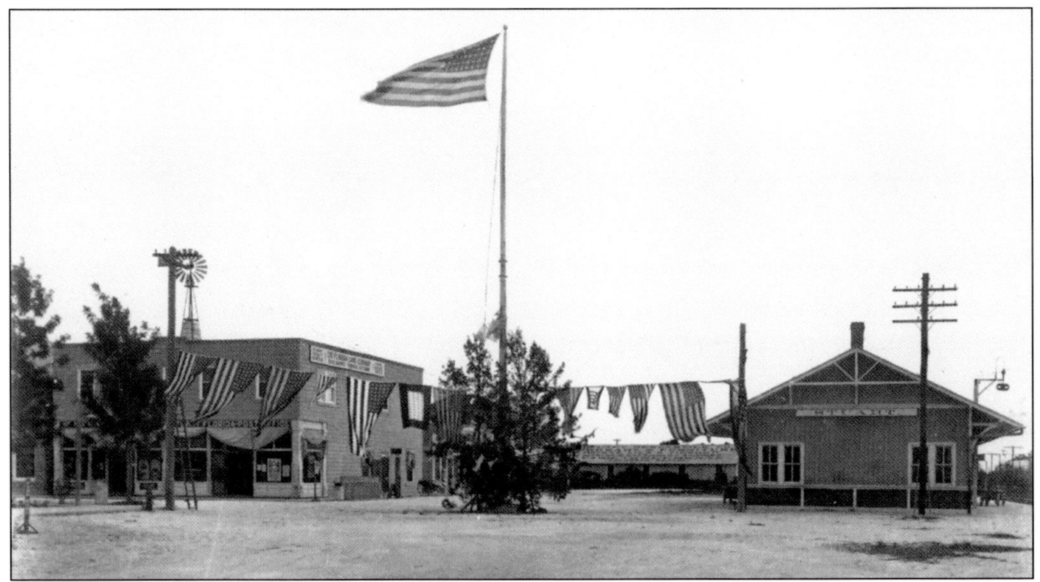
In the opposite direction along Railroad Avenue was the 1913 Feroe Building, which housed the town's post office, the Stuart Drug Co., and businesses such as a real estate office upstairs. It was opposite the passenger train depot. The Stuart Mercantile Company, established in 1913 by George W. Parks and Charles E. Christensen, was adjacent to the road visible in the distance. At center, the city's flagpole and various flags are proudly on display.

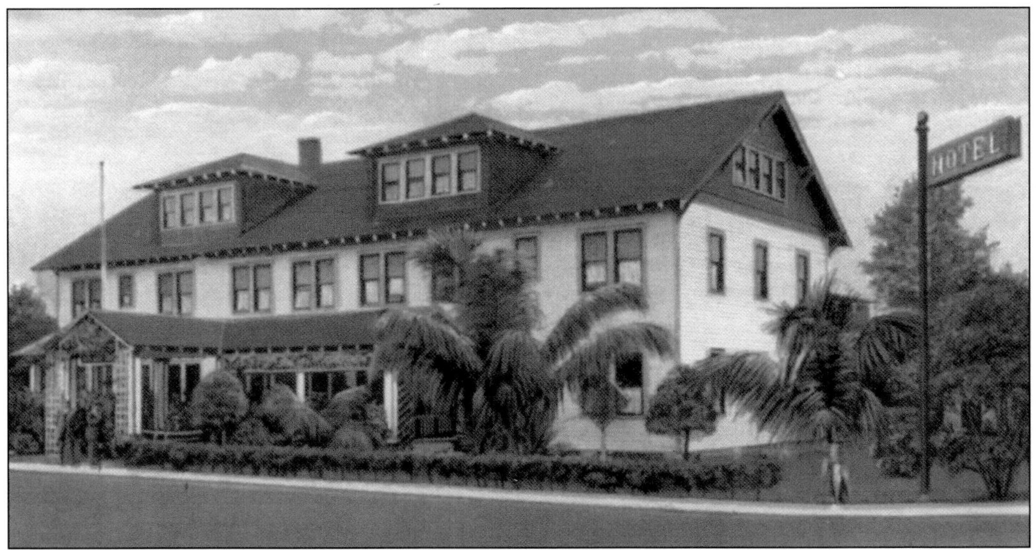

The Stuart House-Hotel, later just named the Stuart Hotel, continued to be a popular destination for visitors to Stuart. It persevered by being remodeled and expanded into the 1920s. As people crossed the St. Lucie River into Stuart over the auto bridge, they were drawn to the well-planted grounds of the hotel. Charles and Edith Glass owned the hotel from 1912 until they sold it in mid-1925 to the Roebuck and Clark families.

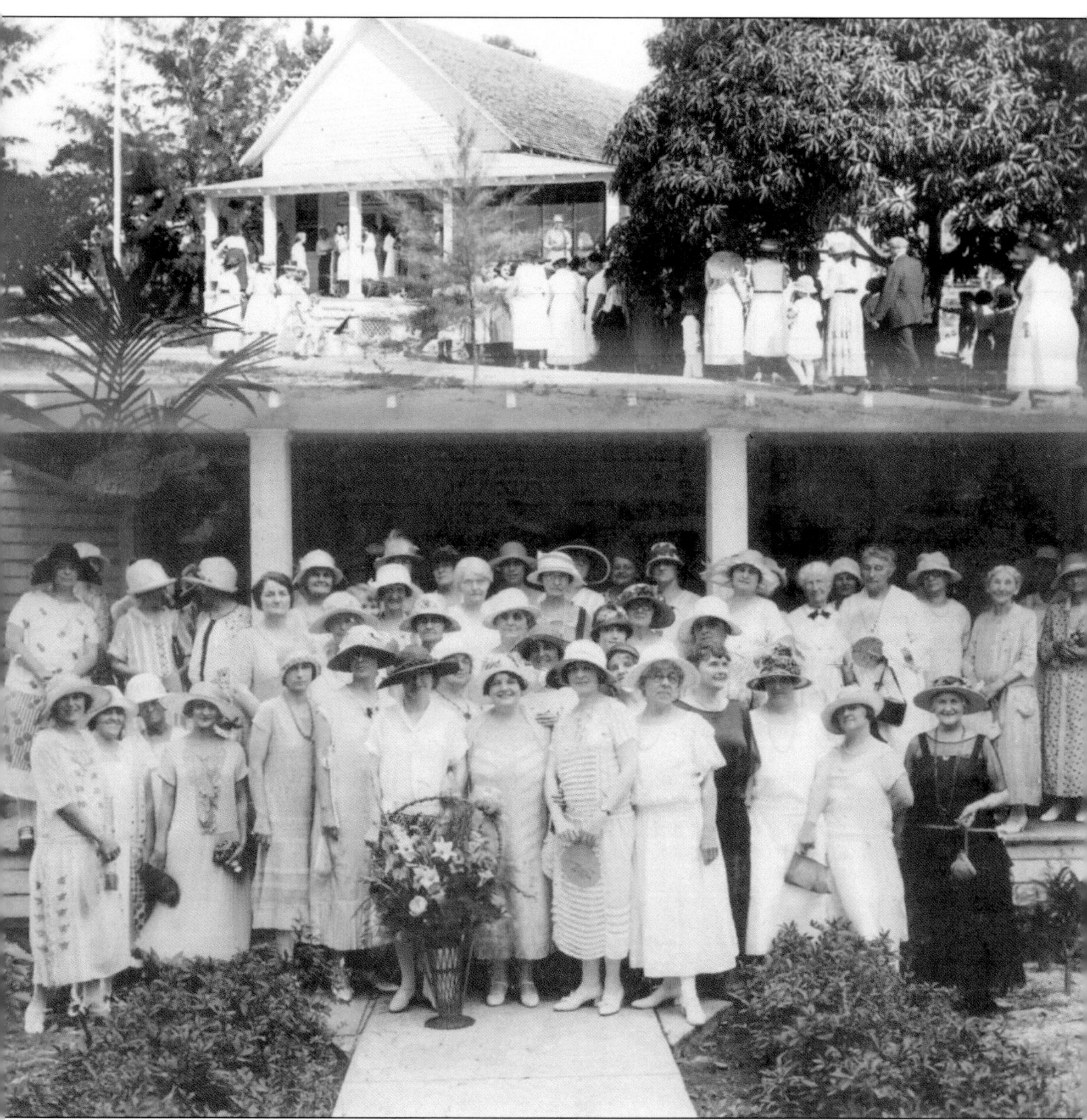

Located along Albany Avenue was the Stuart Woman's Clubhouse (Christian Endeavor Hall). There, the club members held musical performances, programs, shows, and poetry readings for the public. The most notable contribution of the Stuart Woman's Club, created in October 1913, was the establishment of the first free public library in their clubhouse. Membership grew to 160 by 1925, and improvements, including a full kitchen with cupboards, restroom, and a screened porch, were made on the clubhouse. The club sponsored numerous community improvement projects. (Courtesy of Dave Murray and Karen Hartman Malfregeot.)

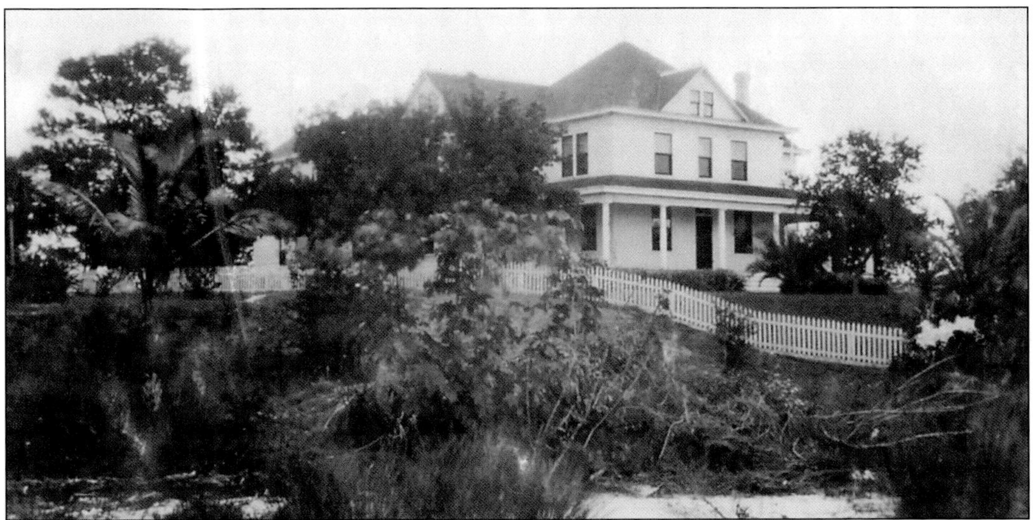

Residences lined the St. Lucie River from the time of the first settlers. Hubert and Susan Bessey's home was on the north bank of Frazier Creek and faced the river. They sold their place, along with four acres, to George W. Perkins in 1910. The property was added to, and a seawall was constructed. With Perkins's death in June 1920, the seven-acre estate was sold to William Henry Shepard in 1923. (Courtesy of Doug Witham.)

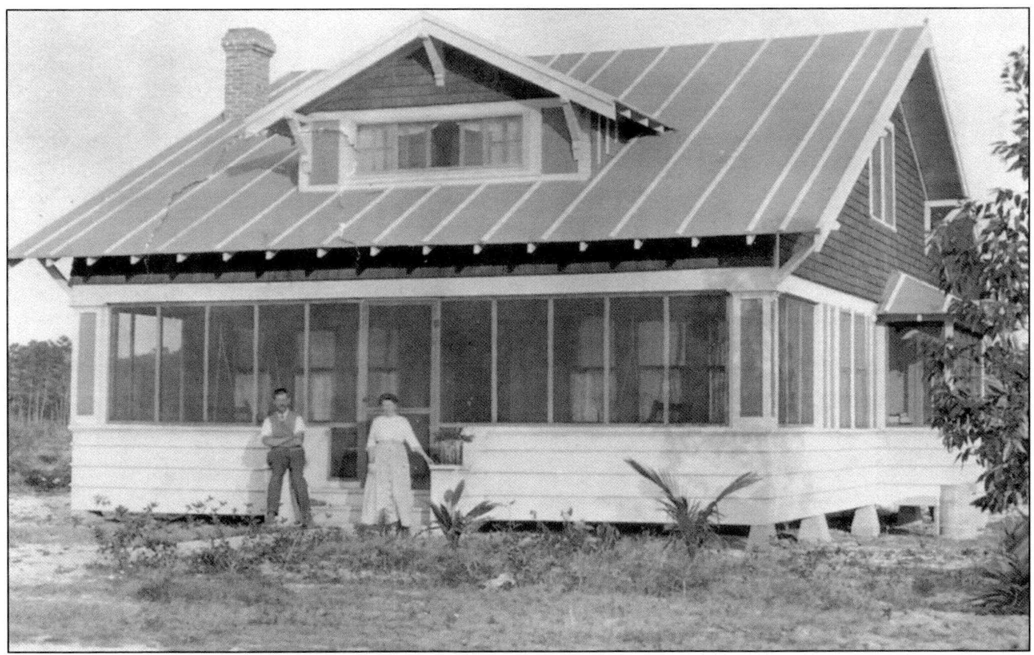

This wood-frame bungalow house, constructed by Sam Matthews in the St. Lucie Crescent neighborhood, was part of the original Hubert Bessey homestead, just blocks from the river. Pictured are Charles E. and Pearl Christensen, who purchased it in February 1917. They lived there for decades. Christensen, along with George Parks, owned the Stuart Mercantile Company, and in 1924, he became the Pure Oil distributor. In 1932, he was elected Martin County sheriff. (Courtesy of Sandra and Tom Thurlow.)

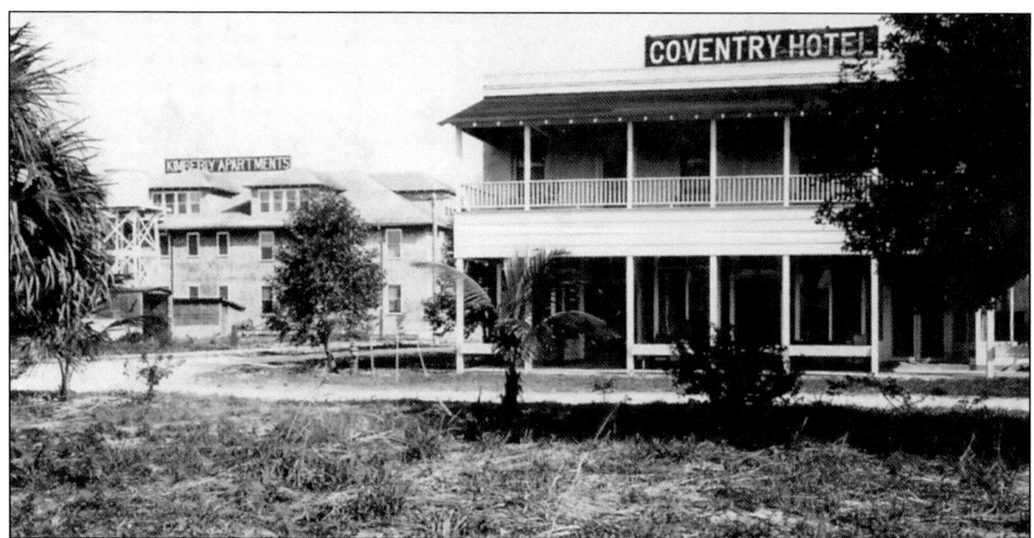

In 1924, the Kimberly Apartments (left) along the St. Lucie River and the Coventry Hotel and Apartments (right) one block away complemented each other in providing homelike lodging for year-round residents as well as visitors to Stuart. With more people coming to Stuart in the first half of the 1920s, housing became scarce. (Courtesy of Doug Witham.)

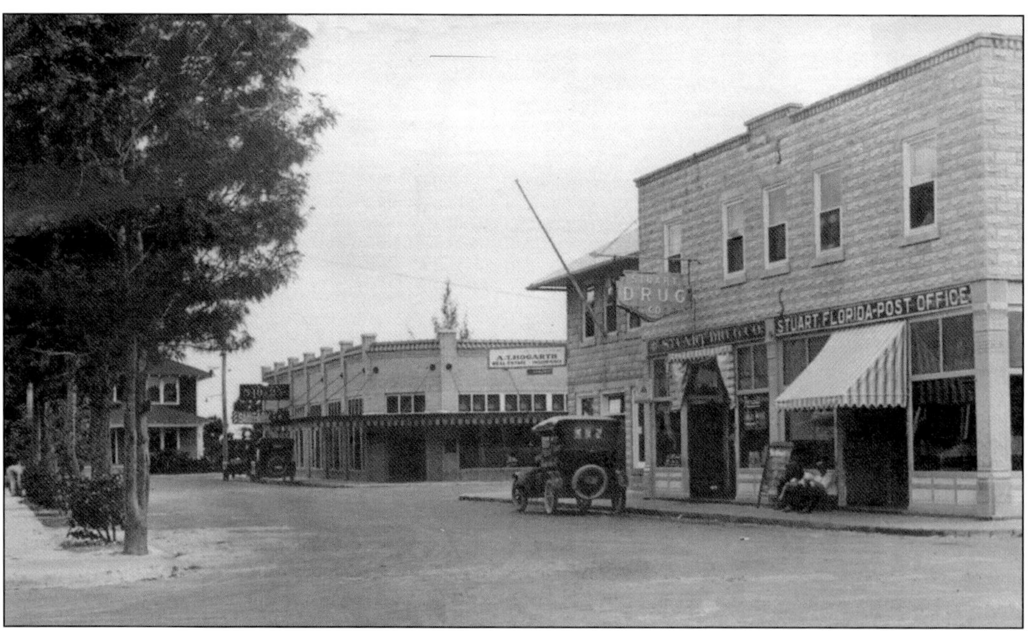

St. Lucie Avenue heads toward the St. Lucie River with the Feroe Building on the right; next is the Seminole Bank, which opened in 1923, and then the new Edward A. Fuge Building, which opened in 1921. The Bank of Stuart moved into the corner location of the new Fuge Building. A park was on the left side of the road, and at the end of the street was the St. Lucie Hotel Annex.

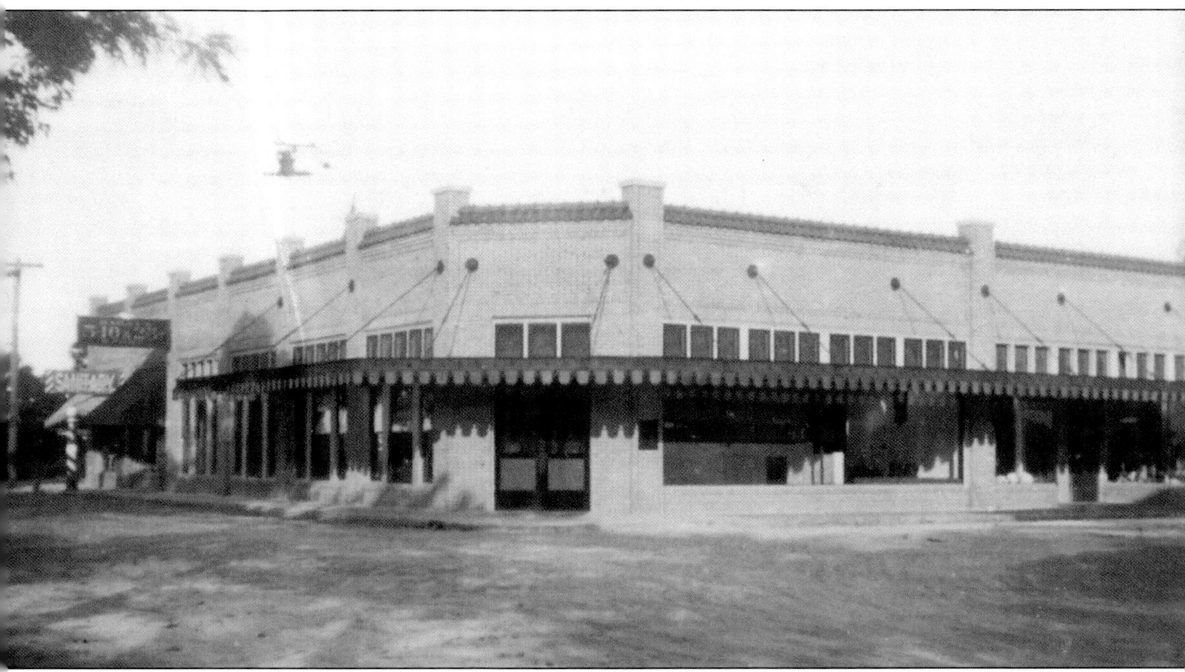

The Fuge Building (Osceola Building) was one story with 13-foot ceilings and measured 36 feet wide by 65 feet deep. It featured two modern fireproof vaults for the Bank of Stuart, which occupied the center section. The vaults may have given a sense of security, but on May 12, 1922, the notorious Ashley Gang robbed the bank for a second time, the first being in February 1915 in its former location across the street. (Courtesy of MCHS, Elliott Museum.)

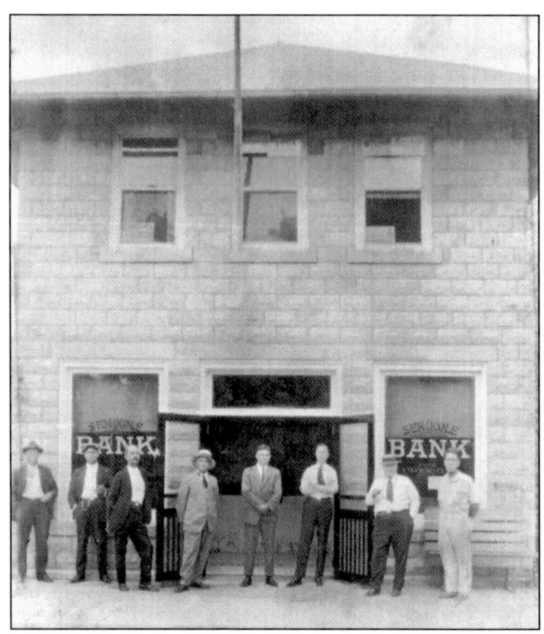

The Bank of Stuart moved to the Fuge Building in late 1921, leaving the former 1912 bank building as the Stuart city clerk's office and council room. The newly formed Seminole Bank leased the first floor from the city and opened April 2, 1923, with John E. Taylor as bank president and Andrew R. Wallace as a cashier. From left to right are Harry M. Speedy, Arthur T. Hogarth, Ernest J. Ricou (vice president), DeWitt C. Ruff (director), John E. Taylor, Andrew R. Wallace, H. Edwin Rogers, and A.L. (Roy) Lane.

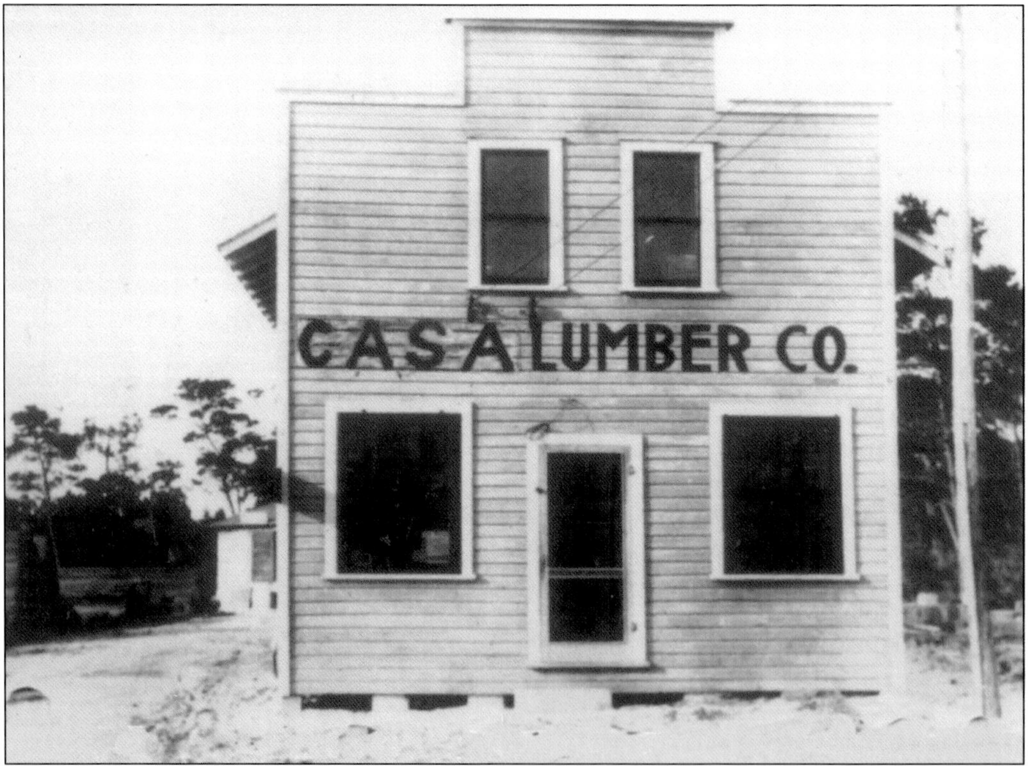

In the early 1920s, Lawrence Dorsey established the small Acme Lumber Company in Stuart, located near Pinewood Street (Martin Luther King Jr. Boulevard) with accessible railroad frontage, not far from its competitor East Coast Lumber and Supply Company. In May 1929, Dorsey changed the name to Casa Lumber Company, which came from the Casa Terrace residential property he had purchased and named. Henry Cabre became the new owner of the company in 1936.

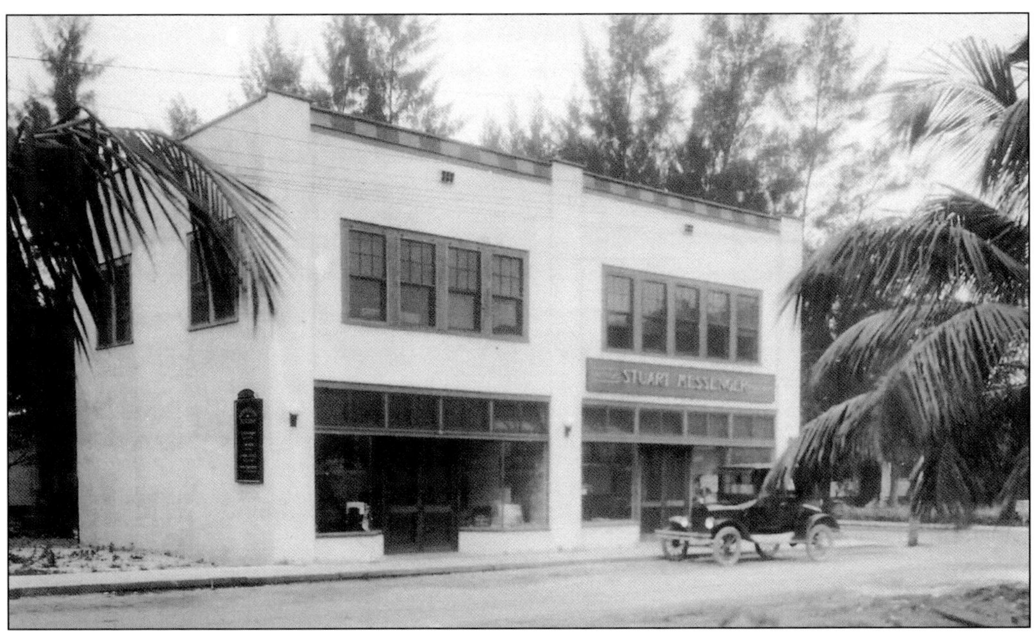

Stuart got its first print newspaper, the *Stuart Times*, on April 18, 1913, with Will Hawley Stevens as owner. The *Stuart Messenger*, a competitor, was founded by A.K. Wilson on November 5, 1915. The two papers were consolidated in March 1917. The *Messenger* was purchased in 1922 by the Clyma family, and in April 1924, a new Messenger Building at First Street and Avenue D (Akron Avenue) was built by Sam Matthews.

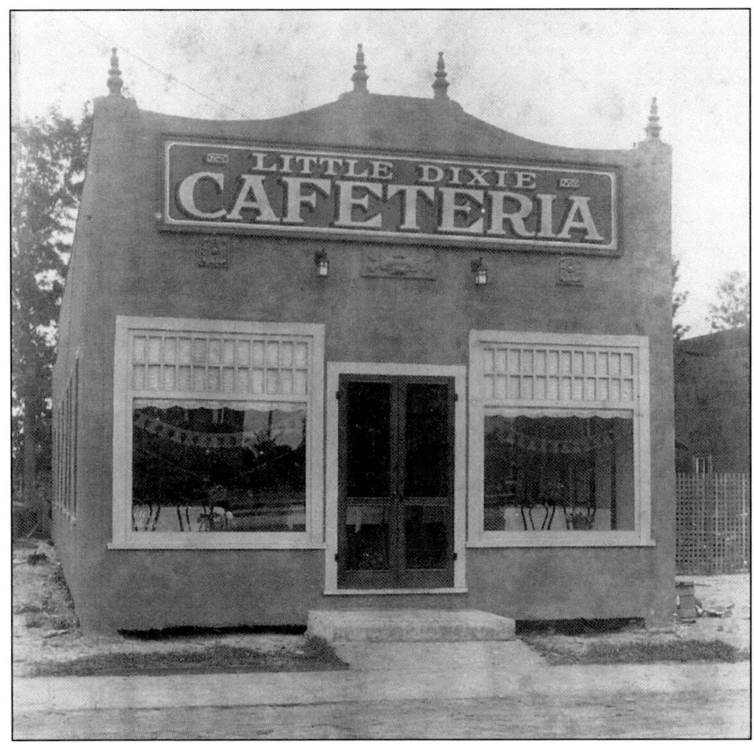

Lizzie Beyer owned and operated the Little Dixie Café for decades. By 1918, she was the second person to receive a license to operate a permanent restaurant. With the building boom, the Little Dixie Café had expanded by 1923, operating as the first 70-seat cafeteria-style restaurant near the train depot with all new equipment and furnishings. A really outstanding cook, Beyer learned that the public wanted their food in a hurry, and the cafeteria style allowed her to provide hot and cold dishes at the lowest cost.

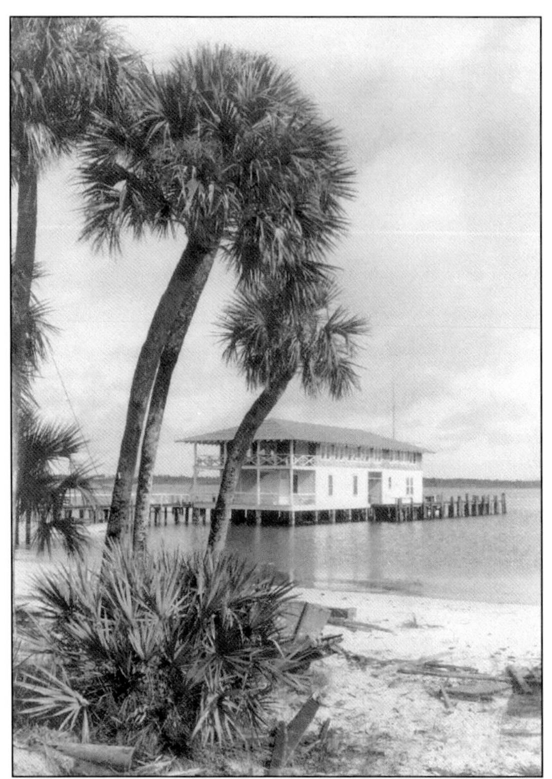

The 1918 St. Lucie River Yacht Club off the St. Lucie River shore was so popular that expansion was necessary by the early 1920s. Its size was doubled, offering a larger dining room, improved reception room, new bedrooms for overnight guests, and additional restrooms and dressing rooms. The Roaring Twenties were truly fun at the yacht club, with music and dances in the elegant ballroom. That ended with the September 16, 1928, hurricane, which ripped the building to pieces. (Courtesy of Martha Penhale Cuthbert.)

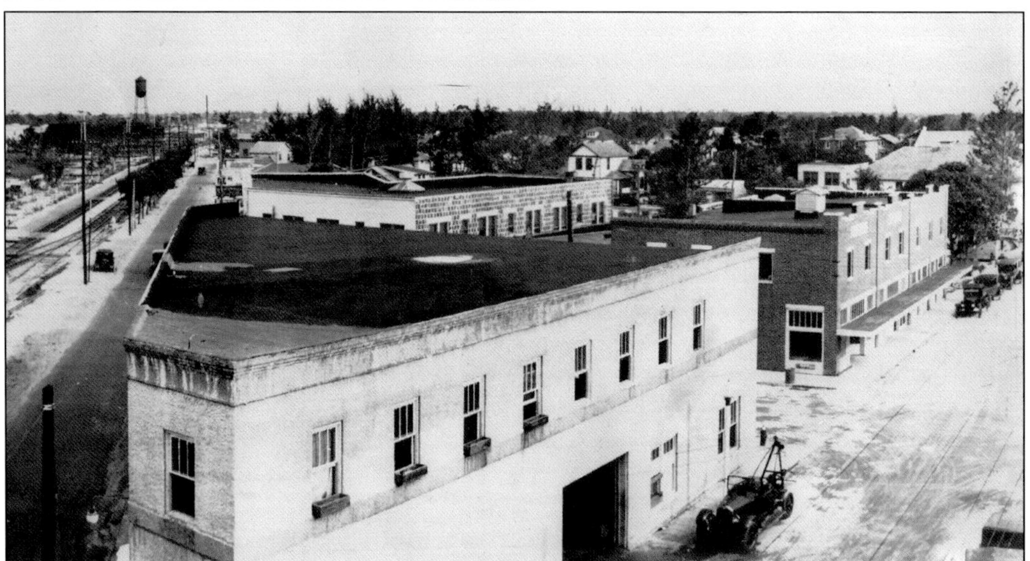

This 1920s view of Stuart shows the new buildings, businesses, and homes constructed on the west side of the railroad tracks. Bert Babcock had owned a one-story garage along Dixie Highway and Second Street since the late 1910s, to which he added a second story by 1923. This transformed structure, known as the Flatiron Building, added storage space, allowing the first level to become a showroom and workshop. It also featured an electric freight elevator. Just to the right was the St. Lucie Building, with rental offices and retail spaces. (Courtesy of the Lockwood Collection, SHM.)

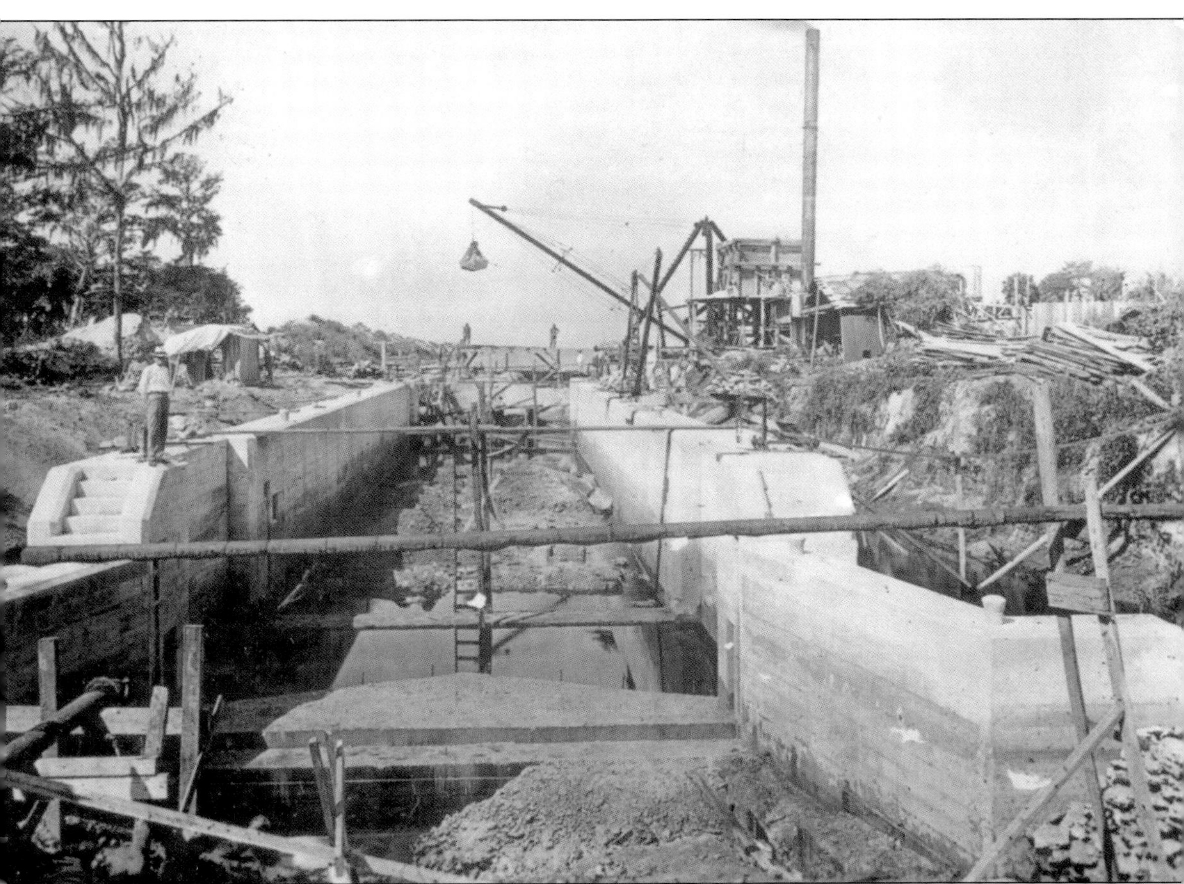

Being a port city was the goal of many people in Stuart. One way was to have a canal system across the state from the east coast of Florida to the west. Construction for such a massive undertaking started in the late 1910s and accelerated in the 1920s. A canal (C-44) was dug from the east shore of Lake Okeechobee and came across the land west of Stuart to eventually connect with the South Fork of the St. Lucie River.

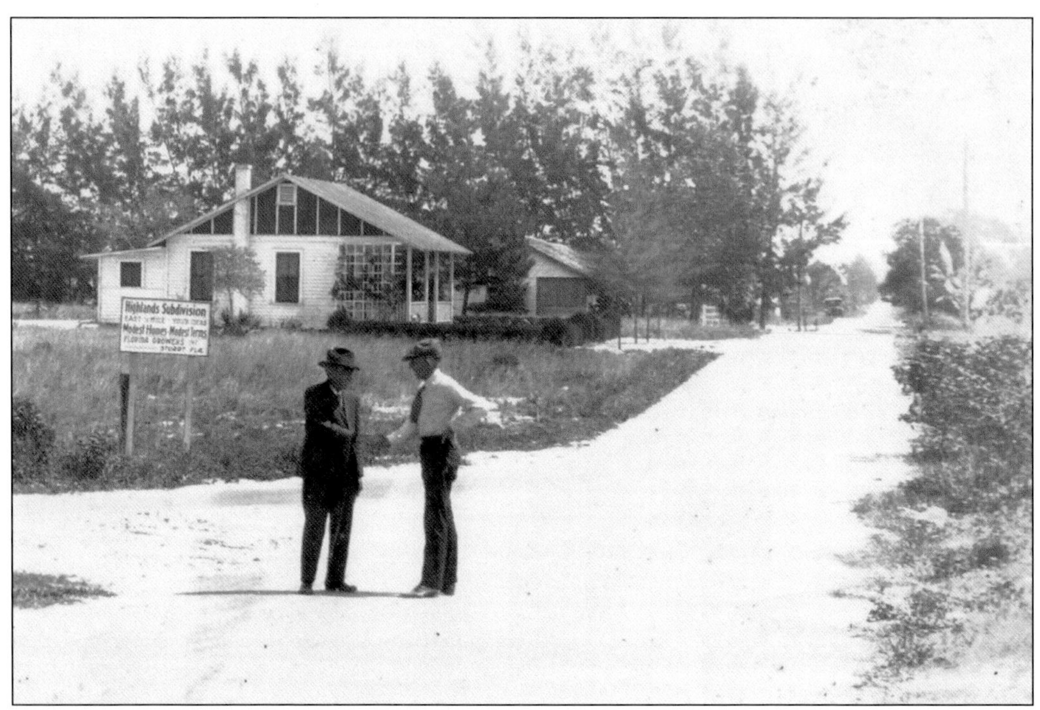

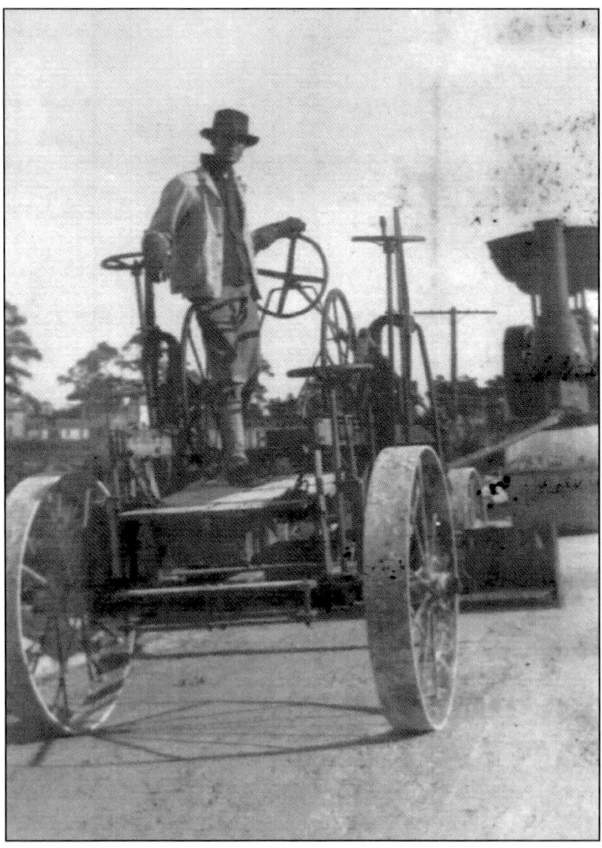

There was a major land boom in Stuart and other parts of Florida during most of the 1920s. Many were involved in real estate as land speculators or developers, all looking to make a quick fortune. This new Highlands neighborhood development of the 1920s is being shown to a prospective buyer on the left; the promoter on the right is Harry Lyons. (Courtesy of Sandra and Tom Thurlow.)

With new neighborhoods created, new roads were also necessary. Employment was steady for those in road and building construction, house painting, and architecture. (Courtesy of the Edith Coventry Collection, Elliott Museum.)

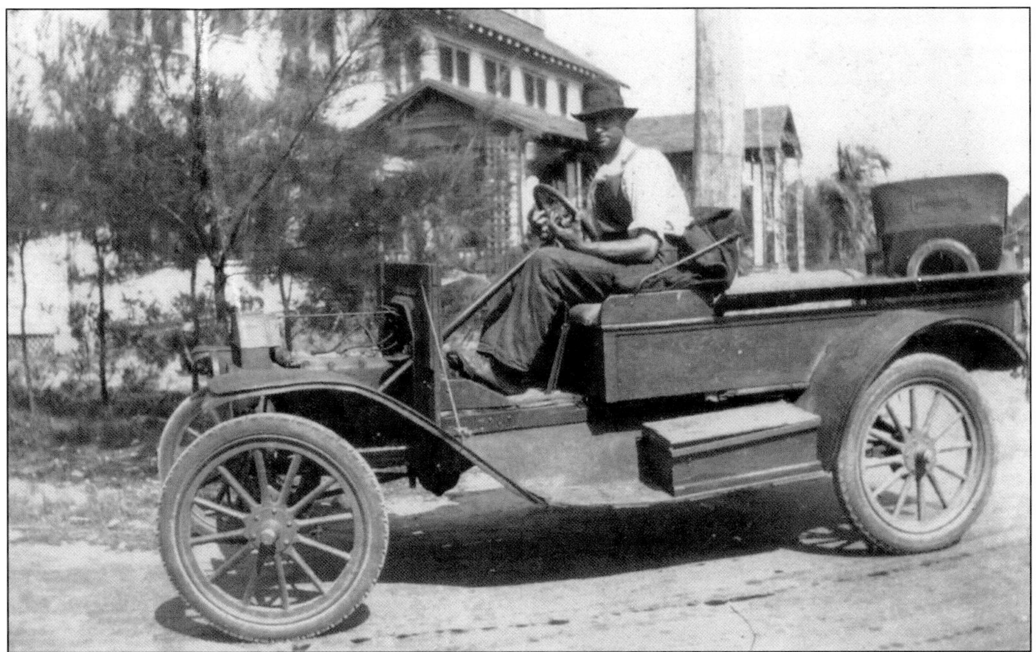

With improved roads, the number of automobiles and trucks increased. George William Pendarvis, a carpenter, could use his truck to haul necessary work supplies and tools to different jobs. In this photograph, Pendarvis was traveling near the Stuart Hotel on his way to a carpentry job. (Courtesy of Harry Lyons, Thurlow Collection.)

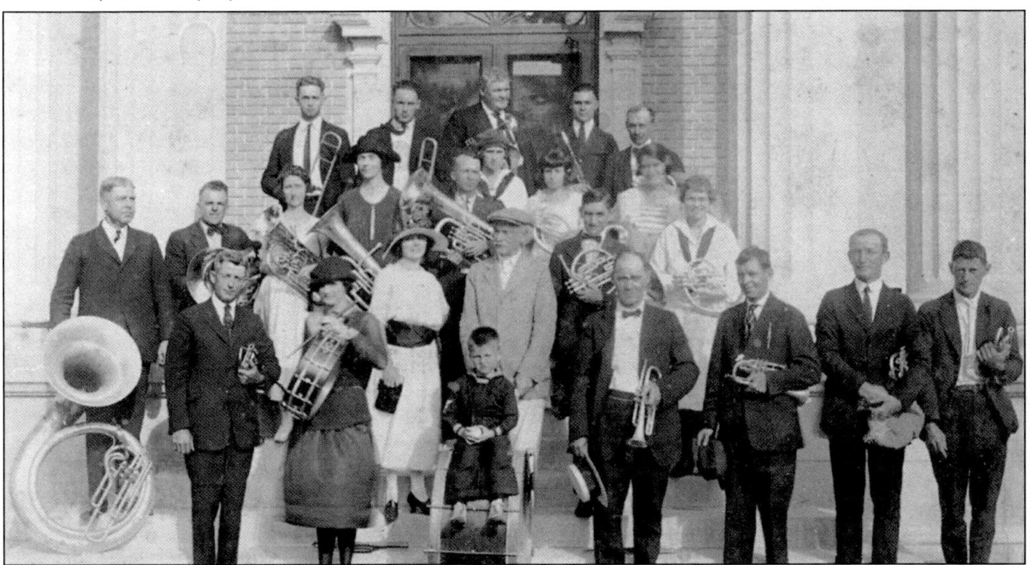

The popular Stuart Band performed for a special occasion in West Palm Beach in 1922. Pictured are, from left to right, (first row) Hershel Worth, Eileen Porter, Vic Worth (on the drum), Charles McPherson, Cy Fox, Toley Engebretsen, and R. Fred Kummer; (second row) J.N. Dunham, Lewis Kreps, Frances Merwin, Harry "Pop" Allen, unidentified, and Marcia McPherson; (third row) Maud Worth, Maud S. Smith, Walter Johns, E. Aspinwall (behind), Silvia Worth, and Belle McPherson; (fourth row) Merle Smith, Darrel Smith, Harvey Merwin, Henry P. Stevenson, and unidentified. (Courtesy of Sandra and Tom Thurlow.)

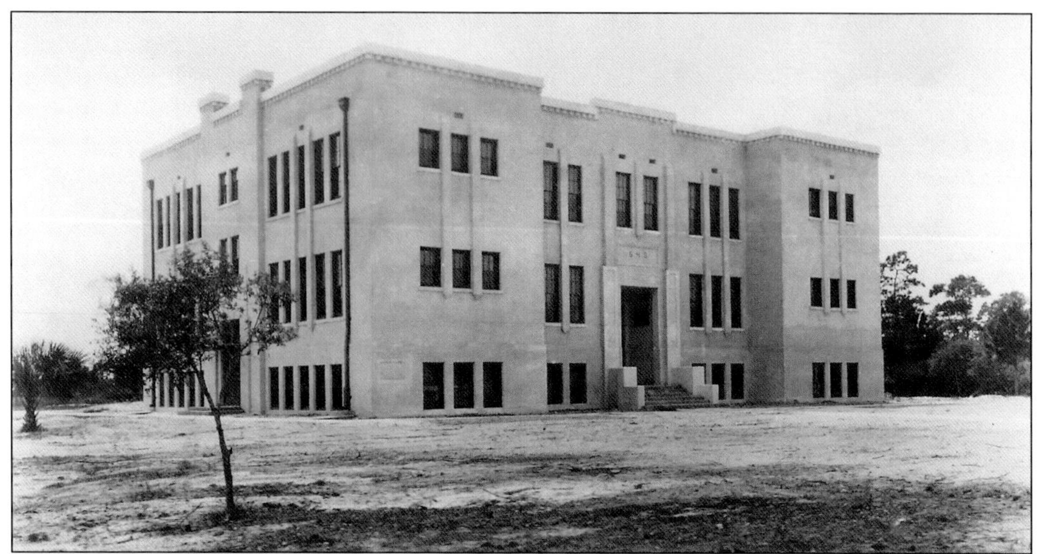

With increased population in 1919, the school board purchased a 10-acre site several blocks west of the 1909 school for $600. In 1921, voters approved a bond issue for a new school building on the site costing $40,000. Ground was broken in October 1922, the cornerstone was laid the next month, and the new school was completed on Friday, September 21, 1923, with principal Ethel C. Youngblood and 300 students covering all grades. (Courtesy of Martha Penhale Cuthbert.)

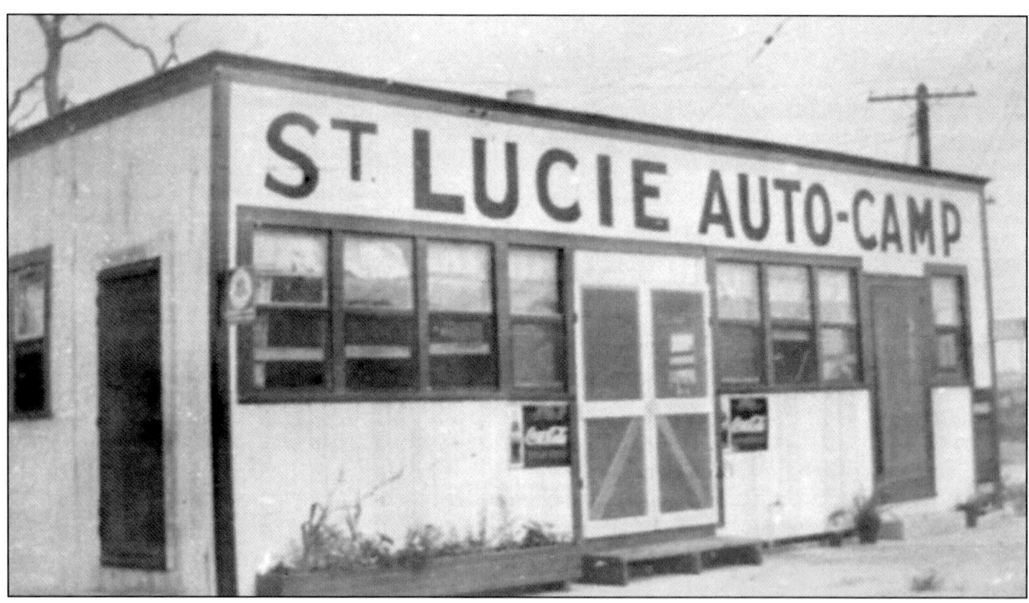

Housing was at a premium in Stuart. One temporary solution was the development of auto camps, which provided basic temporary lodging with cottages and grounds for tents or trailers. The St. Lucie Auto Camp, established in 1924 on a 10-acre tract on Dixie Highway, near Frazier Creek, was operated by brothers Charles and John Woodrum. There were 55 one- and two-room screened wood cottages, along with a bathhouse and laundry facility for the tenants. (Courtesy of the Wiley family.)

Six

Creation of Martin County

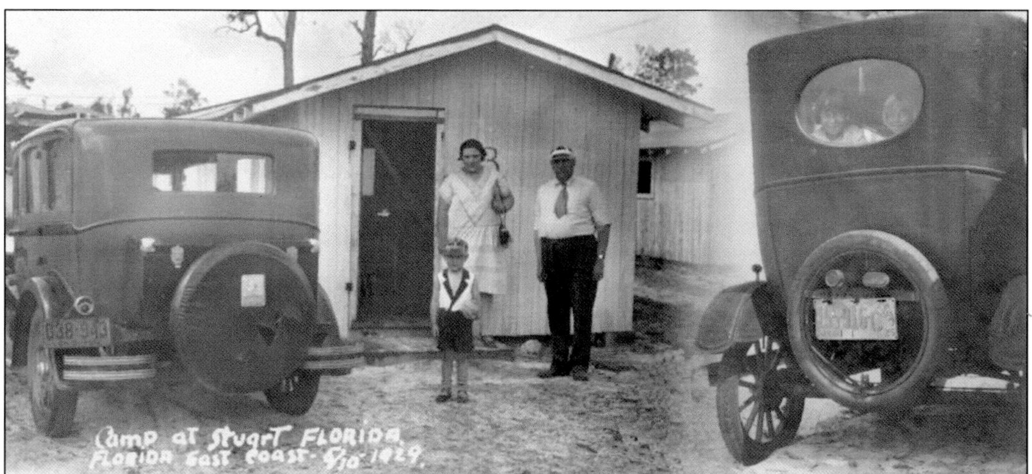

Leaving northern homes for the tropical paradise along the St. Lucie River became the norm in the 1920s. The Rue family from Michigan were settled in Stuart by 1925, staying in the St. Lucie Auto Camp for a few months until better quarters could be located. Their old Michigan tag was immediately hung at the cottage door. The two youngest members of the family pictured in the car at right were Leila (left) and Leona Rue. Those standing outside the cottage are, from left to right, Donald, Kathryn, and Elmer Miller. (Courtesy of the Rue-Luckhardt family and Florida Memory Project.)

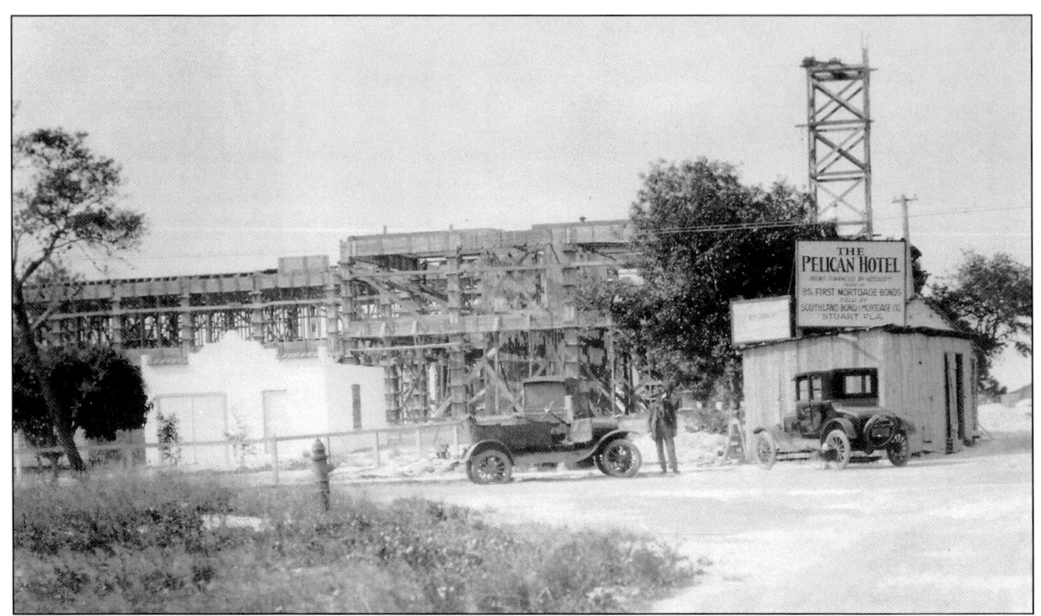

The building boom peaked in the mid-1920s. The 1925 construction of an elegant and enormous new hotel, the Dixie-Pelican, demonstrated the growth in Stuart. This fine hotel on the edge of the St. Lucie River went back a full city block to Osceola Avenue. The price tag for this three-story structure with 50 rooms, each with private bath, was $175,000. On January 28, 1926, the hotel received Florida governor John Martin and his staff, the first to sign the guest registry.

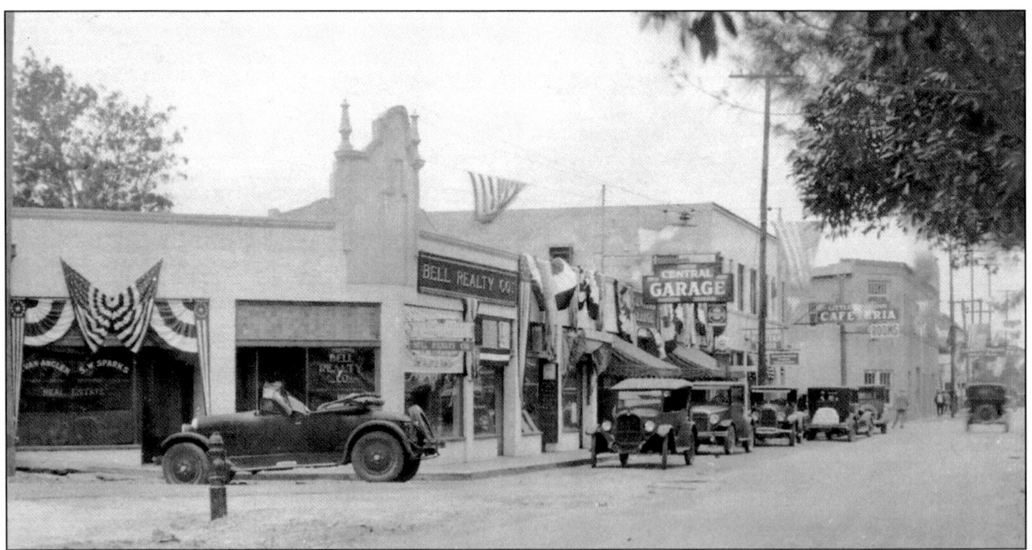

Albert "Bert" Krueger had constructed the Central Garage along Dixie Highway in the early 1920s, and by 1925, turned its operation over to his brother George. In 1925, Bert had completed the Krueger Building at a cost of $100,000, located on Dixie Highway and Second Street, near the garage. This fireproof, Spanish-style structure was two stories in height with 10 stores on the first floor and 18 hotel rooms on the second floor. (Courtesy of Sandra and Tom Thurlow.)

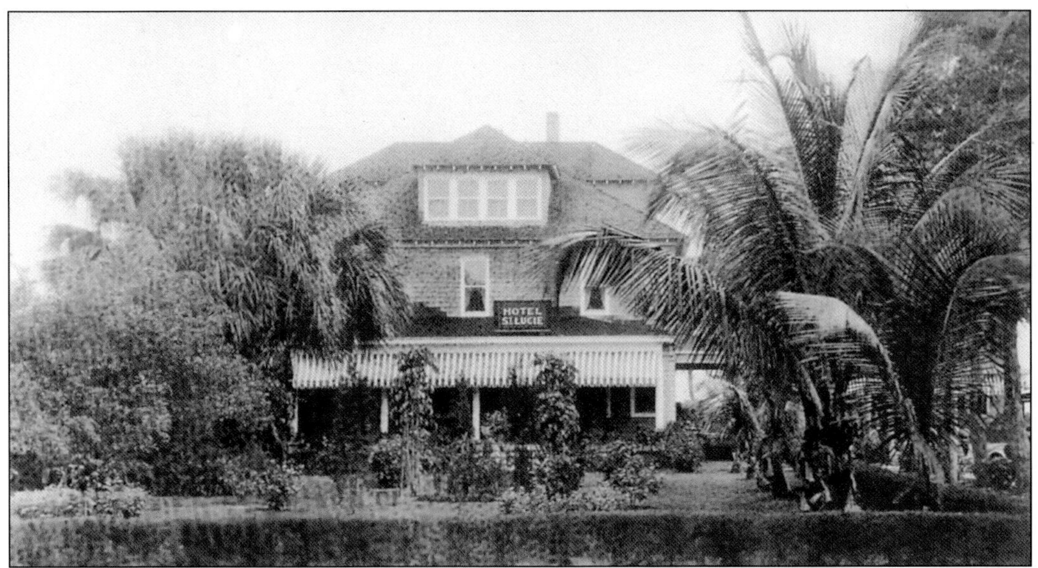

In the 1920s, a popular hostelry along St. Lucie Avenue, in the heart of Stuart, was the 1913 Hotel St. Lucie (St. Lucie Hotel), which so typified the lush tropical paradise along the St. Lucie River with its manicured gardens. The hotel offered fine dining and meeting rooms serving local residents and visitors alike. (Courtesy of Doug Witham.)

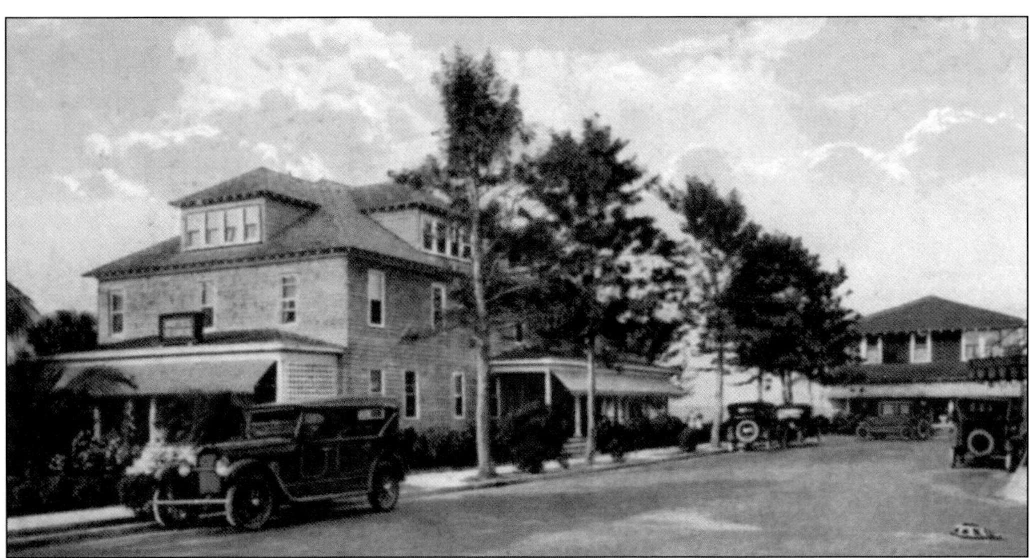

Built in 1916 as an annex for the Hotel St. Lucie, this two-story building was located at the end of St. Lucie Avenue. The annex, seen at far right, served as a popular social gathering place for local civic group meetings, parties, and luncheons during the early 1920s. (Courtesy of Jo Marie Paradise.)

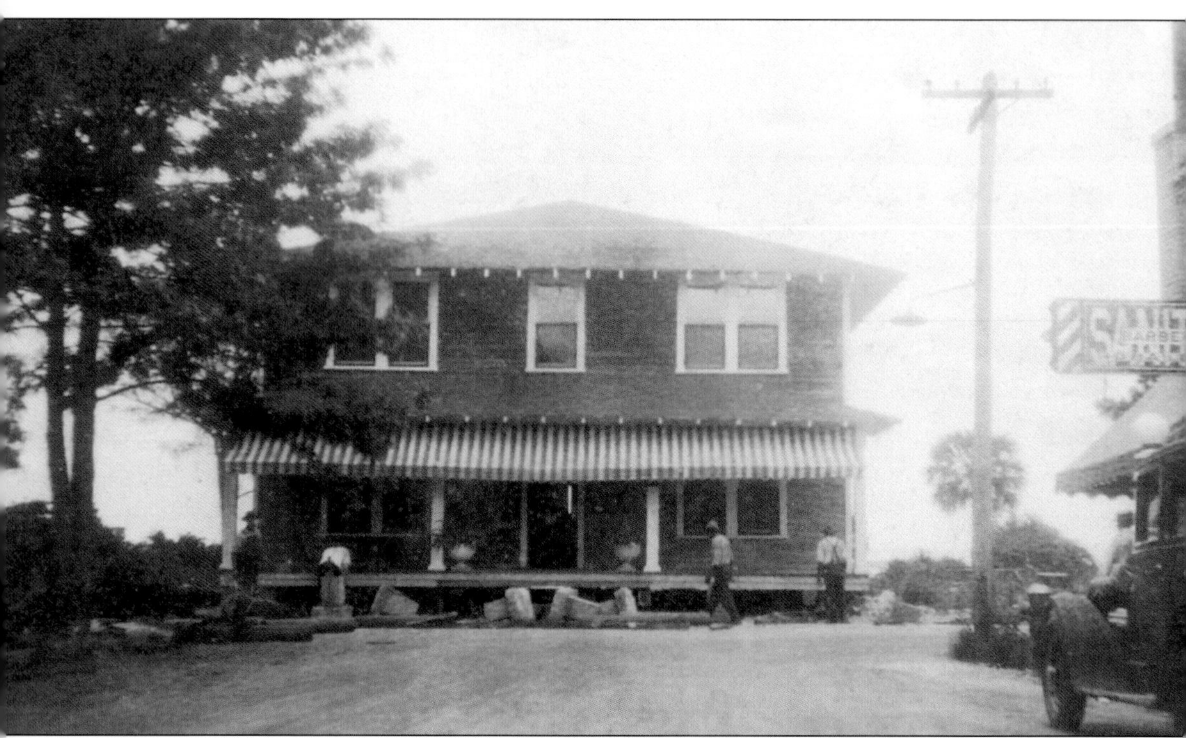

Around late 1925, a Stuart City Dock was built at the terminus of St. Lucie Avenue but proved to be inaccessible to motor vehicles. It was decided that the St. Lucie Hotel Annex would be moved a few yards to the right, as seen here, to the corner of St. Lucie and Seminole Avenues, where it remains to this day.

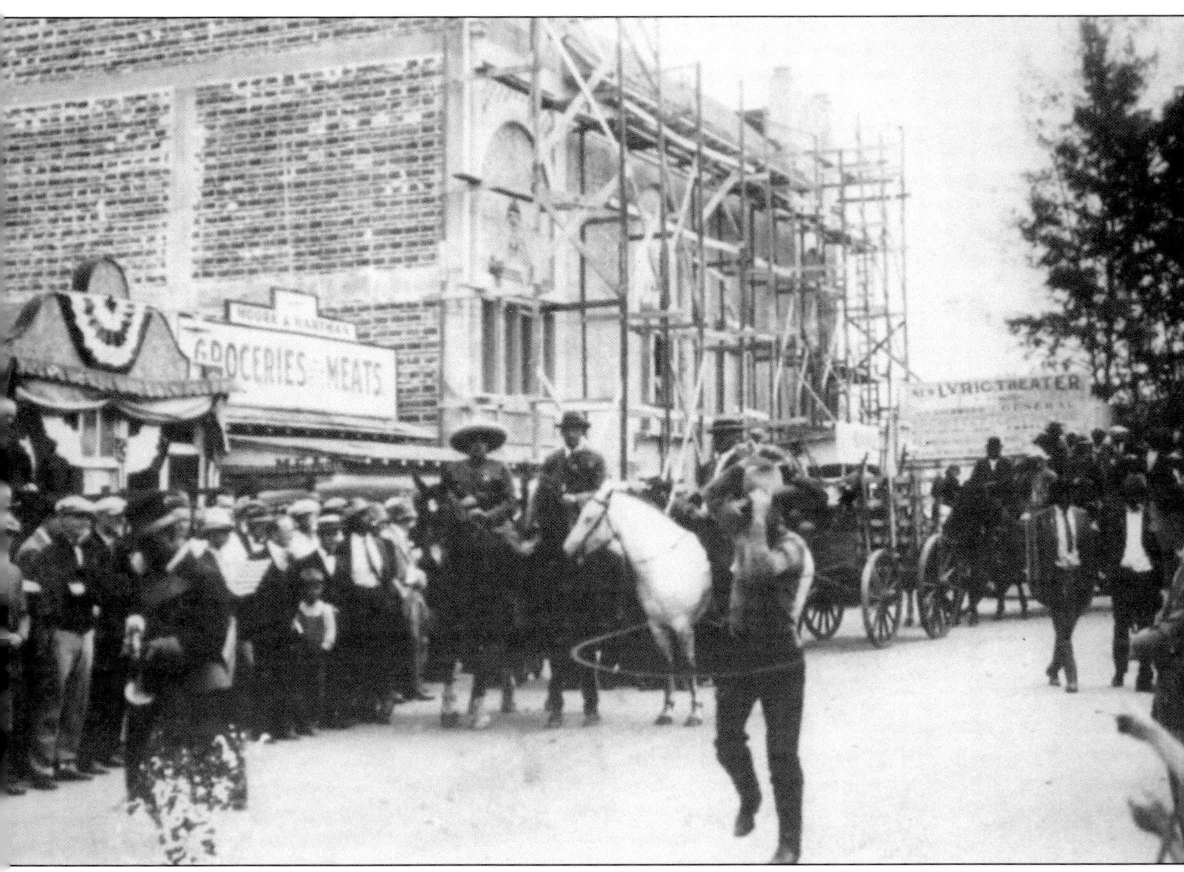

One of the proudest moments for locals was the creation of Martin County in May 1925, named for Florida governor John W. Martin. With the area once part of Dade and later Palm Beach County, the local citizens felt they were ready to govern their own county. To celebrate, on January 28, 1926, there was a stellar event along the streets of Stuart. Leading the parade riding a horse in his uniform and a broad hat was Chief of Police Oren B. Padgett.

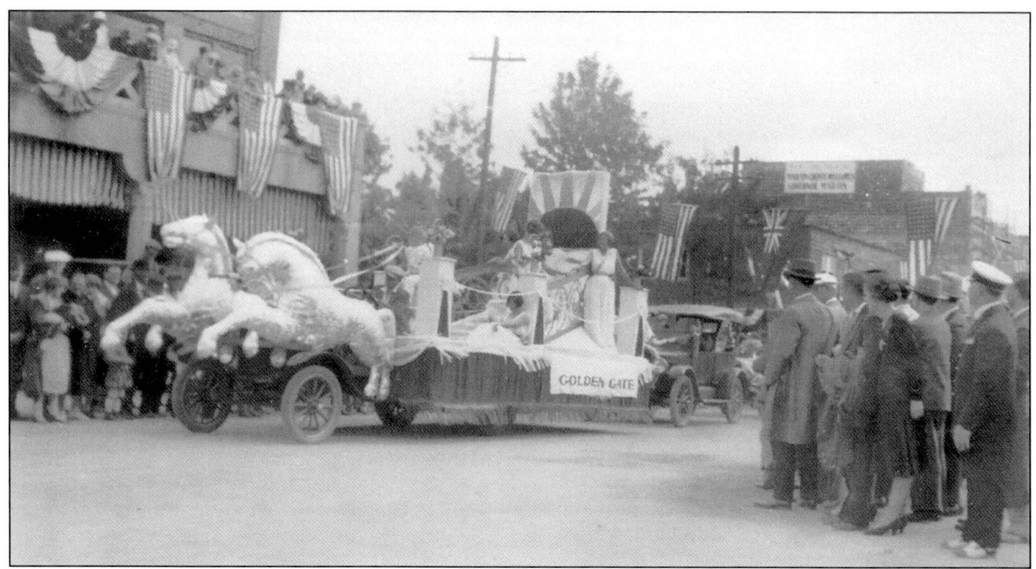

The newest neighborhoods and developments were featured in the parade. Here is the float for the new Golden Gate community, which is located near Port Sewall. Shown in the background to the right is the third Lyric Theatre under construction. At its top level was the theater penthouse for planned VIP parties. (Courtesy of Martha Penhale Cuthbert.)

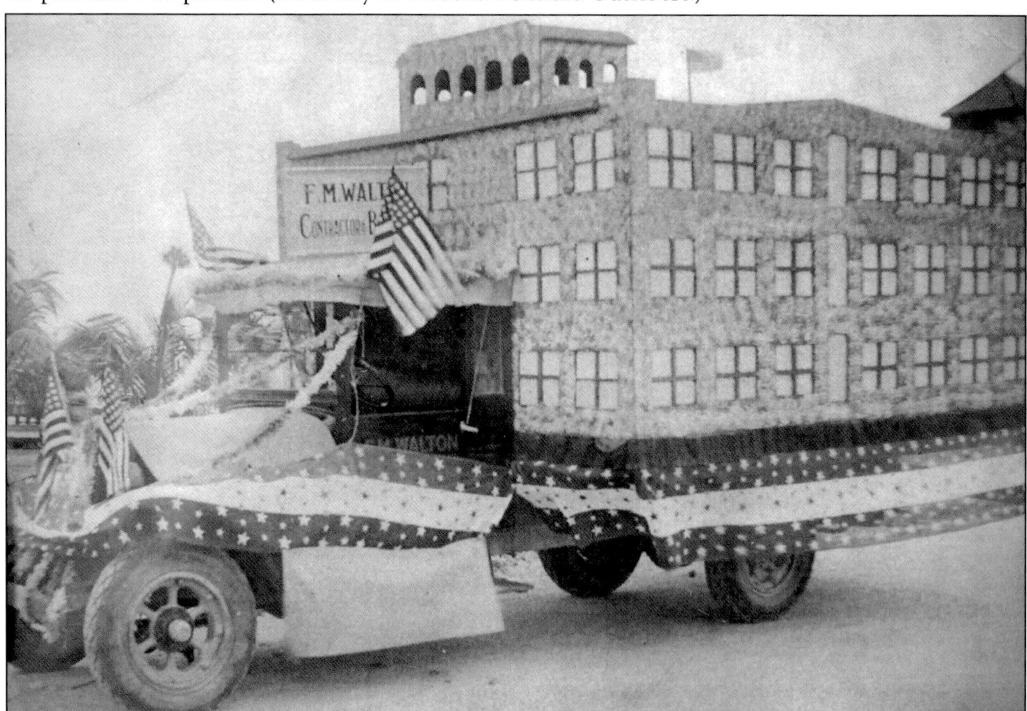

Fred M. Walton, who was one of Stuart's major building contractors, shows off his construction abilities in this mock-up model float of the new El Bit-Lor Apartments. During this year of 1926, Walton was near completion of the newest Lyric Theatre and the Hibiscus Apartments and was working on the impressive three-story El Bit-Lor Apartments, which would open in May. Later in 1926, Walton also constructed the France Apartments building along Frazier Creek.

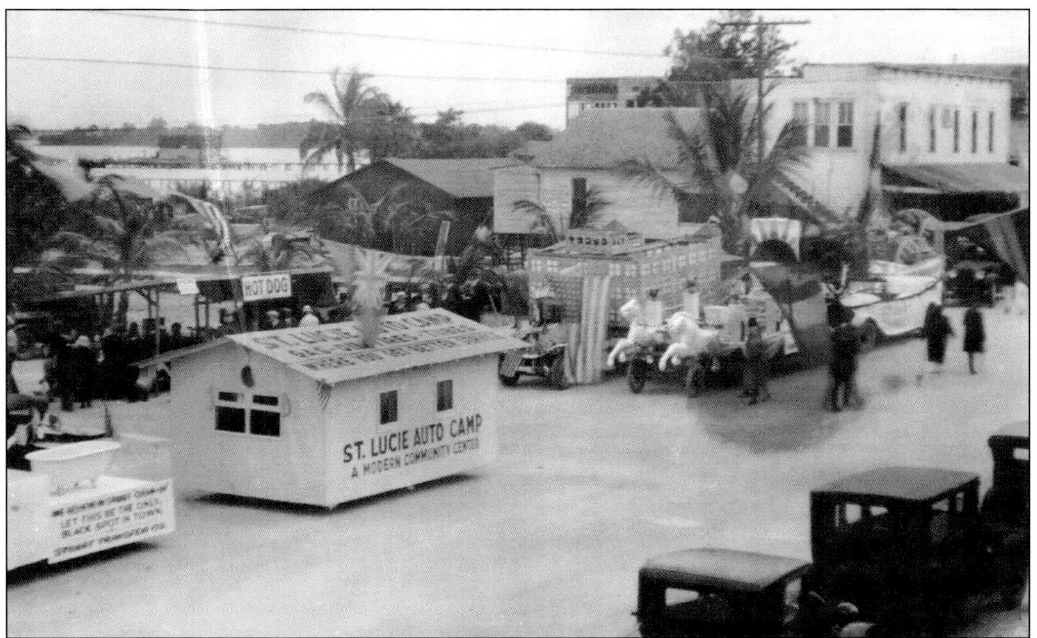

The two-mile parade through town in celebration of the new Martin County was attended by thousands of local citizens and out-of-town visitors. Florida governor John W. Martin was the special guest of honor and later spoke before the crowds. Over 500 cars and floats participated in the parade. (Courtesy of Jo Marie Paradise.)

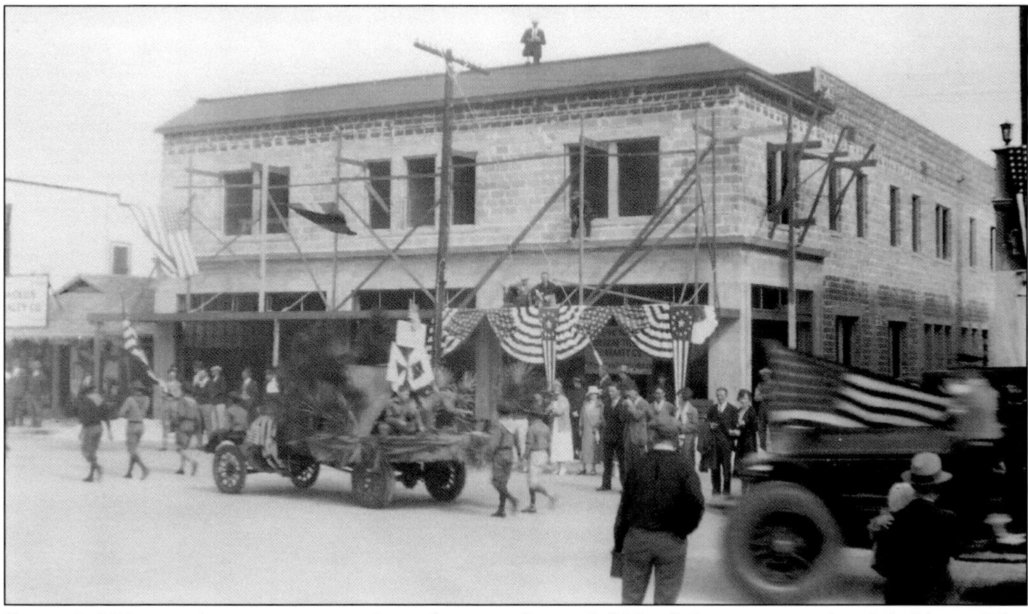

Some 2,000 marchers participated in the parade, and 500 of them were schoolchildren. The children were dressed to represent people from Florida's past, such as early pioneers and the Seminole Indians. Stuart's local Boy Scout troop is featured in this photograph. In the background along the parade route is the Peacock Arcade, which was still under construction by contractor Sam Matthews. This building would offer shops that opened onto a covered arcade, allowing protection from the weather for shoppers. (Courtesy of Martha Penhale Cuthbert.)

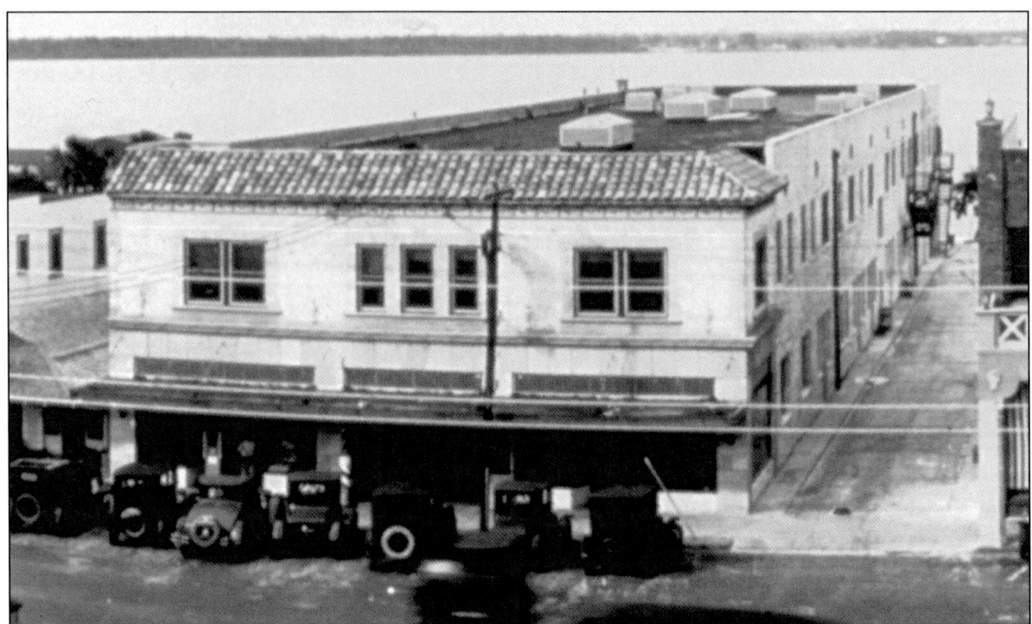

Developer Charles Peacock envisioned centralizing a variety of shops, businesses, and a hotel into one large building located on Flagler Avenue, near the St. Lucie River, in the heart of Stuart. This two-story stucco-and-tile, Spanish-style structure, named the Peacock Arcade, was completed in April 1926 and featured a 14-foot-wide arcade extending 190 feet through the building. On the ground floor were 12 shops and a beautiful restaurant at the rear with a dance pavilion overlooking the river. The top floor had hotel rooms and offices.

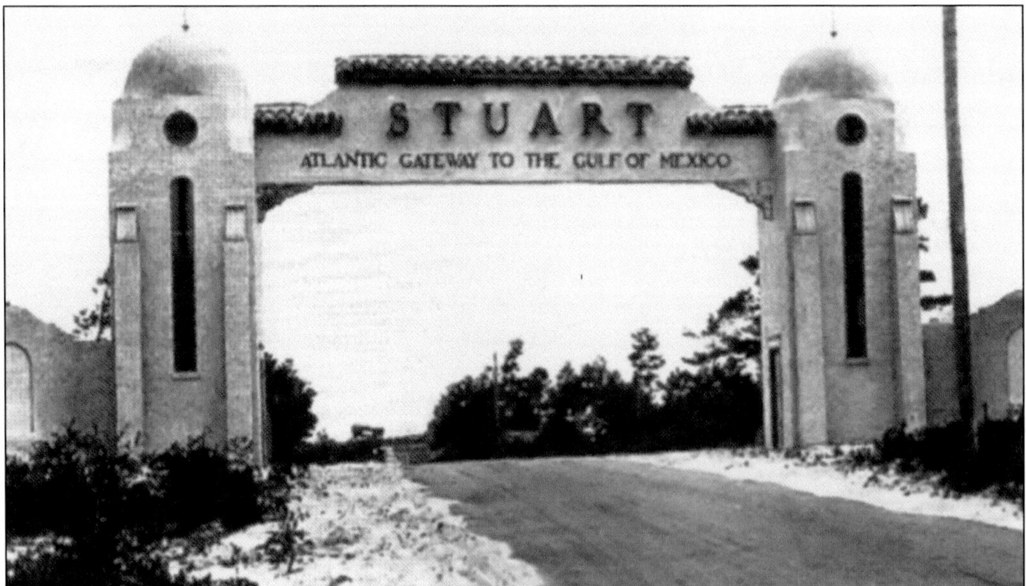

The words "Stuart: Atlantic Gateway to the Gulf of Mexico" on the welcoming archway at Stuart's northern boundary represented the great expectations of local business and government leaders in 1926. They had worked at making the St. Lucie Inlet larger and deeper, and having the South Fork of the St. Lucie River connect to the St. Lucie Canal, so boats could cross Lake Okeechobee and continue on the Caloosahatchee River west to the Gulf, some 154 miles away.

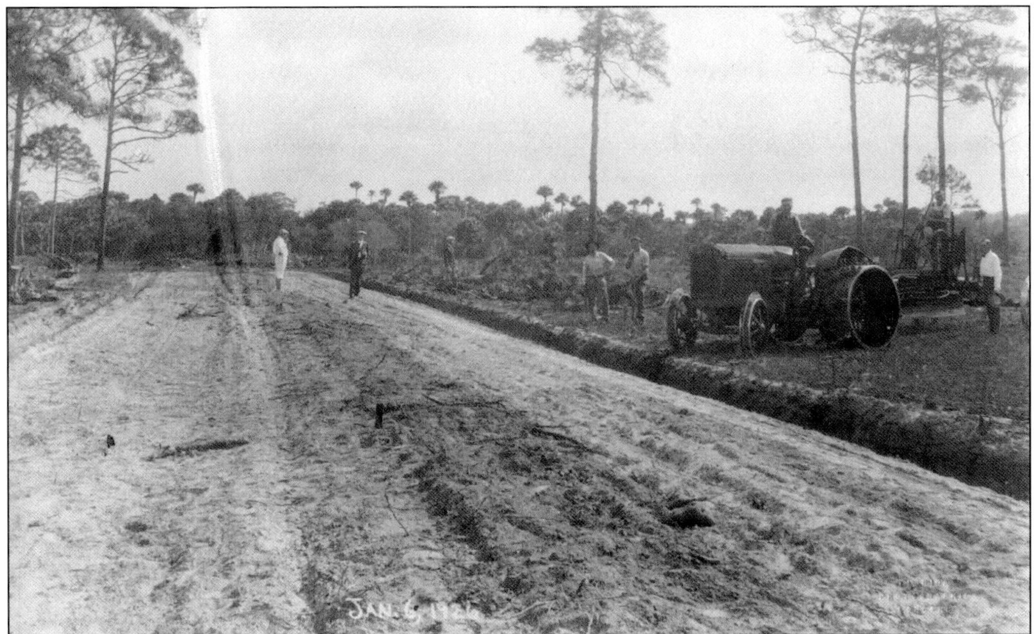

Besides new homes and buildings, the clearing of native vegetation for road construction became essential. This provided employment for residents. What were once wilderness lands in and around Stuart were being tamed. (Courtesy of Harry Lyons, Thurlow Collection.)

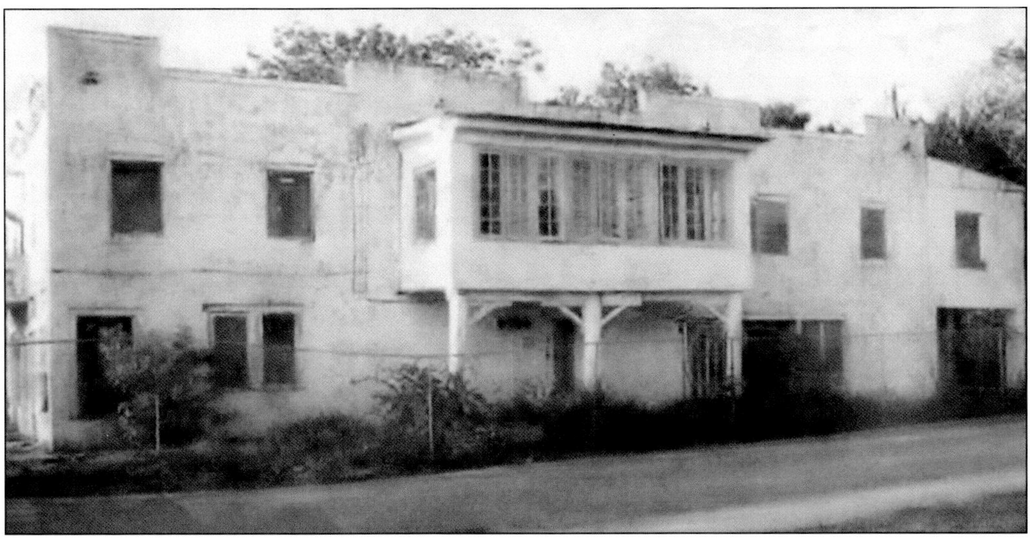

Thriving expansion in the town included Little Dixie, a self-contained neighborhood southwest of Stuart's downtown, home to most of the African American population. This white, two-story 1926 structure along Church Street, right in the heart of the busy commercial scene in Little Dixie, was owned and operated by George and Bessie McHardy. A pharmacy with an ice cream parlor was on the first floor, and rooms were rented out on the second.

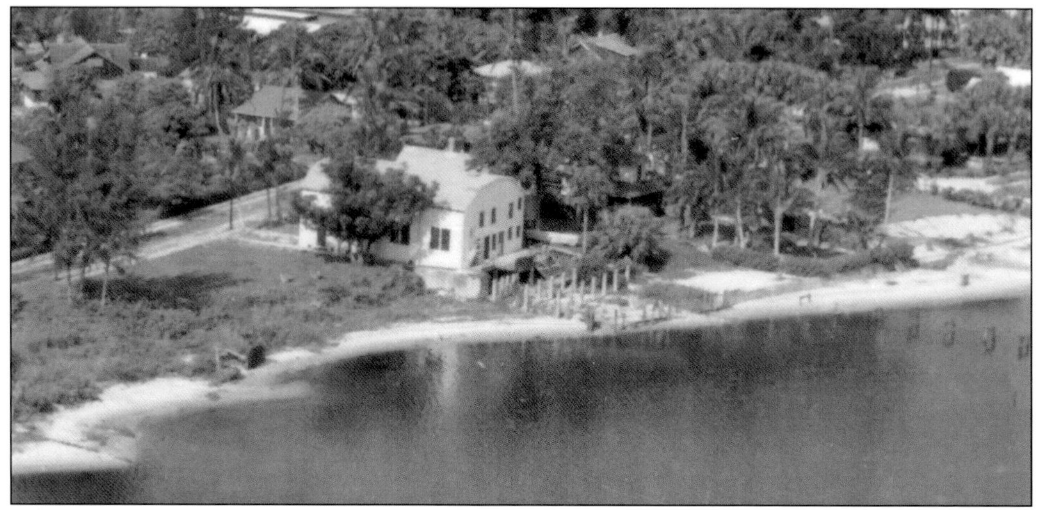

In June 1927, the new American Legion hall provided an auditorium and stage for various kinds of entertainment including dances, vaudeville and talent shows, musical comedies, and plays, as well as an arena for live boxing and wrestling matches. Its highly polished maple dance floor was considered one of the finest in Florida. Located on the St. Lucie River shore near the grand Dixie-Pelican Hotel, the Legion hall was near Seminole and Osceola Avenues. (Courtesy of Sandra and Tom Thurlow.)

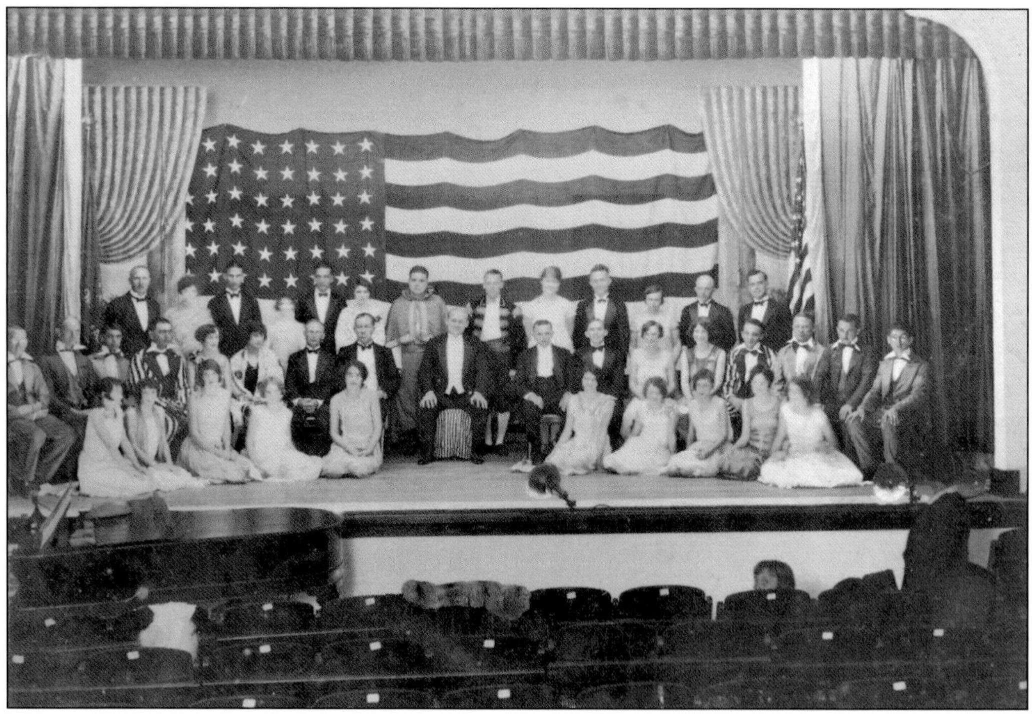

The American Legion hall stage was used for many amateur plays and singing performances by the local residents. There were dressing rooms, lavatories, and showers. The building had four large ceiling fans and two ventilators in the roof that provided ample air circulation for the auditorium and stage. Featured orchestras furnished entertainment with lively music and dancing for over 300 couples on a weekly basis. (Courtesy of the Thurlow and Luckhardt Collections.)

The Martin County Business Men's Association representing the local chamber of commerce saw that brochures were printed and distributed across Florida describing the fine accommodations available in Stuart. With 14 apartment houses and eight hotels pictured and described in the brochure, visitors knew what was available. Pictured in the late 1920s are the Sunrise Apartments, with rates for a four-room apartment at $8 a week. (Courtesy of the Luckhardt Collection.)

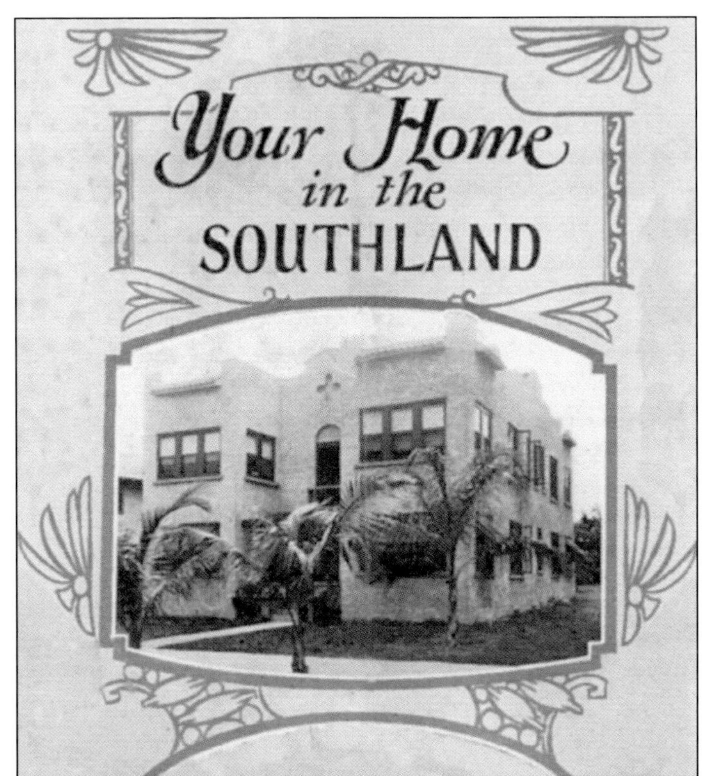

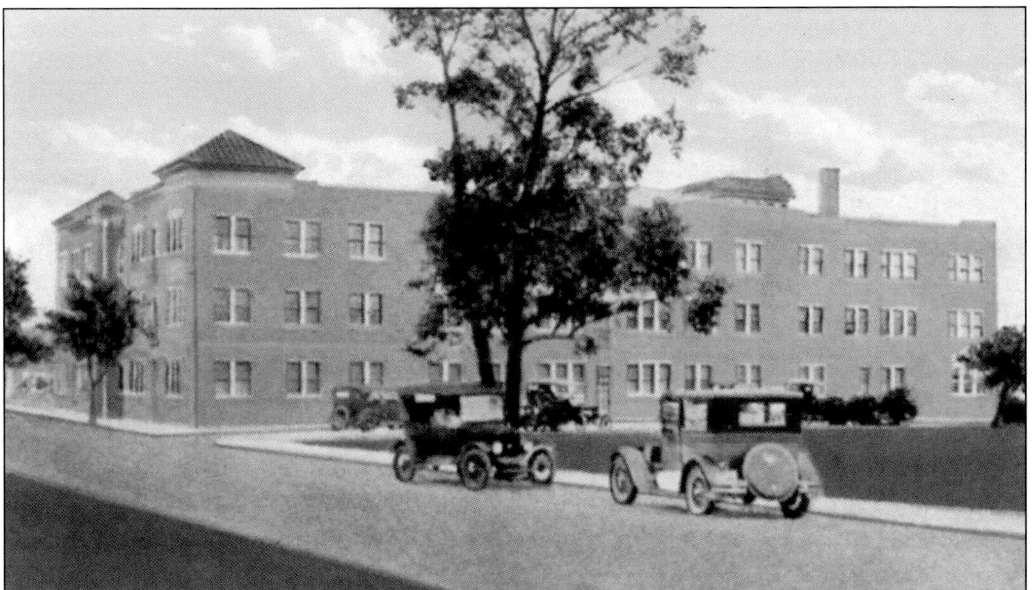

Opulence and grandeur best describe the three-story El Bit-Lor Apartments, constructed on Fourth Street (East Ocean) between 1925 and 1926. Bert A. Bittan and John E. Taylor partnered to build one of the finest apartment buildings on the East Coast. The name El Bit-Lor was derived from their last names. The U-shaped, Spanish Mediterranean Revival, fireproof structure, with a total of 57 fully furnished apartments, cost $225,000 to build with rents starting at $50 a month. (Courtesy of Doug Witham.)

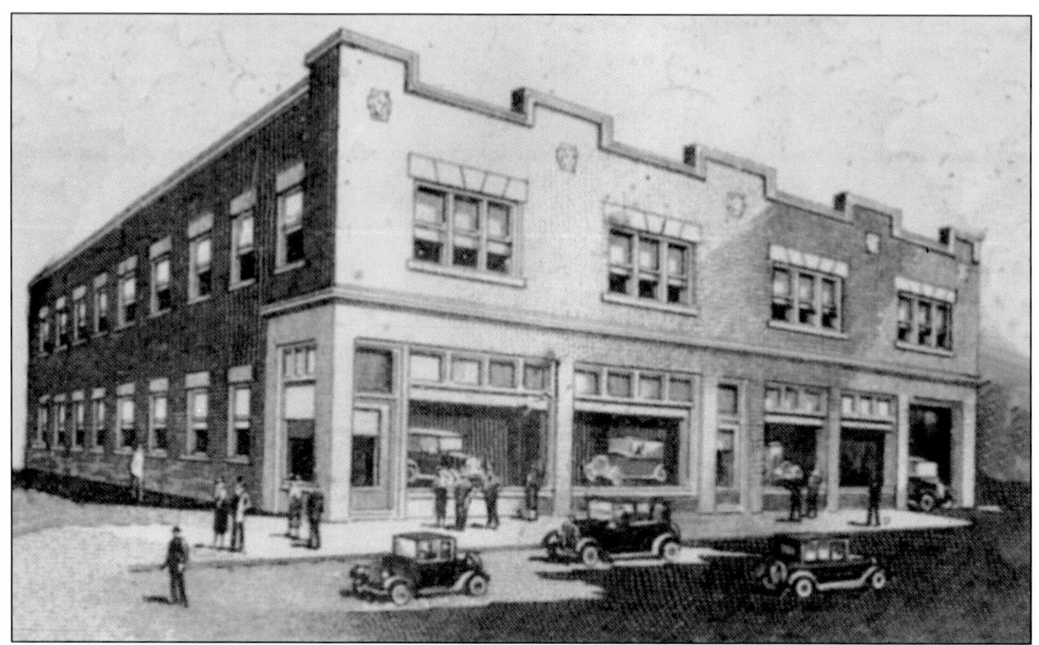

George H. Browning opened Browning Motors, selling Fords in Stuart in late 1922. By early 1925, Browning needed a larger building and purchased the triangular corner of Fourth Street (East Ocean) and Flagler Avenue. He sketched out plans for a new two-story block structure. The impressive first-floor showroom and offices opened in March 1926 with six full-size Fords and Lincoln vehicles. The second-floor repair shop could hold 75 vehicles, which entered the top level using a ramp.

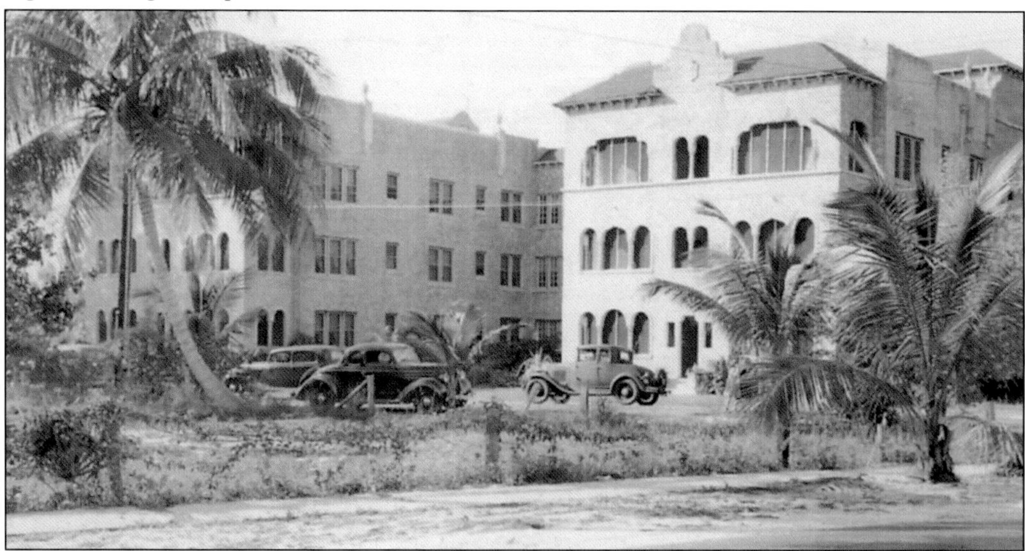

In the Hubert Bessey Addition, part of the original Bessey homestead, Adam W. France purchased property with 300 feet along the south bank of Frazier Creek. France designed a Mediterranean Revival–style apartment building named the France Apartments. It was made of poured concrete and had two wings and three stories. It featured a central courtyard resembling the architecture of a hacienda, offering wonderful cross ventilation. With a boat basin along Frazier Creek, it had river access. Ready for rent by 1927, there were 30 one-bedroom units with a solarium on each floor.

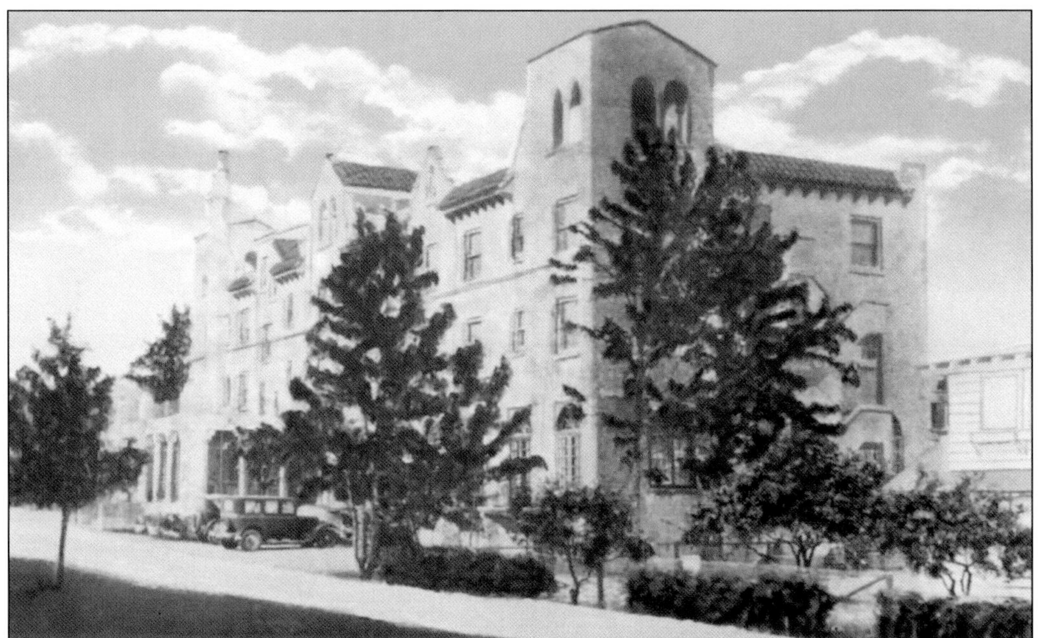

The Dixie-Pelican Hotel opened in January 1926, and by 1929, its name had changed to the Pelican Hotel. It was known for emphasizing four important business principles: hospitality, comfort, service, and courtesy. Along with the name change, a new lessee, Drew W. King Sr., had a pier and dock added into the St. Lucie River to encourage yachtsmen to moor their boats and stay at the hotel. (Courtesy of the Luckhardt Collection.)

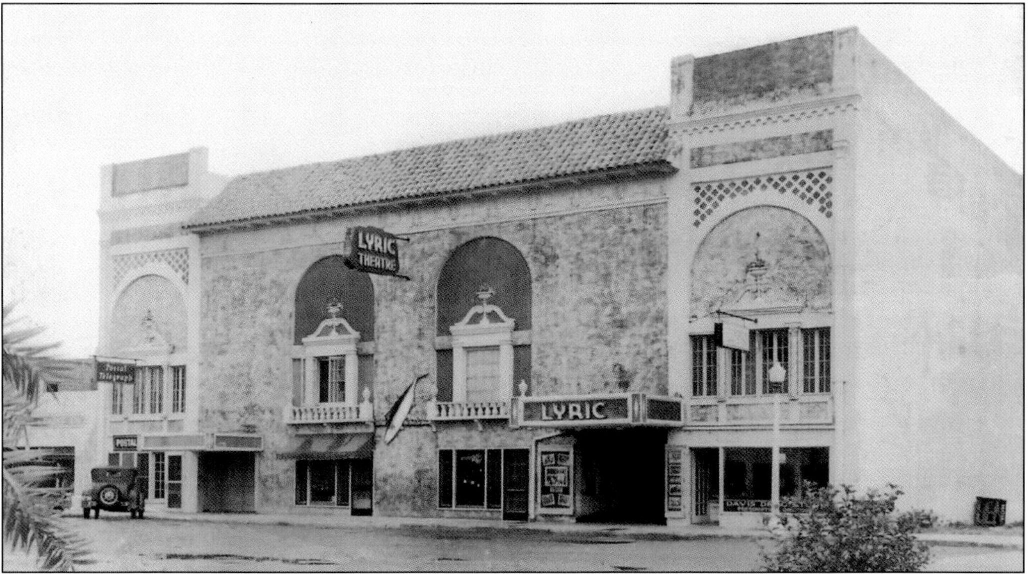

The third Lyric Theatre, opened in March 1926, was the star showpiece of Stuart. The first 1914 Lyric, built by the Hancock family, was along Osceola Avenue. Expansion was later needed, so the second Lyric was constructed, opening in 1919 along Railroad Avenue. With the 1920s boom, this third Lyric would be the grandest. The structure was multipurpose in 1929, with a telegraph office to the left and several different leased shop spaces to the right for a drugstore, key and lock shop, and a tackle shop.

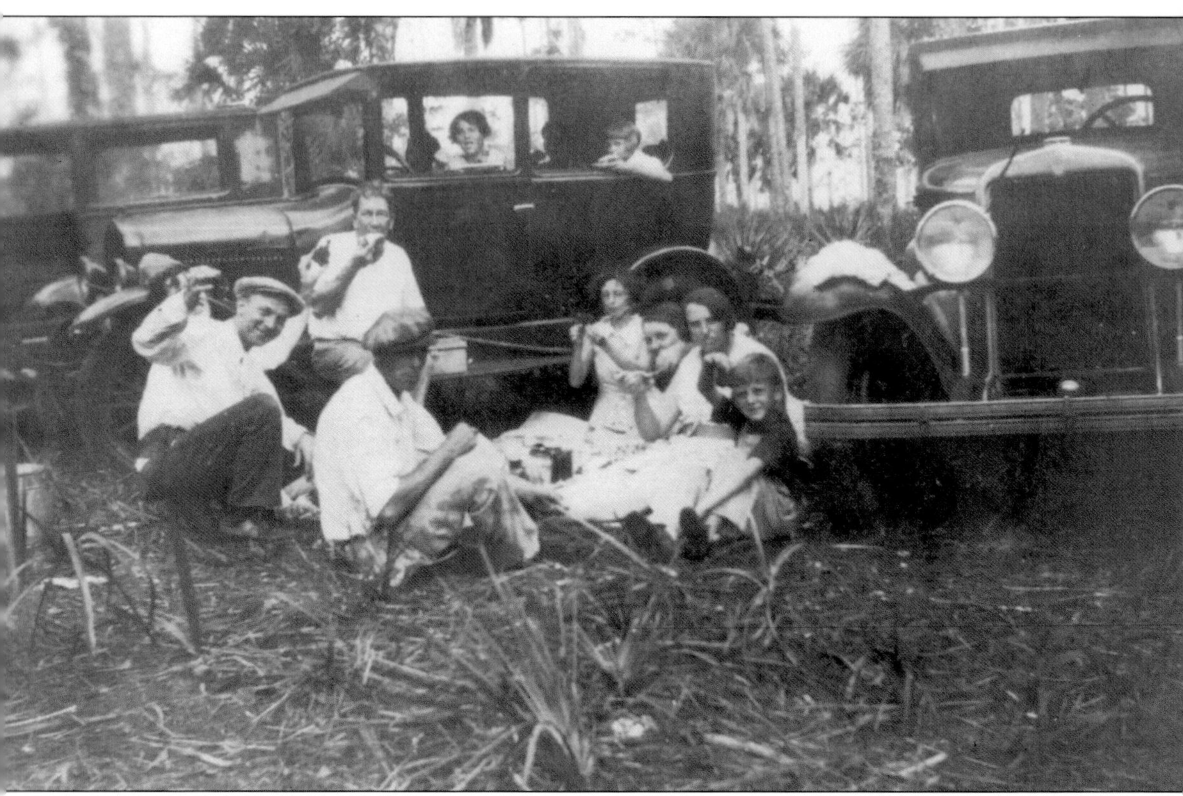

A favorite form of relaxation for Stuart residents was the chance to get back to nature and enjoy their piece of paradise. Just driving a couple miles out of town offered the opportunity for a picnic; nothing fancy, just a pleasant day with family and friends. From left to right are Charles Rue, A.L. "Roy" Lane, an unidentified man with hat, Lois Rue, unidentified, Edith Coventry, and an unidentified boy. Children in the car are Leila Rue, unidentified, and Leona Rue. (Courtesy of the Rue-Luckhardt Collection.)

Seven

Fishing Capital for Presidents

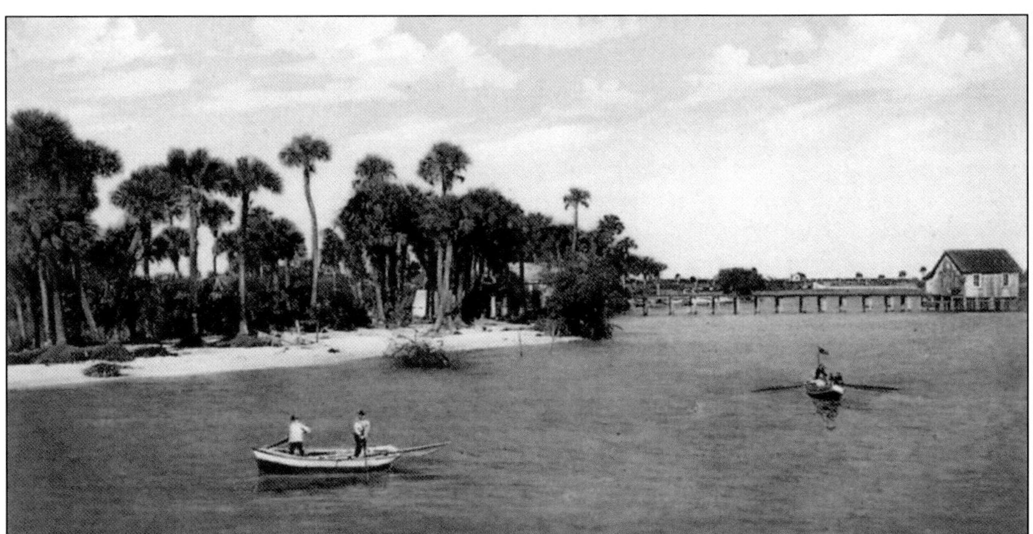

Fishing along the St. Lucie and Indian Rivers has a long history among all the settlers of Stuart. Fish houses for the storage and sale of fish dotted the shoreline. This image from the 1910s shows the Blakeslee's Fish House in the St. Lucie River to the right. (Courtesy of Doug Witham.)

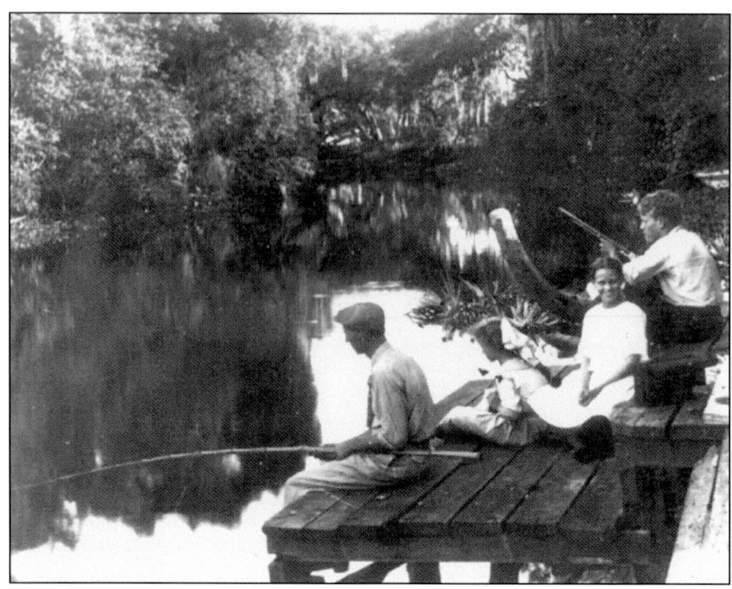

Fishing was not always just in a boat on the St. Lucie River. With the many smaller creeks and waterways lining the shore, there were plenty of quiet areas with a little dock from which to fish. This image from the early 1900s shows the North Fork branch of the St. Lucie River. (Courtesy of Sandra and Tom Thurlow.)

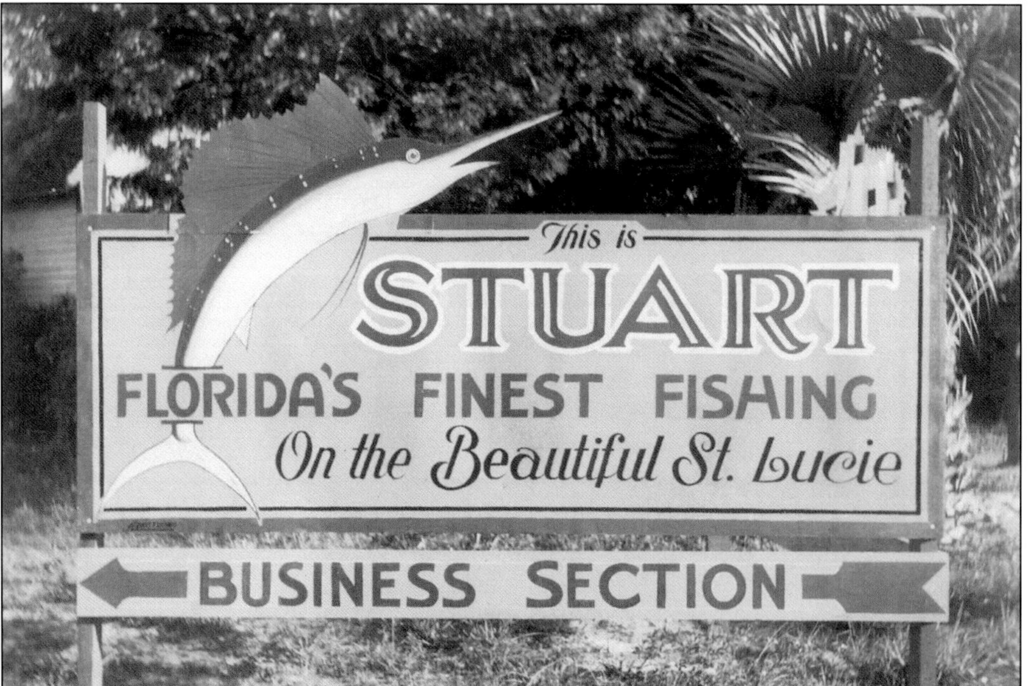

This sign greeted the many visitors and residents in the 1920s as they motored from the north side of the St. Lucie River across the concrete bridge into Stuart. Numerous people were drawn to the fishing in the river surrounding Stuart as well as the abundant sportfishing of sailfish out in the Atlantic Ocean.

To bring in the big ones was always a thrill. Pictured around 1919 are Ernest Fulton "Ernie" Lyons (left) and hunting guide Mac McKibben; they are landing a huge grouper from the St. Lucie River. Lyons later became a local newspaper man and then editor of the *Stuart News*. He wrote of the great beauty of the river and the need for its preservation and became a passionate environmentalist. (Courtesy of Sandra and Tom Thurlow.)

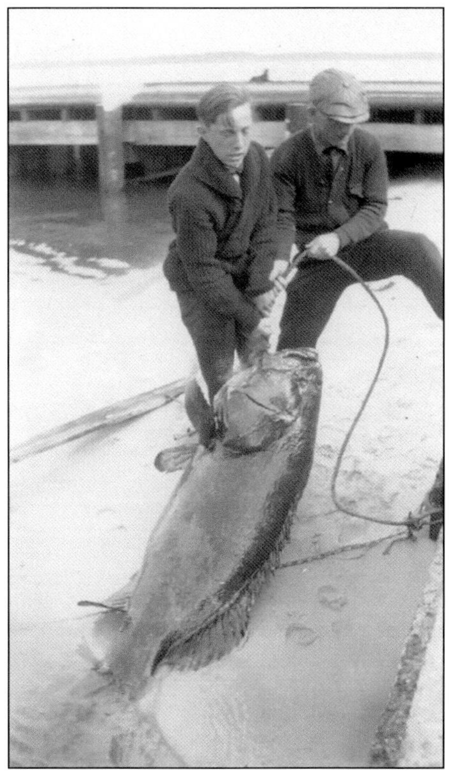

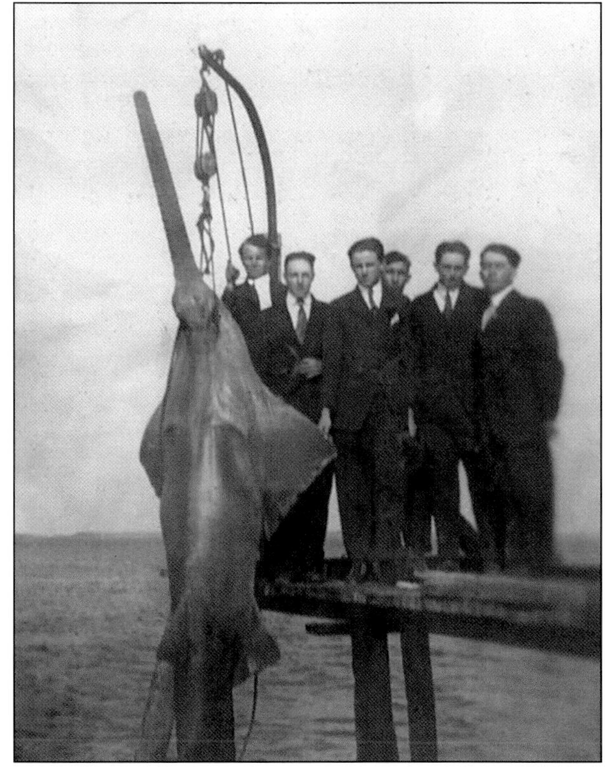

Another prized catch years ago in the Atlantic off the Stuart coast was the sawfish (saw shark). This one was proudly shown off by several locals in 1916, all dressed in their fine suits for the photograph. (Courtesy of Karen Hartman Malfregeot.)

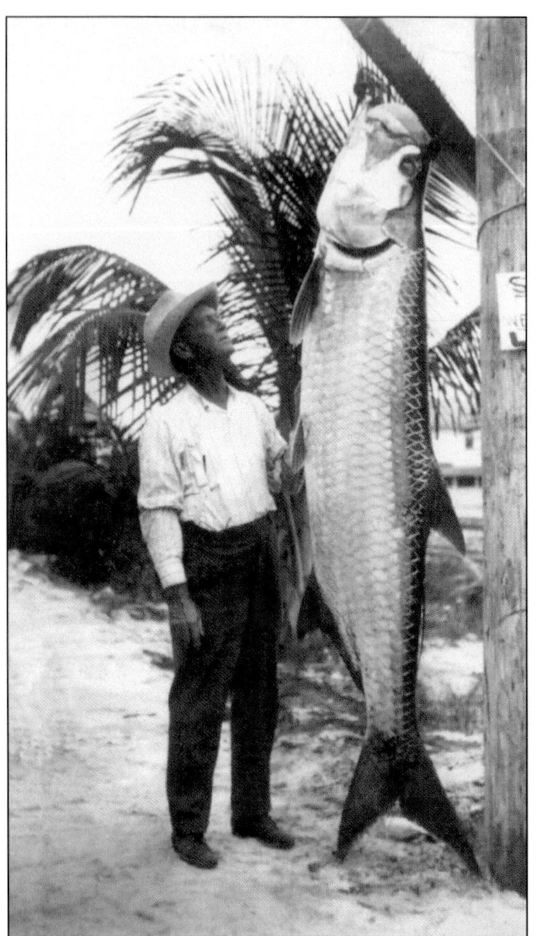

Morris Johns was pleased with his tarpon catch in the St. Lucie River around 1920. Such a fish might have weighed in at about 180 pounds. As Stuart developed over the coming decades and the water drained into the St. Lucie River from Lake Okeechobee to prevent overflow, the river became less tolerant for these large tarpons. (Courtesy of the Coventry Collection, Elliott Museum.)

Charter fishing vessels in the 1930s left the docks nearly daily in the winter season, taking sportfishermen out into the Atlantic Ocean in search of the plentiful sailfish and marlins, some seven to eight feet long. Capt. Toley Engebretsen established Toley's Boatyard south of Stuart in Salerno. To maintain the sportfishing of sailfish, in 1941, the release system was established, where the sailfish caught would be released and the fisherman got a prized pin designed by Curt Whiticar stating "Release."

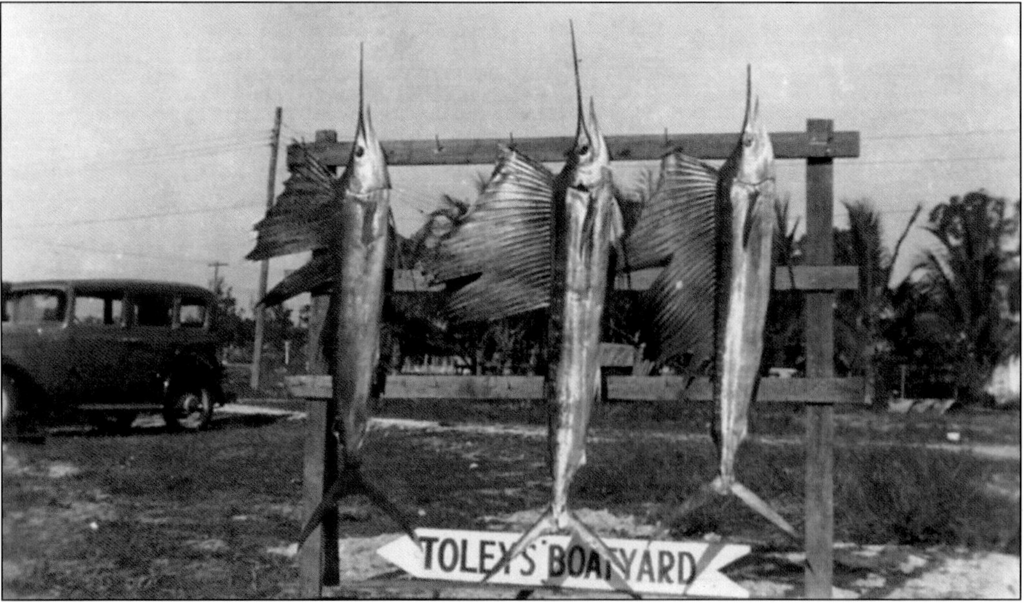

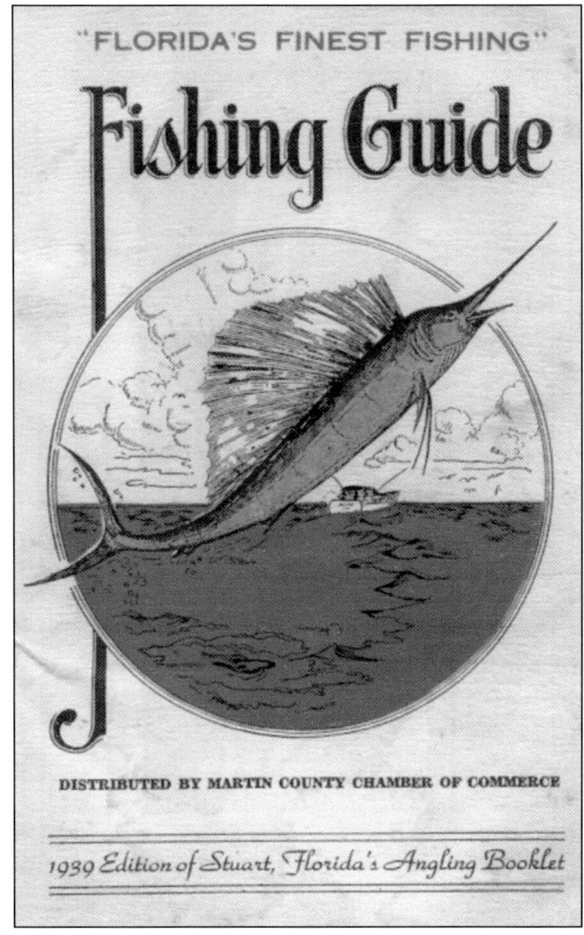

The *Fishing Guide* booklet, illustrating game and sportfishing in Stuart's rivers and the Atlantic Ocean, was first published around 1933. The guide was printed annually, with thousands of copies going to tourists as well as local fishermen. Sponsors included the Martin County Chamber of Commerce, which could see to it that the fishing guides were sent all across the United States. In 1935, over 20,000 copies were printed and distributed. This cover is from the 1939 edition.

Entrance signs praised the great fishing around Stuart. The Stuart Sailfishing Club, formed in 1936, promoted the city as the prime fishing region in the country. The motto "Sailfish Capital" was adopted by the early 1940s. This new 1954 entrance sign proclaimed the motto, only the sign maker used the wrong spelling of "capital," which was soon corrected. The title of "Sailfish Capital of the World" was officially declared in 1957 by the Florida secretary of state, giving the city the exclusive right to use the slogan for advertising. (Courtesy of MCHS, Elliott Museum.)

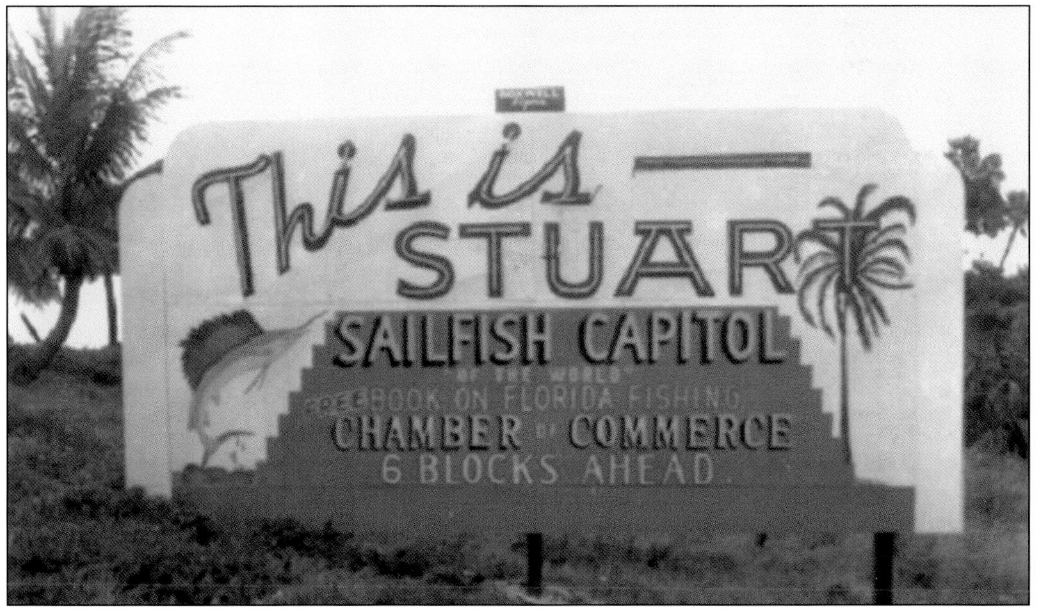

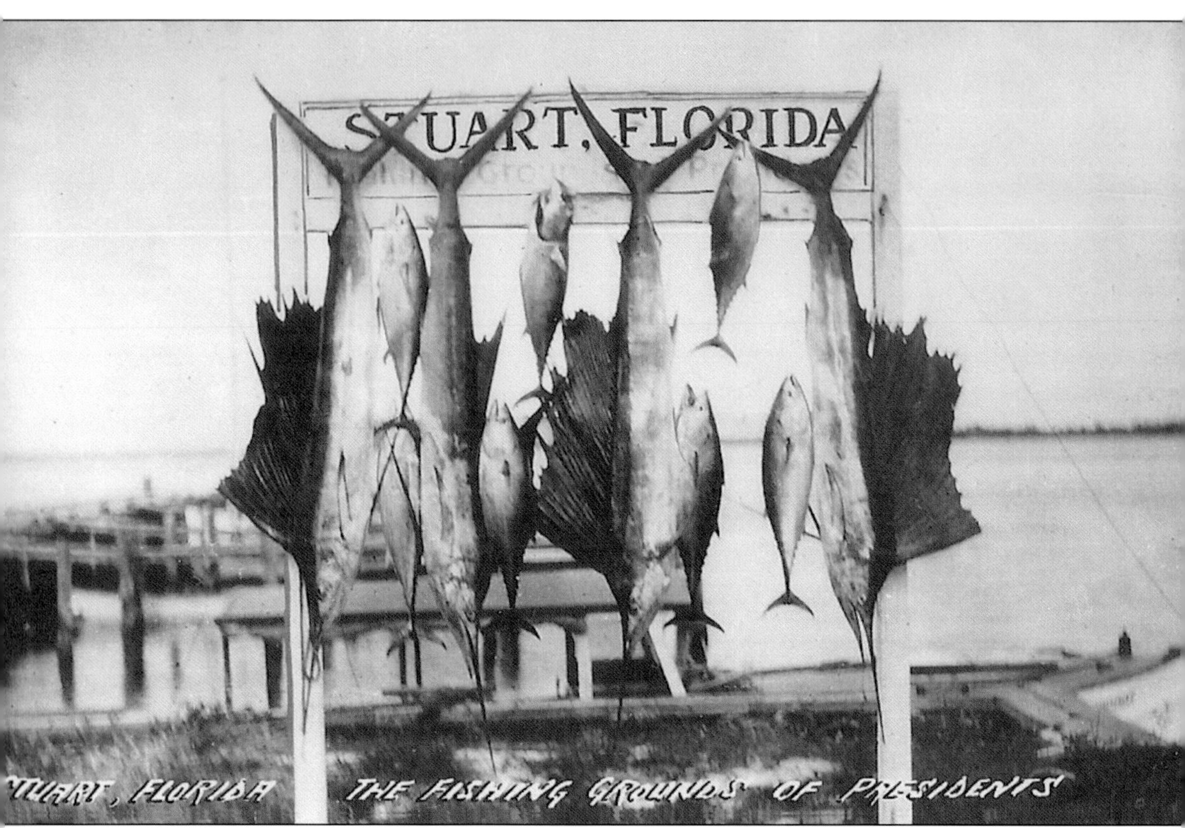

"The Fishing Grounds of Presidents" was a popular slogan that referred to the fact that five famous angler presidents came to the area to fish: Grover Cleveland, Chester Arthur, Theodore Roosevelt, Howard Taft, and Warren G. Harding. It began in 1899 with Cleveland, who praised the great fishing he experienced in Stuart and enjoyed it so much that he continued fishing here until his death in June 1908.

Eight

Economy Crisis of the 1930s

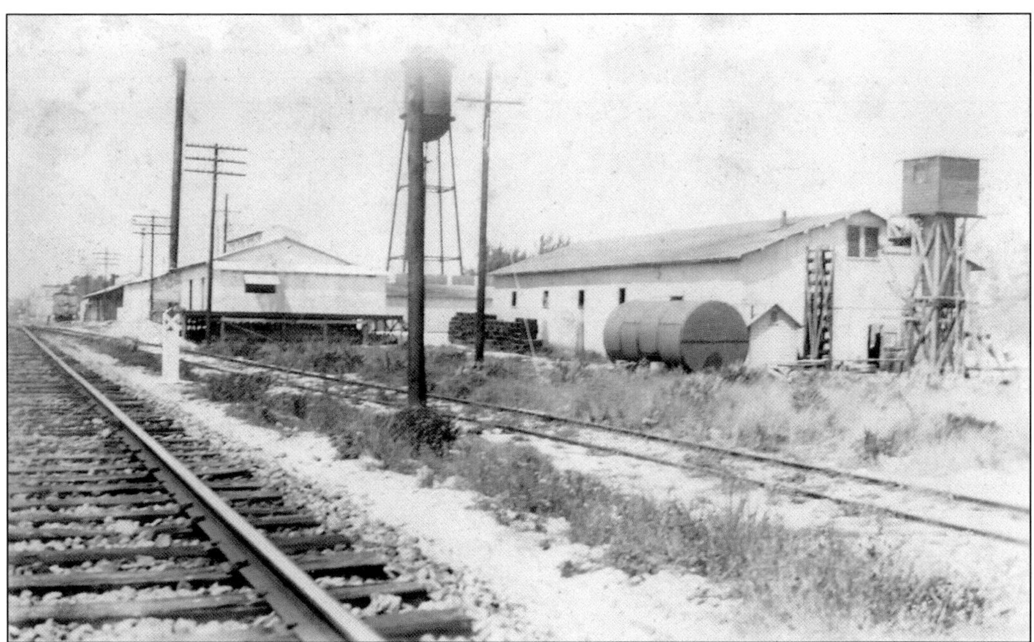

Along a dirt road off South Flagler Avenue was the Stuart Ice Company. In 1924, Fred E. Murphy built it just north of Casa Lumber Company. In the background are the Southern Utilities Light and Power plant, the town's first electric generating facility, and the water tower. The ice building, pictured at right, cost $50,000 and was Stuart's largest and finest ice plant. About 25 tons of ice could be produced per day with a storage capacity for 70 tons. (Courtesy of Ted Huf.)

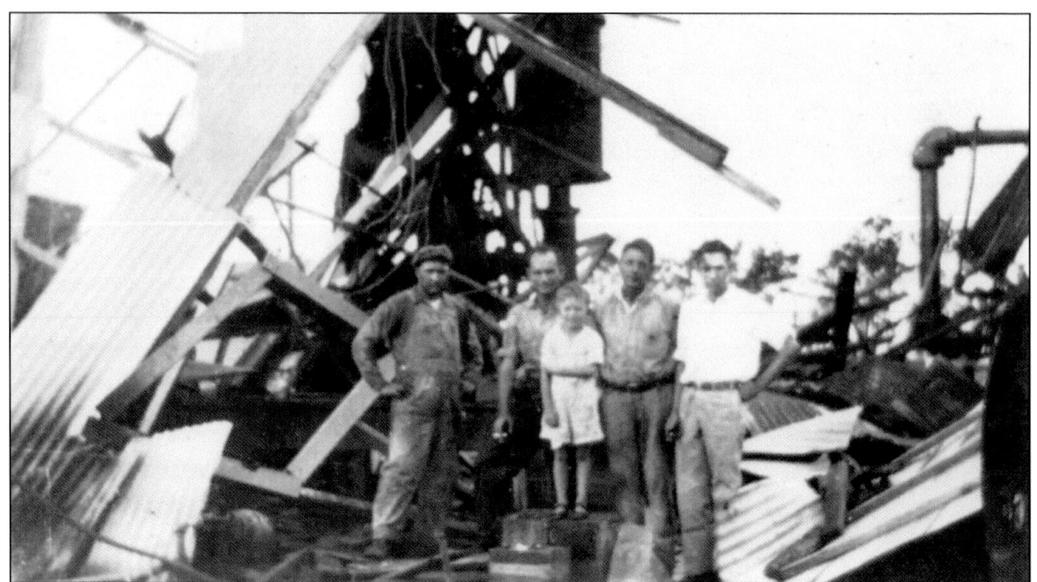

There was a change of owners in 1927 for the Stuart Ice Company, and then on September 16, 1928, a hurricane severely damaged the plant facility. It was rebuilt with a new flat roof and with poured concrete to produce a thick-walled ice plant, approximately 50 by 75 by 20 feet. The 1928 hurricane was only the first of several major storms to strike Stuart as the town moved into the 1930s. From left to right are two unidentified, Allen Andrews, unidentified, and Bill Andrews. (Courtesy of Ted Huf.)

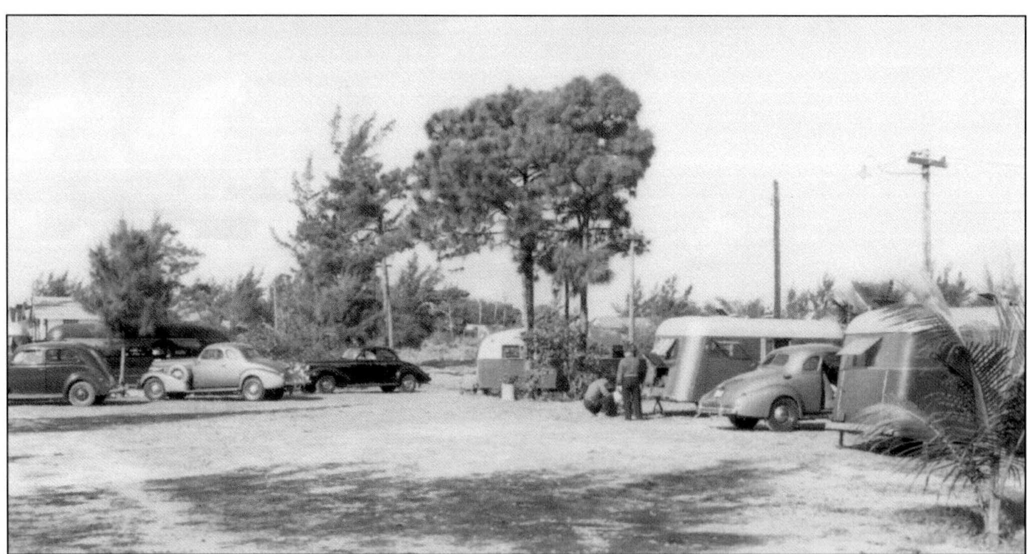

Even with the major economic crisis across Florida after the land bust of the late 1920s and then the Great Depression of the 1930s, people still managed to travel to Florida. The St. Lucie Auto Camp remained a popular destination in Stuart, offering winter tourists an affordable place to stay with many amenities on the premises. Those who had their own tents paid just 25¢ a night, and a four-room furnished cottage rented for $15 a month.

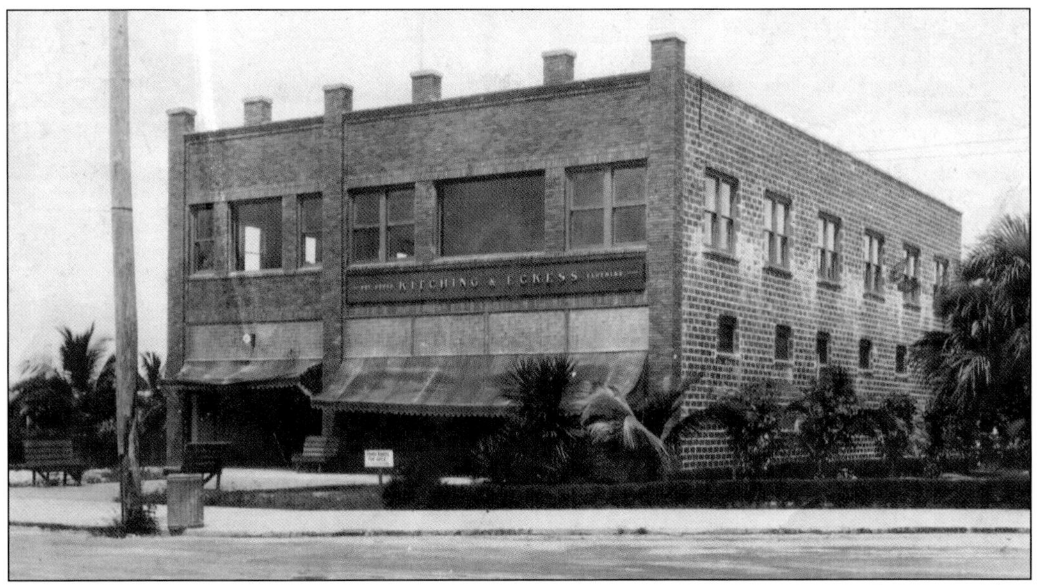

From the simple Stanley Kitching store of the 1910s, Benjamin Eckess and Kitching joined to create a new and larger brick department store, which opened in March 1922. A special attribute was a balcony that provided shade for the first-floor commercial space and a reviewing stand for parades. The balcony was removed by the 1930s, with only cloth awnings for shade. Eckess became sole owner of the business by 1934, but Kitching remained the owner of the building. (Courtesy of Jo Marie Paradise.)

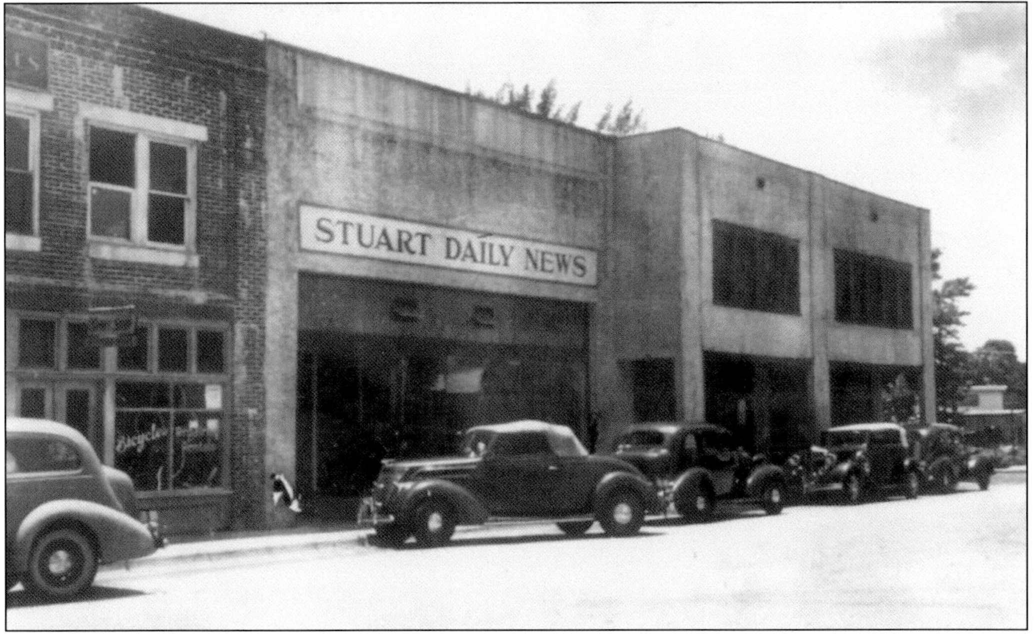

In September 1925, the *Stuart Messenger* became a daily newspaper, and the name changed to *Stuart Daily News*. In 1928, it was purchased by Edwin Menninger and continued as a daily paper in the former Messenger Building. The name was changed to *Stuart News*, and due to economic conditions, Menninger was forced to change to a weekly paper by September 1938, coming out every Thursday. (Courtesy of MCHS, Elliott Museum.)

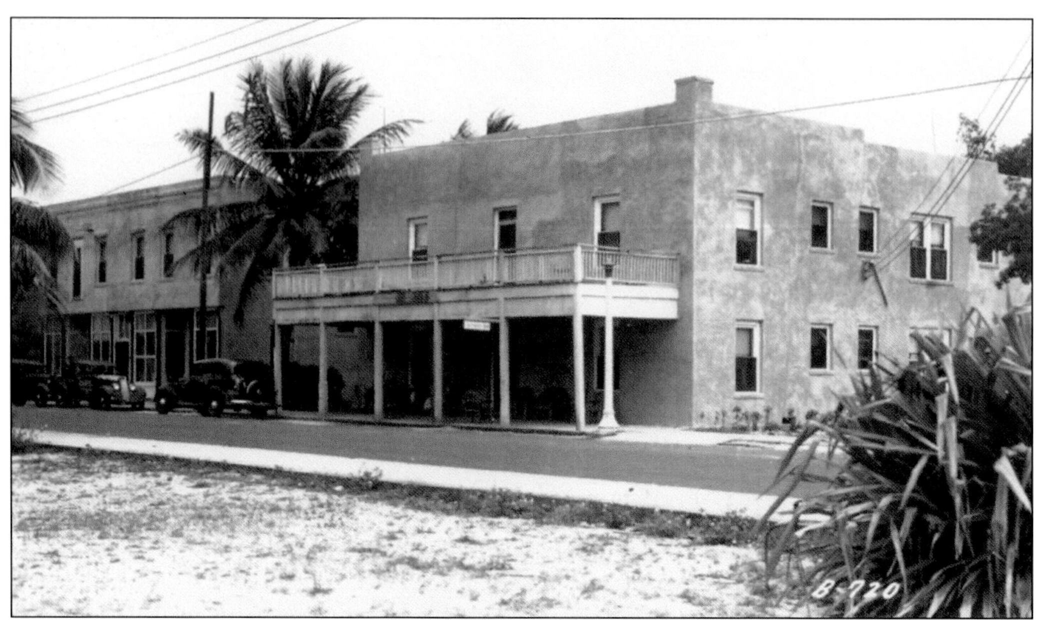

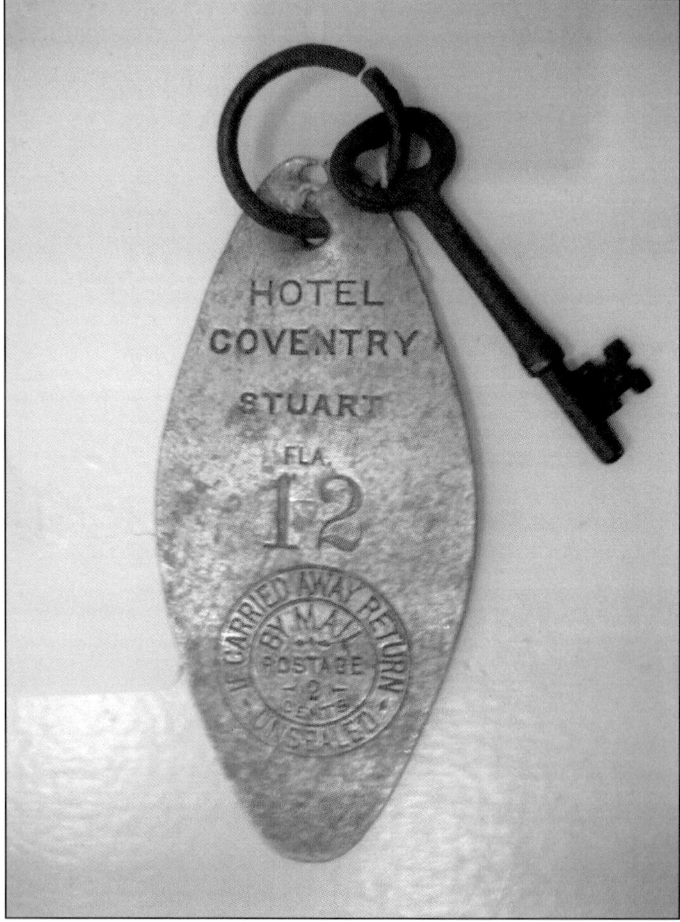

Even during the depths of the Great Depression in the 1930s, the Coventry Hotel (left) and Coventry Apartments (right) operated by John Coventry, his wife, Charlotte, and their daughter Edith, kept up their longtime high standards. By October 1936, the two Coventry buildings had been sold to Maurice P. Payette. A new roof, modern bathroom fixtures, and extensive redecorating were done, at a cost of $4,000, and the apartments were renamed the Majestic Apartments. (Courtesy of Sandra and Tom Thurlow.)

The new owner of the Coventry Hotel, Maurice P. Payette, kept that name for the hotel. John Coventry, the original owner and proprietor, died in 1938. This hotel key and its holder for room No. 12 are reminders of a time long ago.

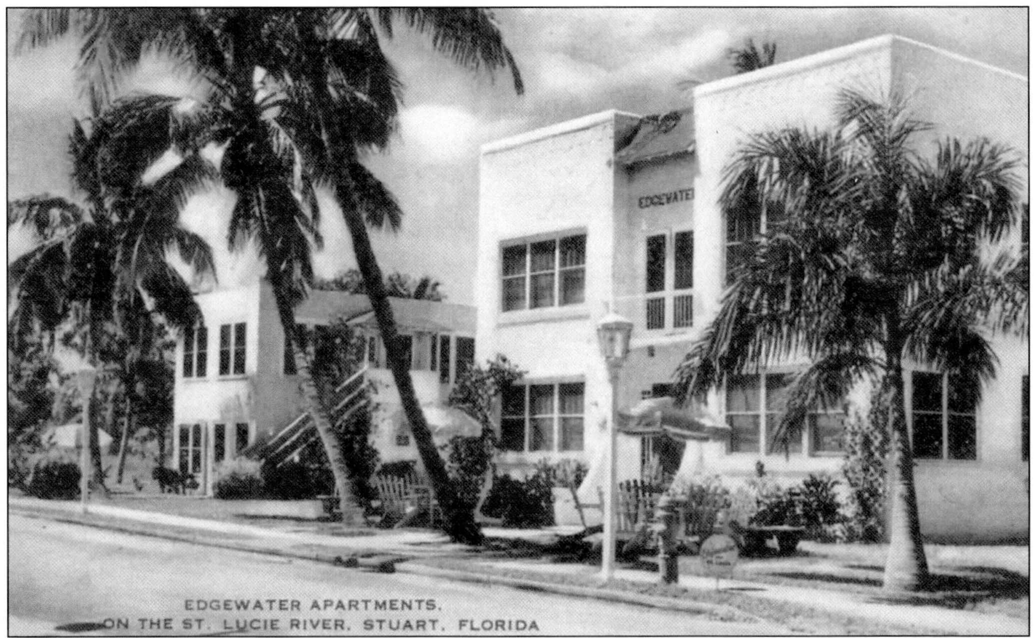

One of the 1920s boom structures still popular in the 1930s was the Edgewater Apartments, located in Stuart's St. Lucie Crescent neighborhood, south of Frazier Creek and along the St. Lucie River. The two-story concrete-and-stucco structure featured eight two-room apartments for $30 a month and eight three-room apartments for $50, each with a kitchen and bathroom.

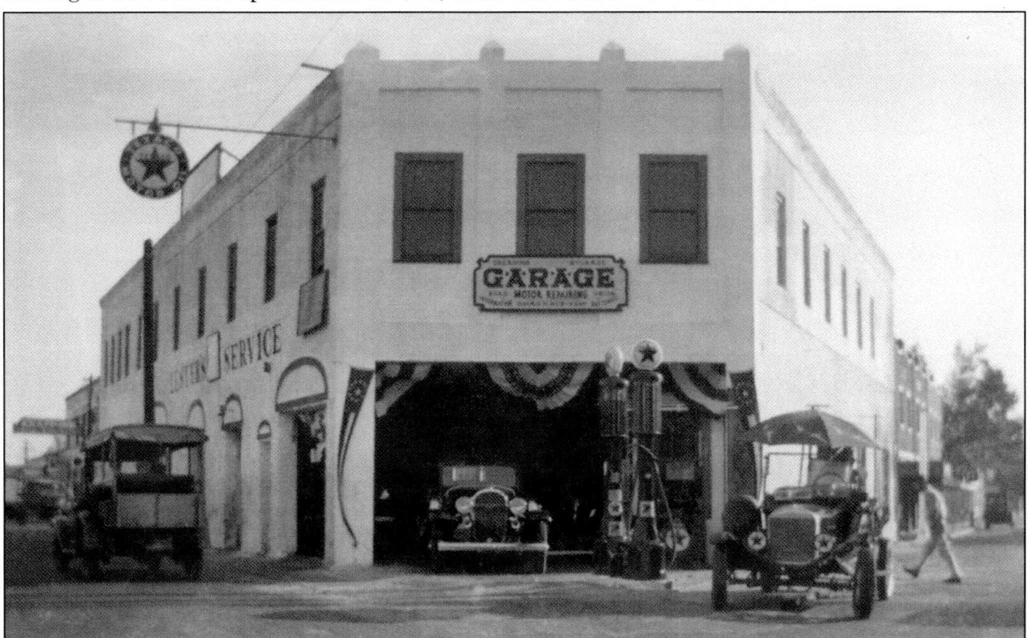

The original Babcock Garage (Flatiron Building) from the 1910s, rebuilt in the early 1920s, was still going strong in the 1930s. It was now the Andrew Lester Service Garage, a very distinctive triangle-shaped building on the corner of Dixie Highway and Second Street near the railroad tracks. All types of auto repairs could be done at the facility. Since many people were not purchasing new cars in the 1930s, repairs became vital. (Courtesy of the Rue-Luckhardt Collection.)

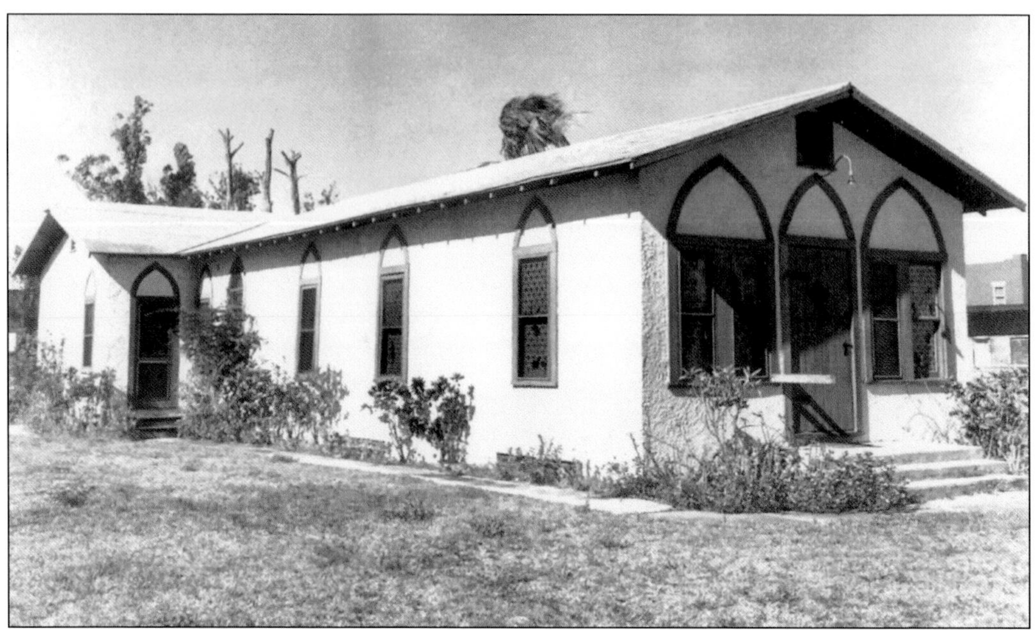

The original 1895 community church building along the railroad tracks had served many purposes, including as a restaurant, fruit store, newspaper office, chamber of commerce, and a real estate office. A major move and transformation occurred in 1930 when a new Episcopal congregation needed a building. This vintage church, purchased for $300, was moved to Third Street and was renovated by the church members. In January 1932, it was ready for services and named St. Mary's Episcopal Church. (Courtesy of the Rue-Luckhardt Collection.)

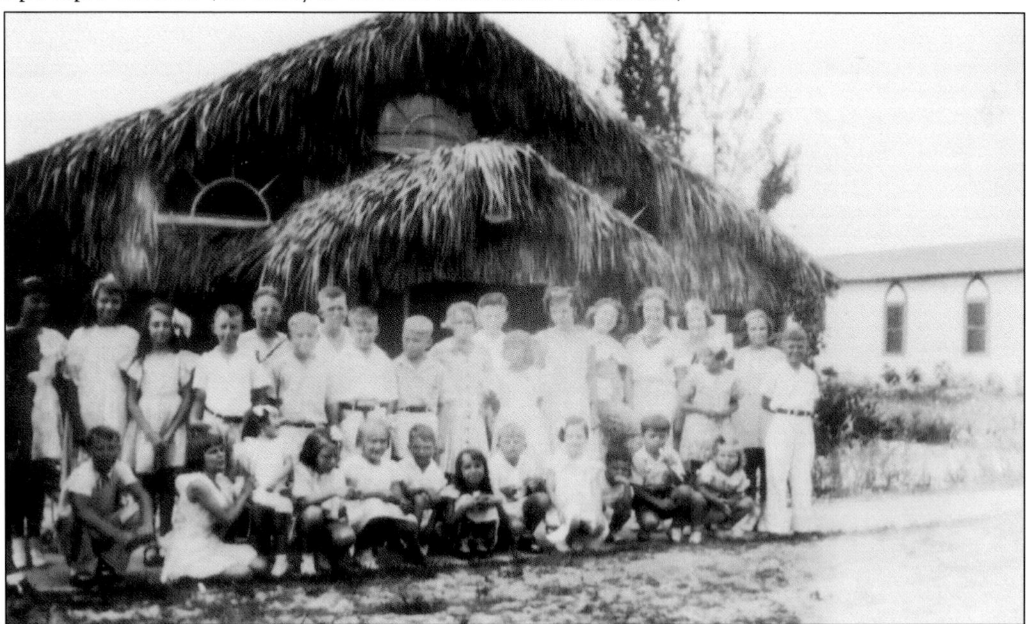

Added next door to the new St. Mary's Episcopal Church was a special thatched structure that could be used for large church meetings, pageants, and shows put on by different members of the congregation. This mid-1930s photograph shows children in front of the structure and the church to the right. (Courtesy of Dale Hipson.)

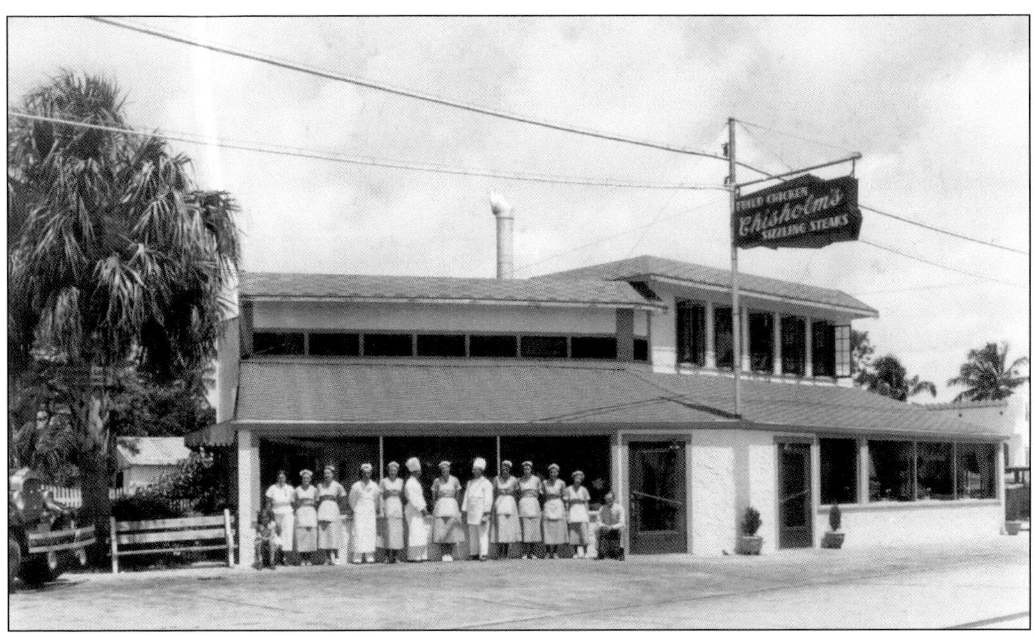

William and Anna Chisholm established Chisholm's Grill in 1928, which was first located in a small trailer parked south of the concrete auto bridge over the St. Lucie River. Later, a new and larger restaurant was constructed, with an advantageous spot along the highway convenient to the traveling public, especially the bus lines. It became a very popular eating establishment during the 1930s. Air conditioning was installed by July 1939, making it the first business in Stuart to do so.

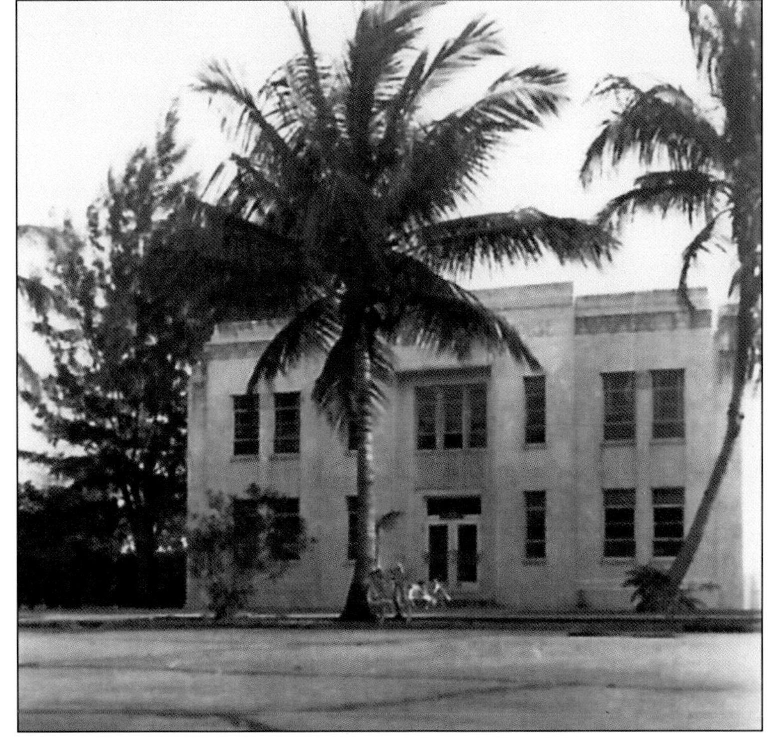

In 1925, the new county's courthouse was the former 1909 two-story school building. By 1937, to provide additional office and courtroom space, the federal government under the Public Works Administration provided the money to have a large addition built on the front of the former school building and to have renovations done to the inside. This also provided work for many men who had been unemployed. The dedication ceremonies were held in June 1937.

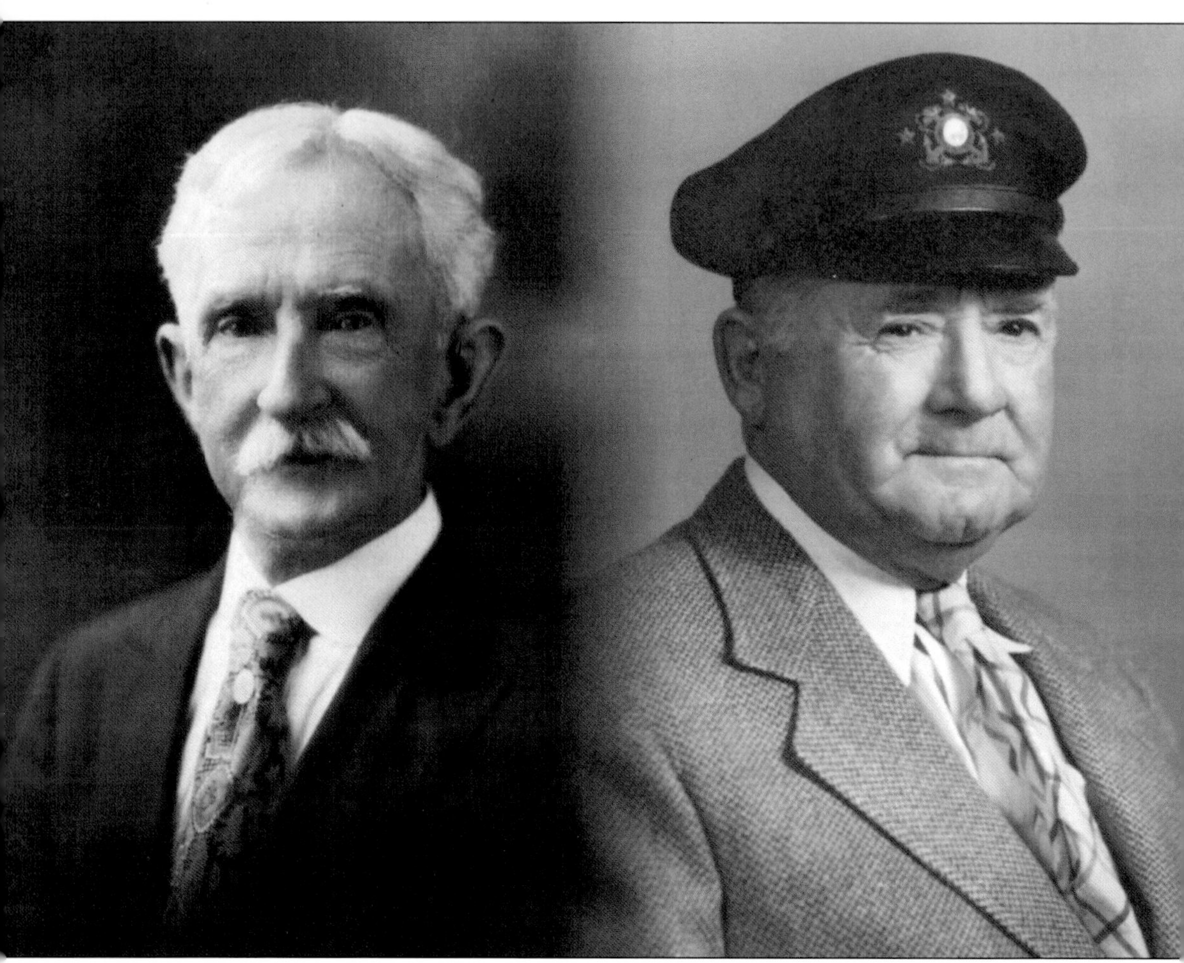

Two men worked tirelessly to improve the economic and civic life of Stuart: Walter Kitching (left) and his nephew Stanley Kitching (right). Walter arrived in 1894 and went on to be the town's leading merchant and the Bank of Stuart's president. He also donated land parcels to the community and planted mangoes, Australian oaks, and coconut palms across Stuart. Walter died in August 1932. His nephew Stanley arrived in 1902 and worked as a merchant, but he mostly was a Stuart "booster," encouraging new churches, organizing civic and social groups, developing the St. Lucie Inlet, and creating waterway improvements. His nickname was "Mr. Stuart." (Courtesy of Jo Marie Paradise, Sandra and Tom Thurlow.)

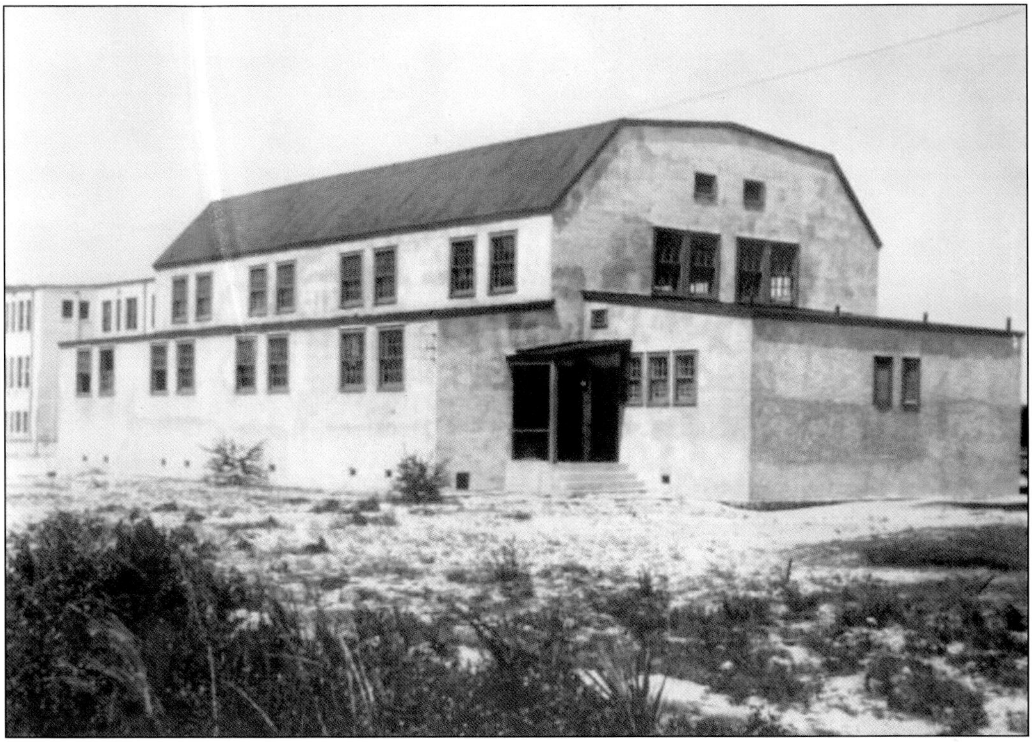

A major structure needed for the Stuart High School in the 1930s was a gymnasium. Through Federal Emergency Relief Administration funding, a $13,500 gymnasium, with seating for 450, was built in 1934 north of the football field. Another addition to the main school building came in 1937 with a railed, steel-stepped fire escape, anchored to the back outside wall, and side entrances with concrete steps into the auditorium. (Courtesy of Florida Memory Project.)

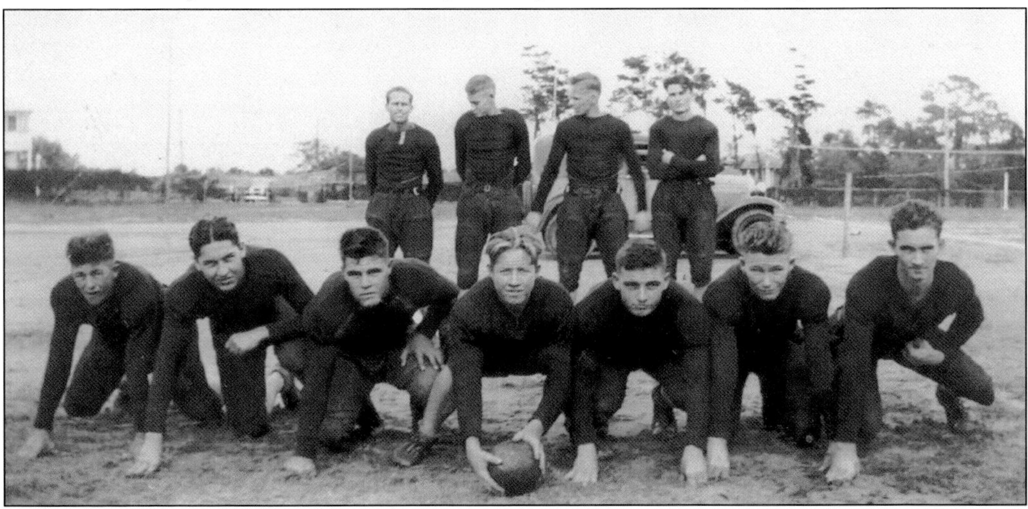

Sports have long been of major interest to students and citizens of Stuart. The 1934 Stuart High School football team proved to be ready for any opponent. Many of these students went on to be leading citizens in Stuart. Team members are, from left to right, (first row) Pete Robertson, Siylvia ?, Bohen Bowmen, Walter Fultz, Duncan John Dunscomb, Ross Witham, and Reg Kitching; (second row) Buster Ulmer, Homer Witham, Chuck Kindred, and Harris Lowery.

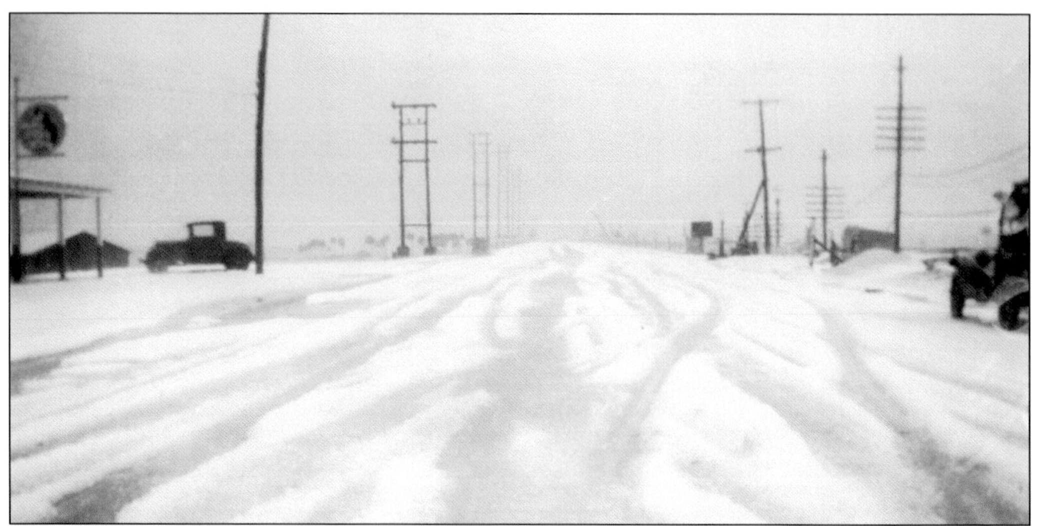

An unprecedented hail storm of great intensity struck Stuart and nearby Palm City the morning of February 10, 1934, leaving behind about six to eight inches of hailstones piled in icy drifts all over. The hail was accompanied by 60-mile-per-hour winds followed by heavy rains. Besides multiple broken windows, roofing material was torn off and screens were shredded. The new 1934 Roosevelt Bridge, which opened in January, appeared to be covered in "snow" after the hailstorm. (Courtesy of Dale Hipson.)

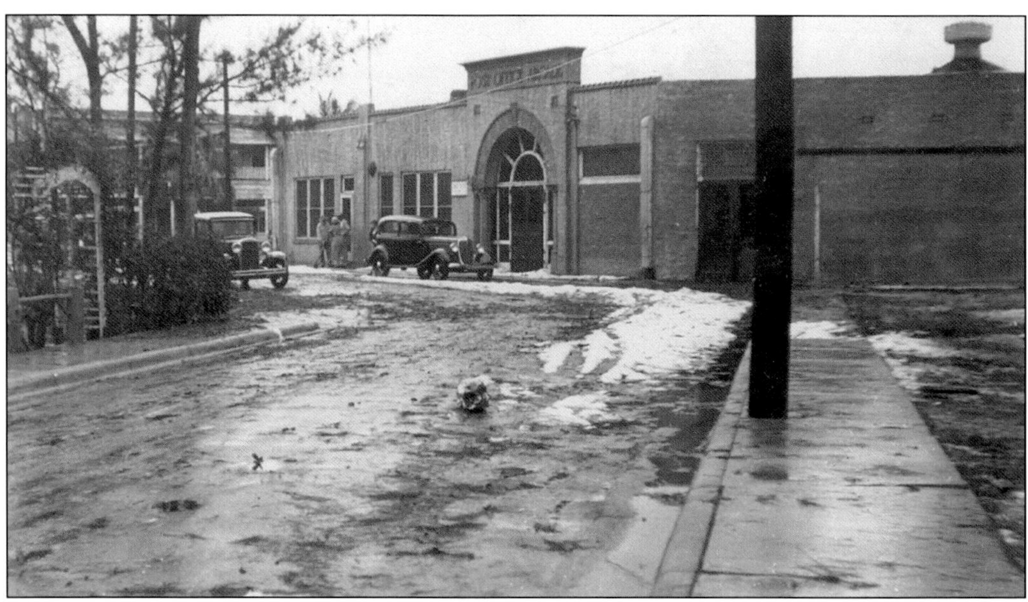

Every area in Stuart had similar scenes of piles of hailstones following the sudden, freak storm. Many plants and crops were flattened, leaves were ripped off trees, printed numbers on freight cars were stripped off, and two cows were killed by the large hailstones. Within a few hours, the hail started to melt. This scene is along Seminole Avenue with the 1925 Post Office Arcade on the right.

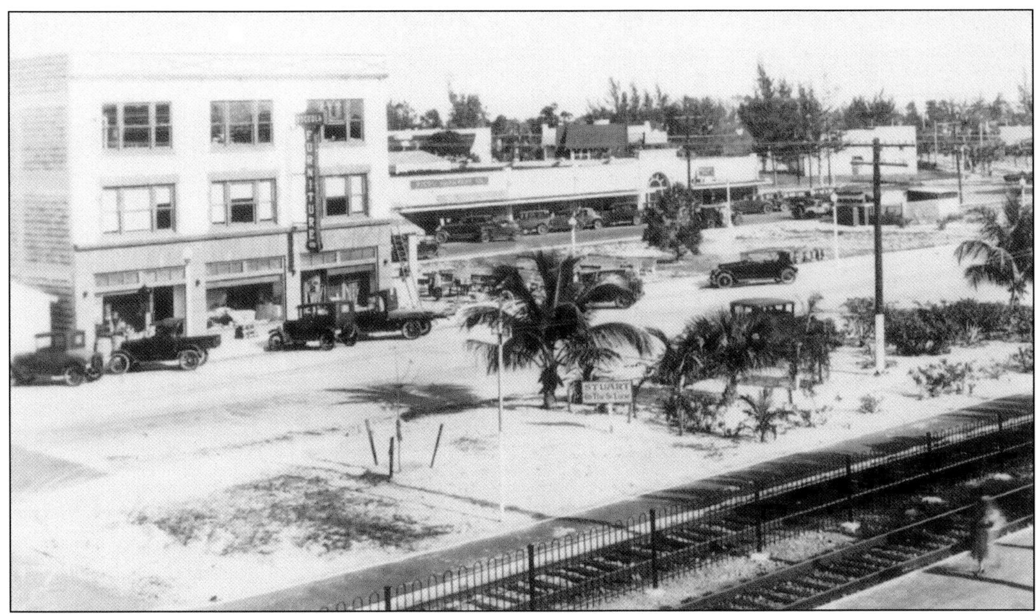

No new buildings were constructed during most of the 1930s. People made do with what they had and did any necessary repairs themselves. Prior to the Florida land bust of 1928, Boleslaw Frank Minschke had opened his new three-story Minschke Building on December 29, 1927, located on five lots between Flagler and Osceola Avenues. The Osceola Furniture Store was one of the main businesses in the building. The properties just beyond remained undeveloped during the 1930s and instead served as a community area named Flagler Park. (Courtesy of MCHS, Elliott Museum.)

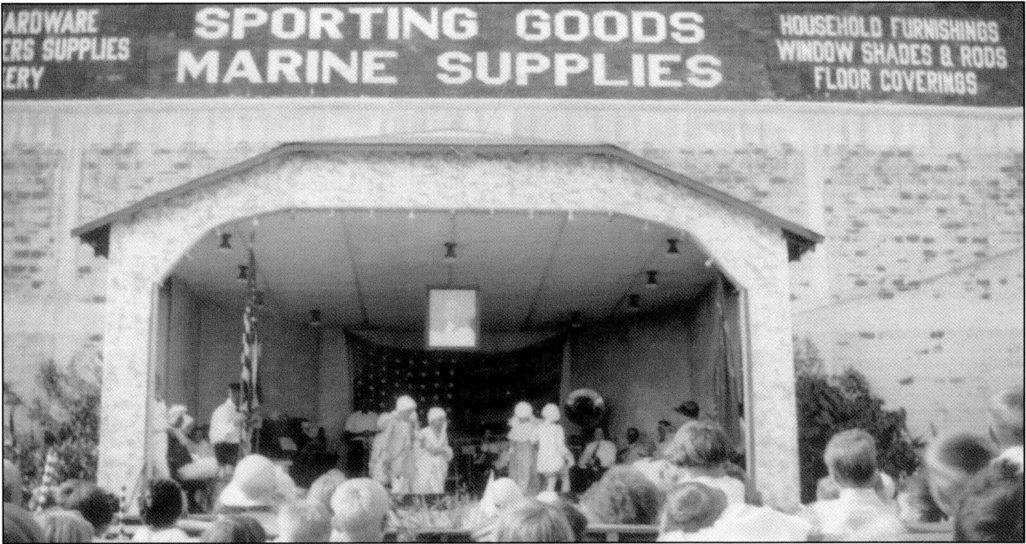

Up against the eastern wall of the Minschke Building (Holleran Building by the early 1930s) was the community bandstand, set up in 1928. This wooden structure was painted, re-roofed, stuccoed, and had a new speaker system. It served during the 1930s as a great location for civic programs as well as the weekly performance of the Stuart Concert Band, made up of local musicians. (Courtesy of Dale Hipson.)

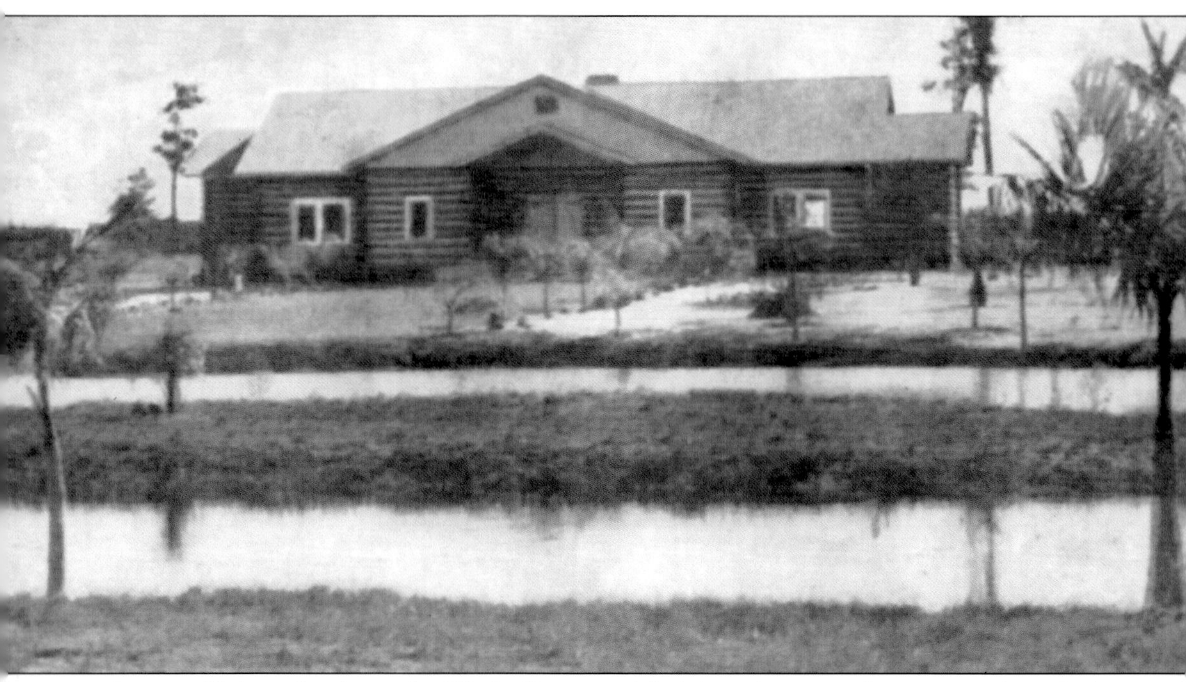

A new addition, thanks to the Works Progress Administration, was the construction of a log cabin community hall in 1936 for public dances, card games, band performances, and other social events. It was located in the Fourth Street Park (Memorial Park), close to Stuart High School. It was made of 412 massive pine timbers, a total of 4,880 feet of lumber. Emilio Cabre built the cabin's special feature, a 12-ton local coquina fireplace. (Courtesy of Jo Marie Paradise.)

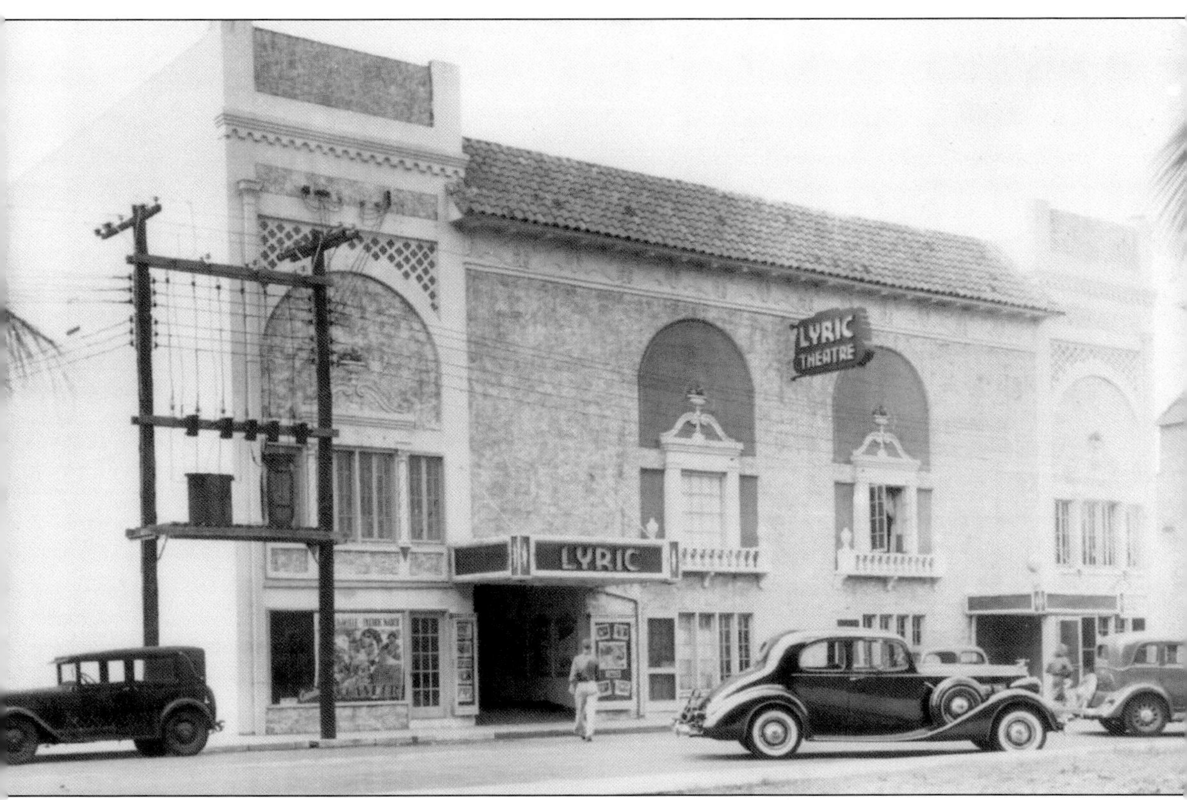

The 1926 Lyric Theatre has two entrances, one on Flagler Avenue and the other on Osceola Avenue, the side shown in this 1938 photograph. The Hancock family continued to operate the Lyric until August 1937; however, due to economic conditions, they had to sell the theater to Eastern Enterprises Inc., owned by the Koblegard family. Under new management, renovations included modern lighting and seats. First-run movies were shown, and special matinee performances were offered. The movie featured at the time of this photograph is *The Buccaneer*, starring Fredric March.

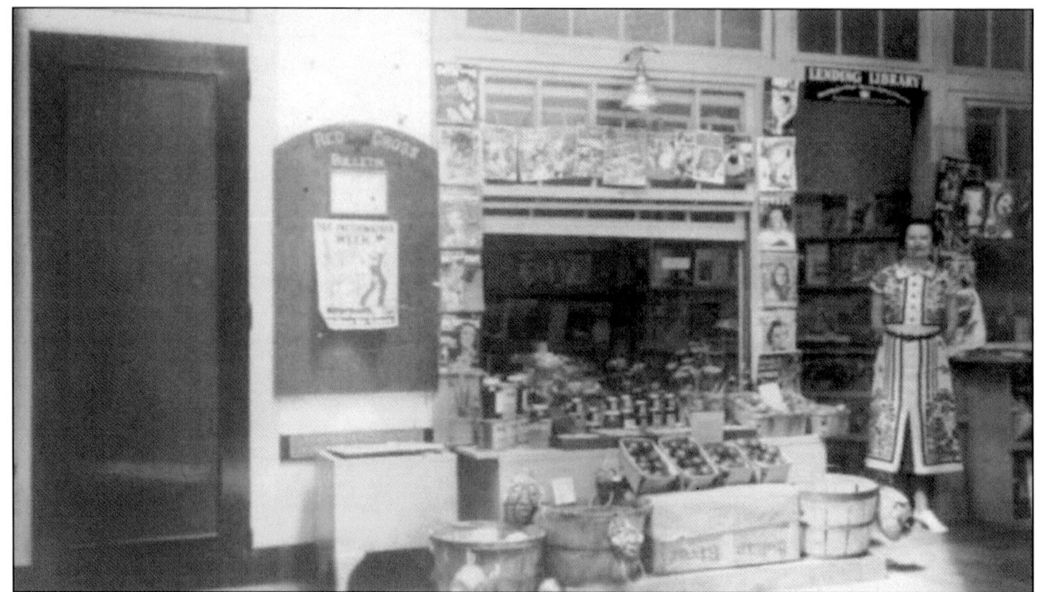

The Post Office Arcade, built in 1925, was home to the Stuart Post Office and several other businesses and shops during the 1930s. One was Dugan's Fruit Stand and Sundries Store, pictured here in 1938. It was owned and operated by Herbert and Lettie Dugan until 1946. The store was known for its honey, fine fruits, jellies, and the latest available newspapers. Pictured to the right is Lettie Wiley Dugan. (Courtesy of the Hall-Strauss families.)

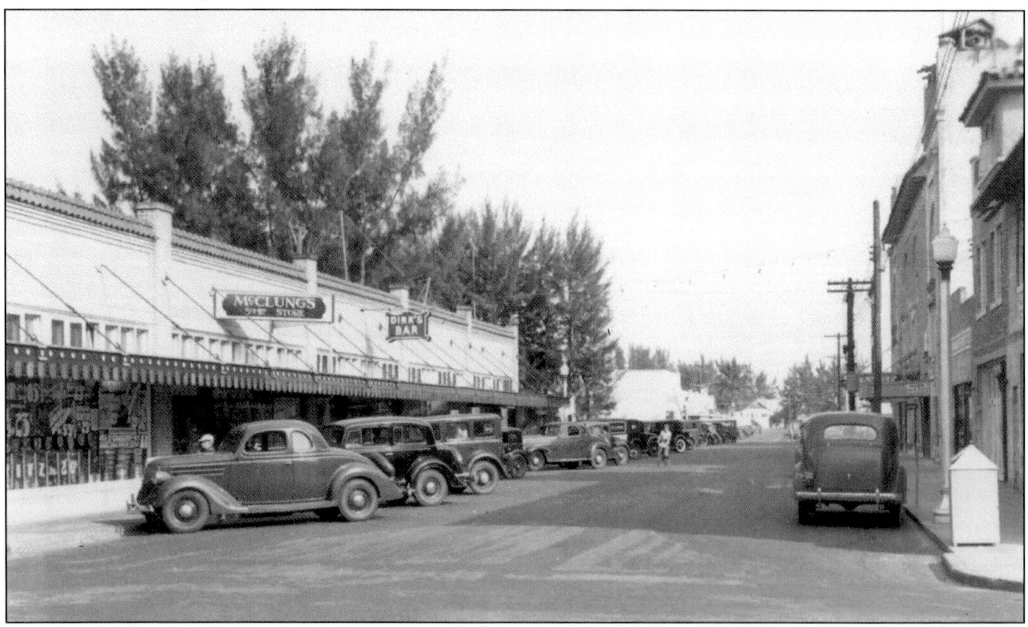

Along Osceola Avenue, a variety of shops existed, but many struggled during the Depression. Having been in the local hardware business since 1921, Earl J. Ricou knew by November 1936 that the time was right to construct the first building along Osceola in 12 years. His $10,000 one-story concrete store was built farther down the street on the left. Ricou stated that he had faith in the future of Stuart. Besides all varieties of supplies for a home, Ricou also carried all types of fishing equipment.

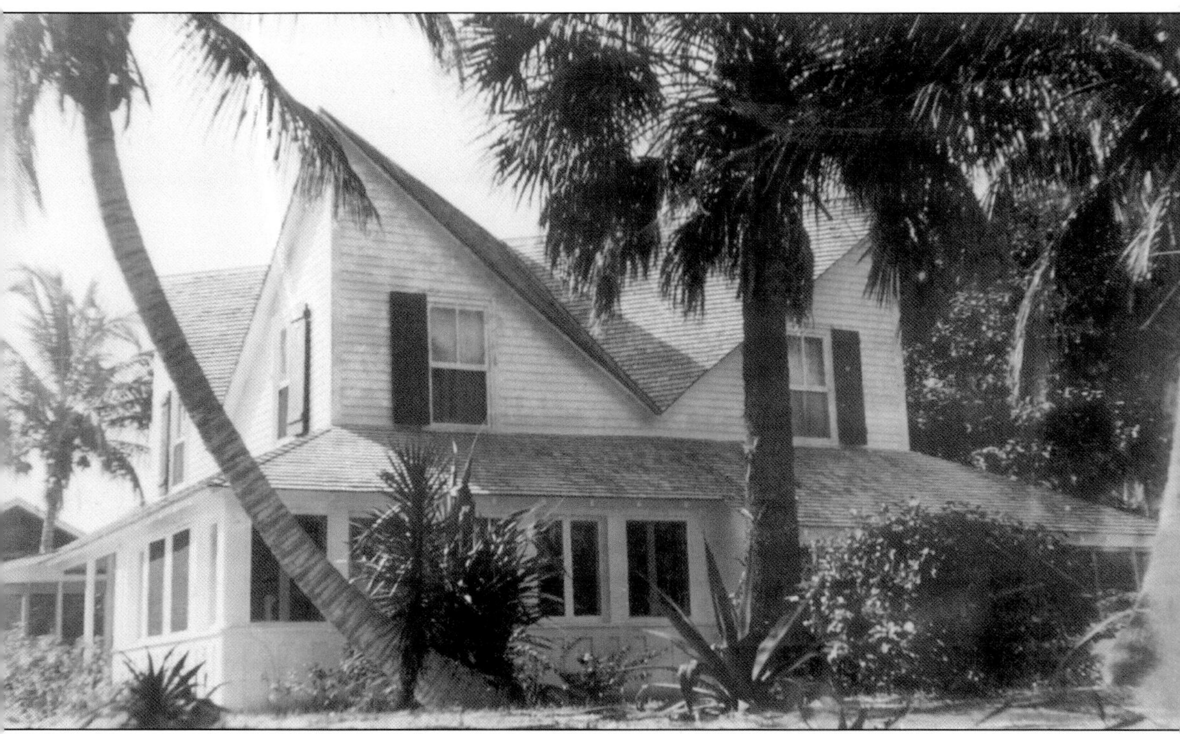

One of the most unusual and symmetrical homes in Stuart is the 1904 Francis Marion and Annie Platt house, which faces the St. Lucie River. It is a two-story wood-and-brick structure with a unique four-pointed gable roof, which resembles the head of an owl, lending the name Owl House to the structure. Charles and Ethel Porter purchased the home from the Platts in 1908, and the Porter family remained in the house for decades. It is located close to the Kimberly Apartments. (Courtesy of the Edith Coventry Collection, Elliott Museum.)

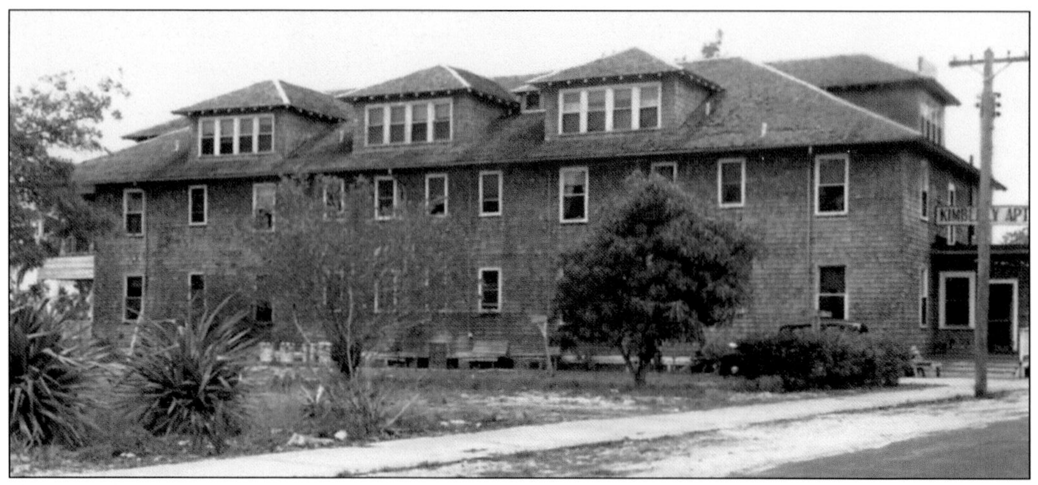

Elmer and Mary Kimberly successfully operated the 1913 Kimberly Apartments. After the 1919 death of Elmer, Mary continued running the residences. The building survived the disastrous 1928 and 1933 hurricanes with only minor damage. Mary sold the structure in 1931 to Fred and Adeline Low, and they painted, redecorated, and refurnished the apartments. With Fred Low's death in 1937, the apartments were sold in 1939 for $4,500 to Joseph and Effie Ahlquist, who renamed it the Riverview Apartments.

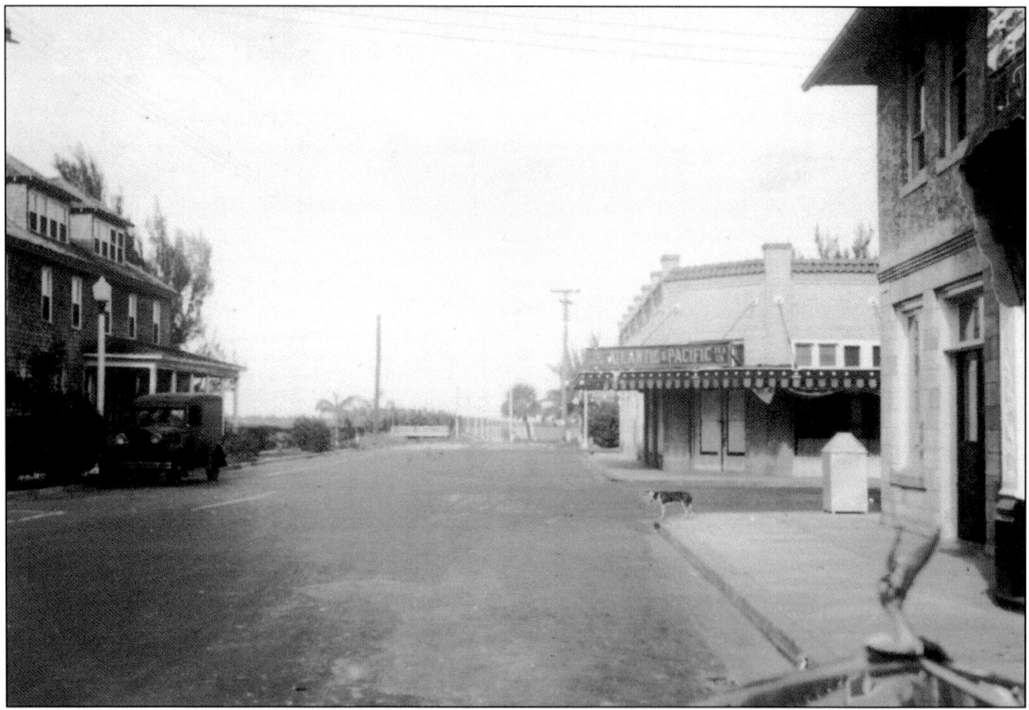

From Flagler Avenue, St. Lucie Avenue took residents into the heart of downtown Stuart. This 1930s scene includes, from left to right, the 1913 St. Lucie Hotel, the city dock at the end of the street, and the Osceola (Fuge Building) on the right with the Great Atlantic & Pacific Tea Company (A&P) grocery. Crossing at Osceola Avenue to the corner was the original two-story 1912 Bank of Stuart (Municipal Building), where the Citizen's Bank began in 1933. (Courtesy of Dale Hipson.)

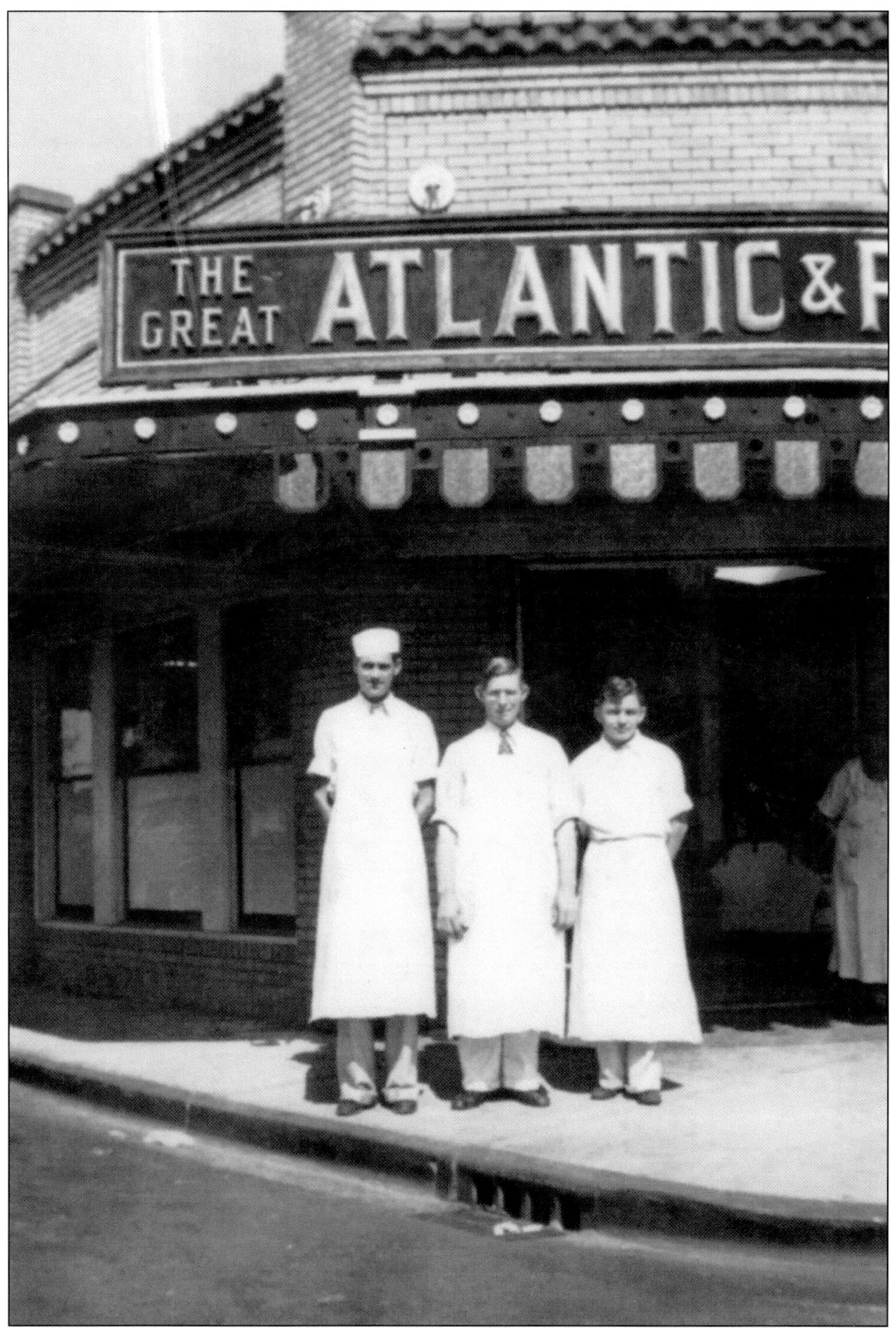

The grocery market was a popular location in town. In front of the Great Atlantic & Pacific Tea Company in the early 1930s are three of the store's employees. From left to right are James Brock, Henry Kindred, and unidentified. Years later, Kindred opened his own grocery store in Stuart. (Courtesy of the Mills, Powers, and McNabb Collection.)

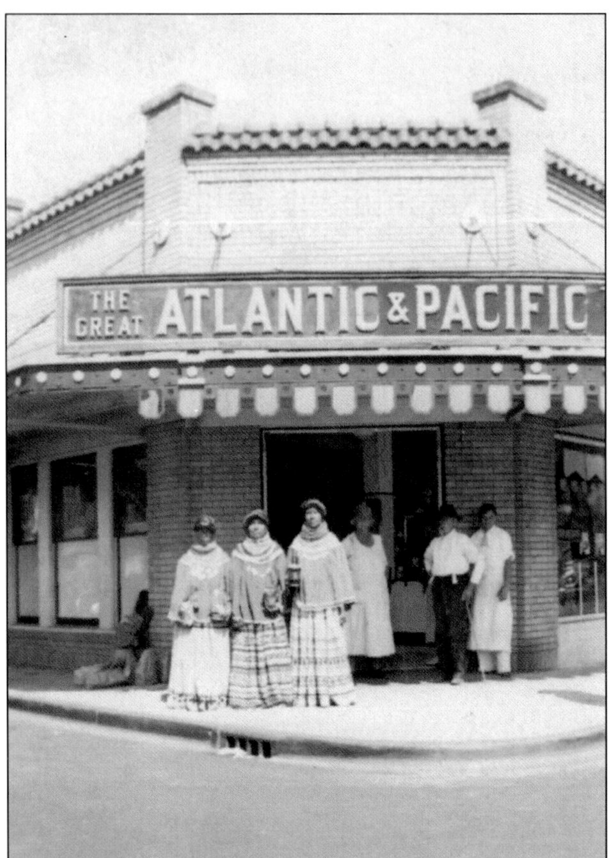

Every month or so, members of the Seminole tribe from around the eastern portion of Lake Okeechobee would come to Stuart to shop or trade for supplies and goods they needed. In front of the grocery store are three Seminole ladies in full traditional clothing. Behind them are two unidentified men and Henry Kindred at far right. (Courtesy of the Mills, Powers, and McNabb Collection.)

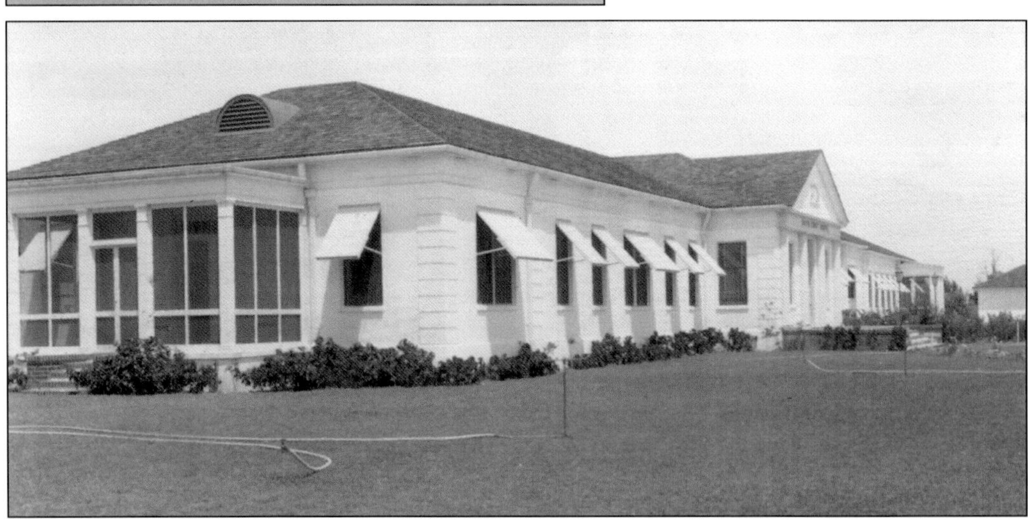

In 1926, Stuart's first hospital, the St. Lucie Sanitarium, was located at Coconut Avenue and Fifth Street and only handled emergency and maternity cases. In 1938, the Barstow and Reed families of nearby Jupiter Island secured a seven-acre parcel along the St. Lucie River near Riverside Drive in Stuart and then contributed the necessary money to have a hospital erected and fully equipped; it was open to all citizens. The new Martin County Hospital, pictured here, held its grand opening on March 8, 1939.

Nine

New Beginnings and the War Years

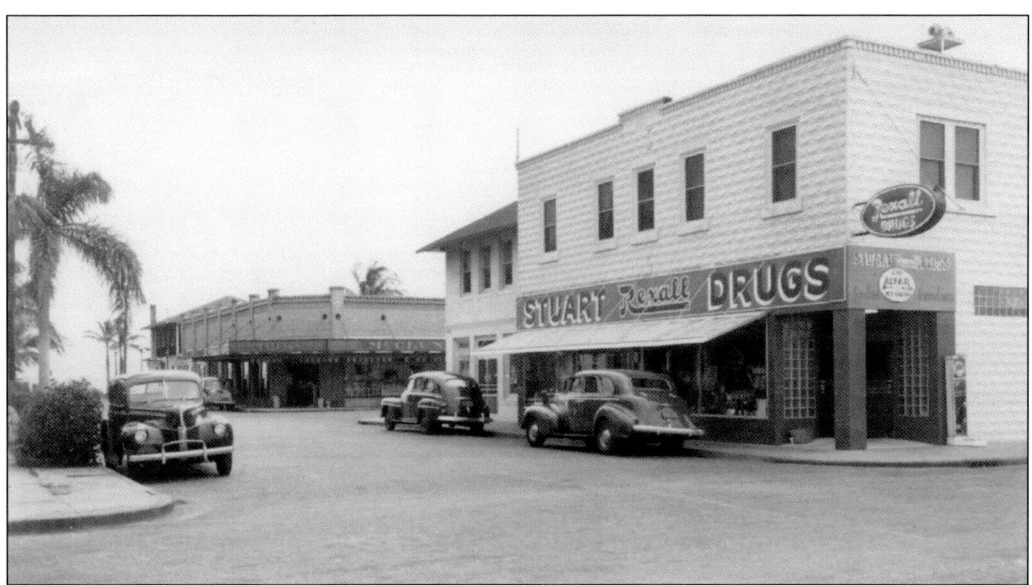

Going down St. Lucie Avenue at the intersection of Flagler Avenue, the business section of Stuart continued. The Stuart Rexall Drugs (Rexall added in the 1940s) in the Feroe Building on the corner was directly across from the train depot. Next to it was the smaller two-story former bank building that housed city hall and the police and fire departments. The corner store in the Osceola Building housed McClung's Five and Dime Store as of 1936. (Courtesy of Martha Penhale Cuthbert.)

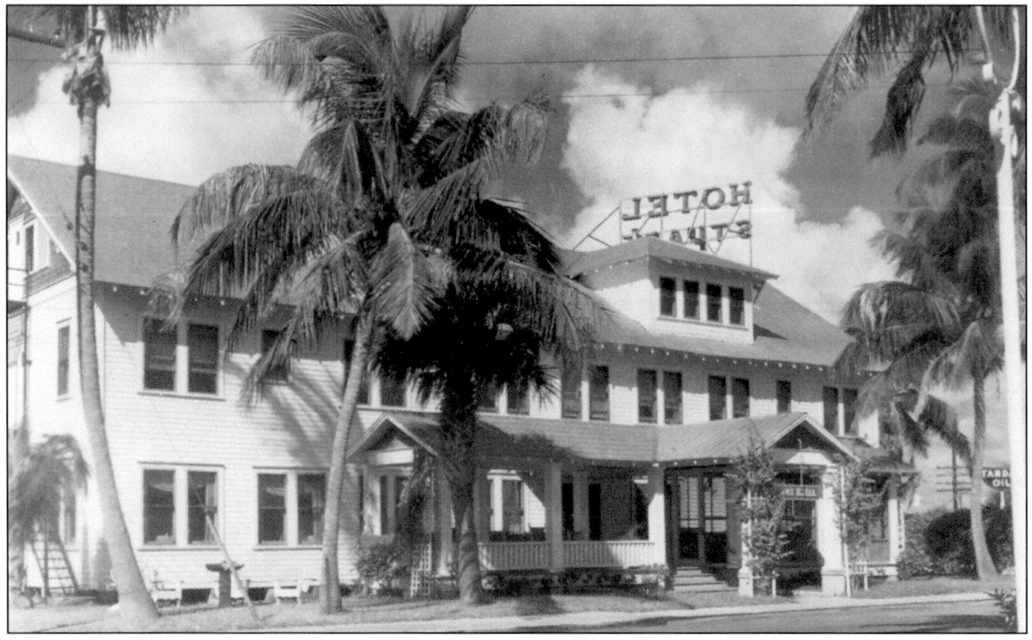

This grand hotel was the Stuart Hotel, which had its beginnings at the turn of the 20th century. Visitors were greeted by this fine hotel close to the south end of the Roosevelt Bridge with large overhead signs. It remained a popular destination for years, especially during World War II, when so many people came through the area. (Courtesy of Jo Marie Paradise.)

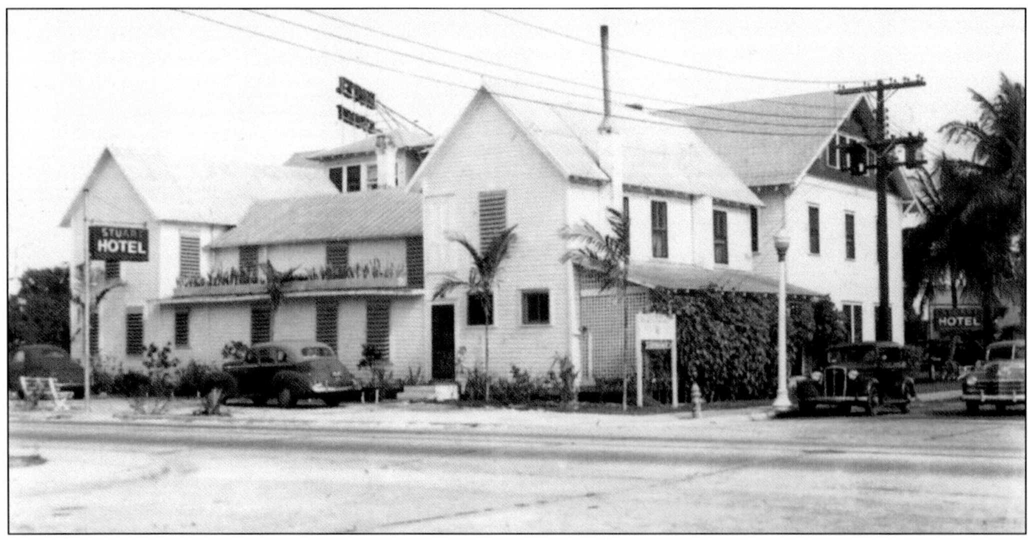

Even the back of the Stuart Hotel showed its character with the multiple sections, which consisted of the original boardinghouse operated by Broster Kitching decades earlier. It was located at Albany Avenue and Dixie Highway. Charles and Mae Clark were the owners since 1925; they sold the hotel in 1946 to investors McQuade and Gagliardi from Connecticut. (Courtesy of MCHS, Elliott Museum.)

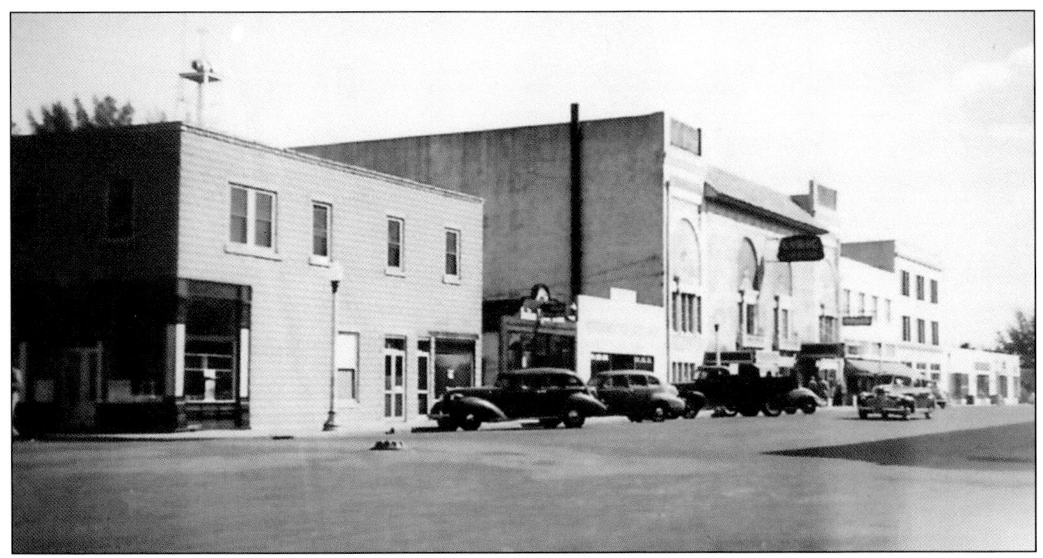

In the 1940s, the length of Flagler Avenue remained the core of the Stuart commercial district. New buildings slowly began to be constructed between Flagler and Osceola Avenues. From left to right starting at the corner were the Feroe Building, Rue's Sweet Shop, a hardware store, the Lyric Theatre, the two-story Greene's Department Store, the Minschke (Holleran) Building, and by 1940, the Pressel Building. (Courtesy of the Coventry Collection, Elliott Museum.)

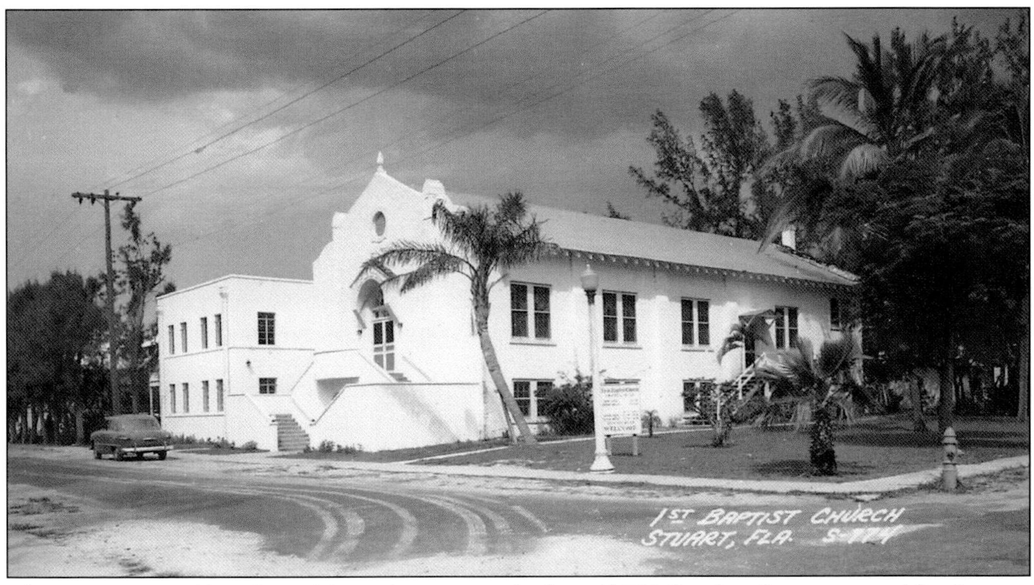

The First Baptist Church on Akron Avenue was built in 1925. The church was unusual for the area in that it had a basement, where many community and civic organizations held their meetings. The church was also the site for numerous Christmas pageants, weddings, and funerals over the decades. (Courtesy of Sandra and Tom Thurlow.)

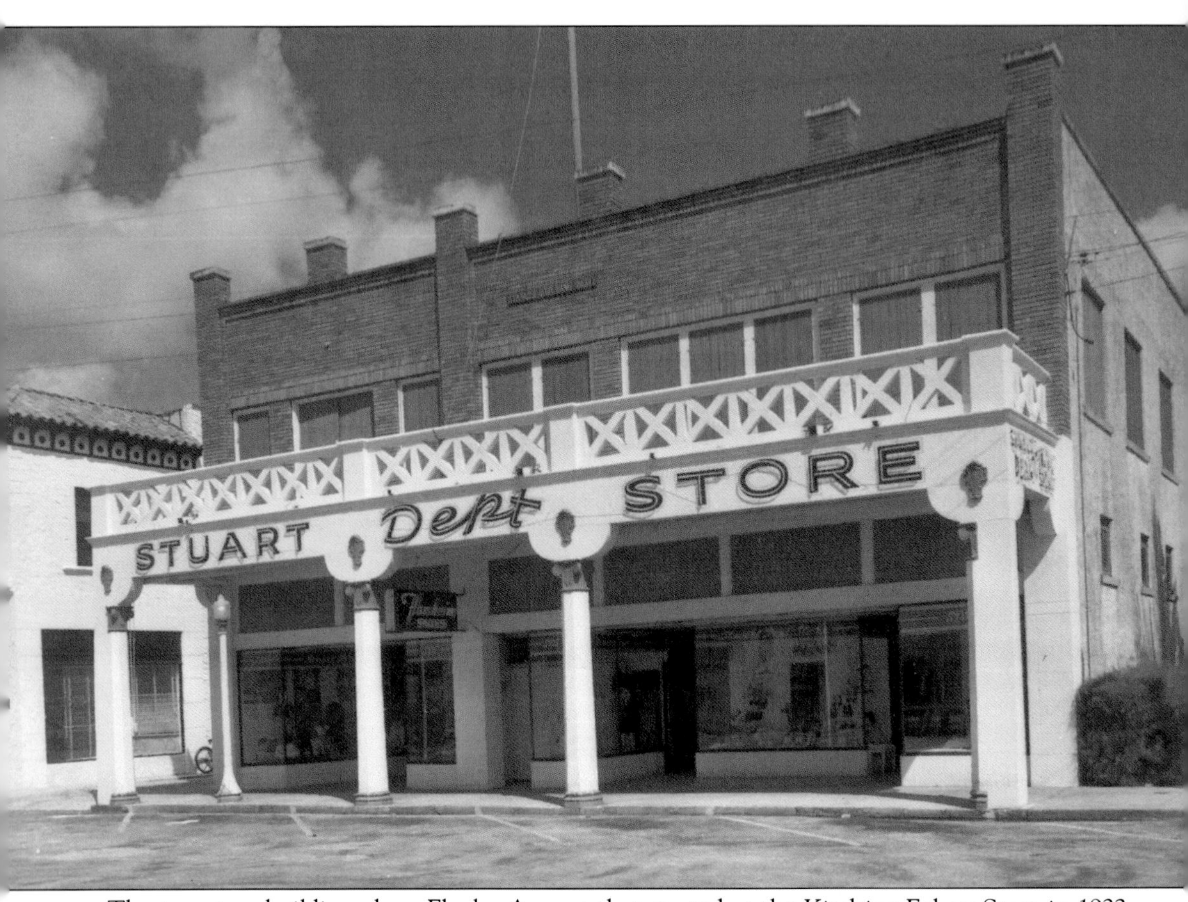

The two-story building along Flagler Avenue that started as the Kitching-Eckess Store in 1922 was sold in 1938 to Oscar S. Kanarek; the store was then renamed the Stuart Department Store. In 1940, Kanarek did a major interior remodeling and exterior refinishing, which included adding back the original balcony design. The Stuart Department Store served as the premier place to shop for clothing and accessories.

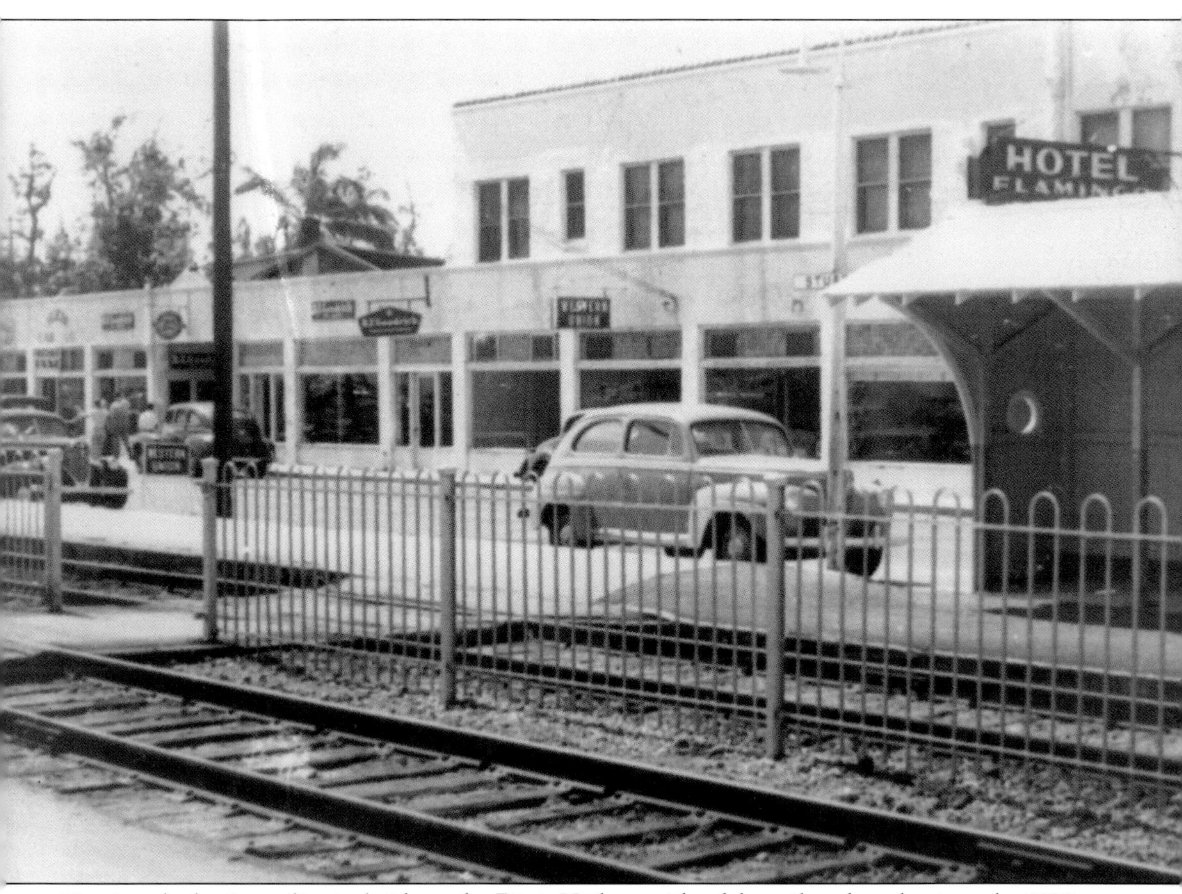

Keeping the business district brisk on the Dixie Highway side of the railroad tracks since the 1920s was the Krueger Building. Having hotel rooms, a restaurant, and various shops such as Western Union, B.F. Goodrich, and a taxi service close to the train depot into the 1940s provided necessary conveniences for locals and visitors. (Courtesy of Sandra and Tom Thurlow.)

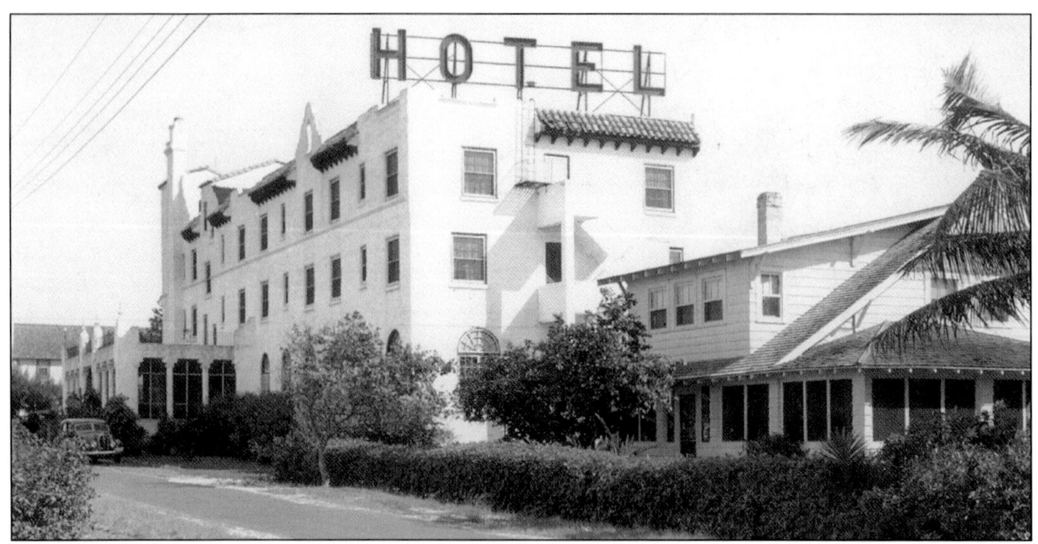

The Pelican Hotel, under the leadership of owner Drew Woodson King, continued full operations during the 1930s and into the early 1940s. He began catering to the sportfishing enthusiasts. After his death on December 23, 1944, ownership and management was turned over to his sons William V. "Bill" and Grover C. King. (Courtesy of the Luckhardt Collection.)

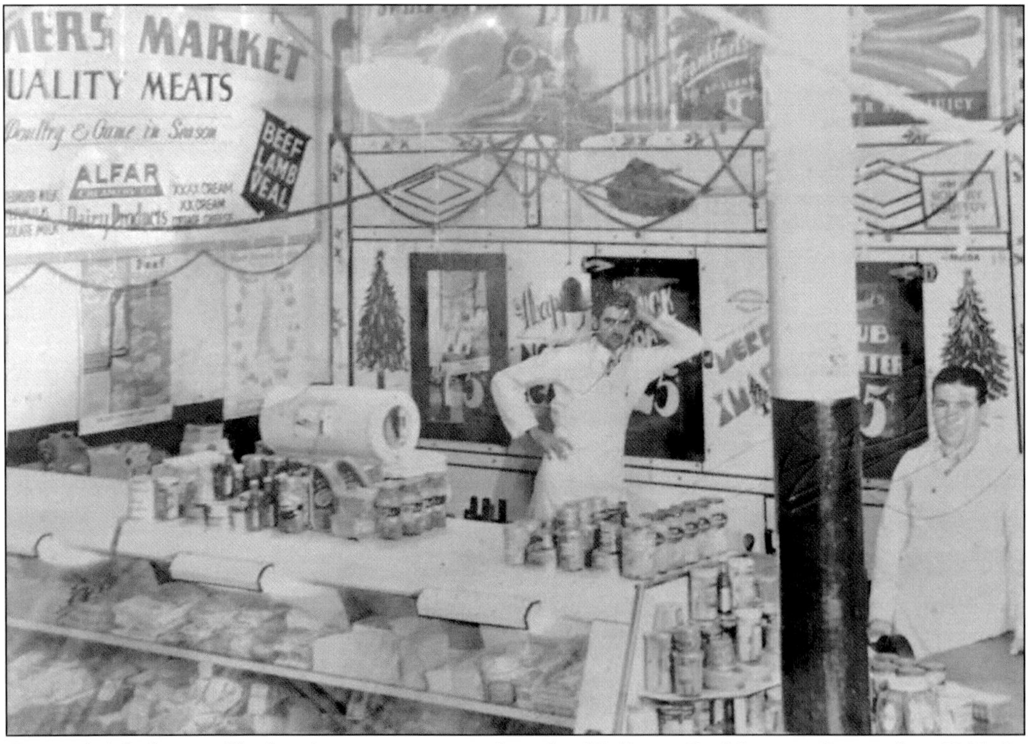

Cromer's Market on Flagler Avenue originated in the Holleran Building in September 1935. In 1941, the popular grocery store was moved to the new Pressel Building, which also faced Flagler Avenue. Jim Brock (left), manager of the market division, is pictured here with John N. Mann, market assistant. Mann later worked as a meat market manager at St. Onge's Grocery in Hobe Sound. (Courtesy of Todd Laraway.)

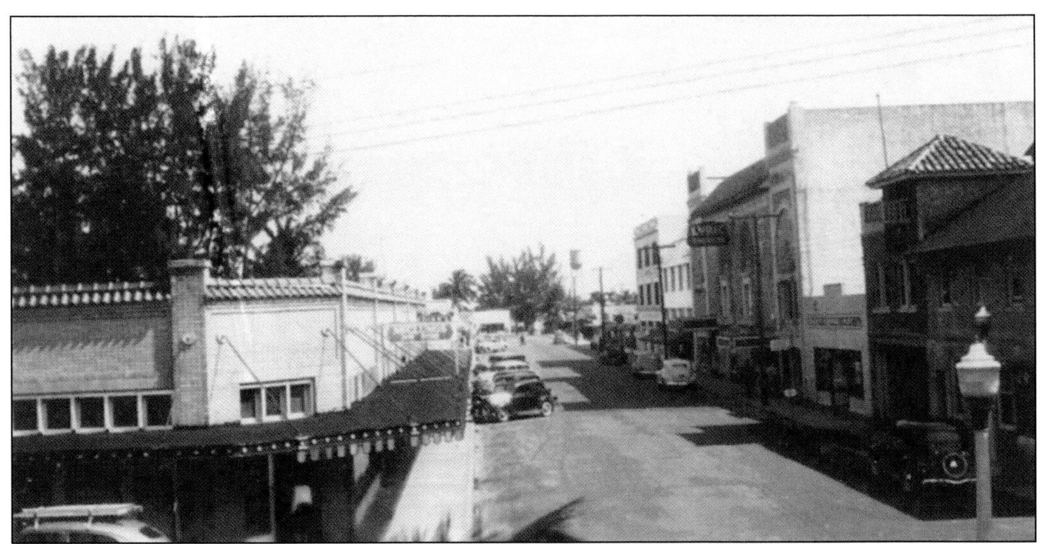

Taken approximately in 1942, this was the view looking east on Osceola Avenue. Note the numerous businesses and shops on both sides of the road. On the right was the one-story Meggett Hardware and Paint Company, started by William Meggett around 1925. The two-story building beside it housed the City of Stuart Police and Fire Departments. Beyond the hardware store was the imposing Lyric Theatre. Osceola Avenue was a popular route for holiday parades. (Courtesy of the Mae Coventry Axwell Collection.)

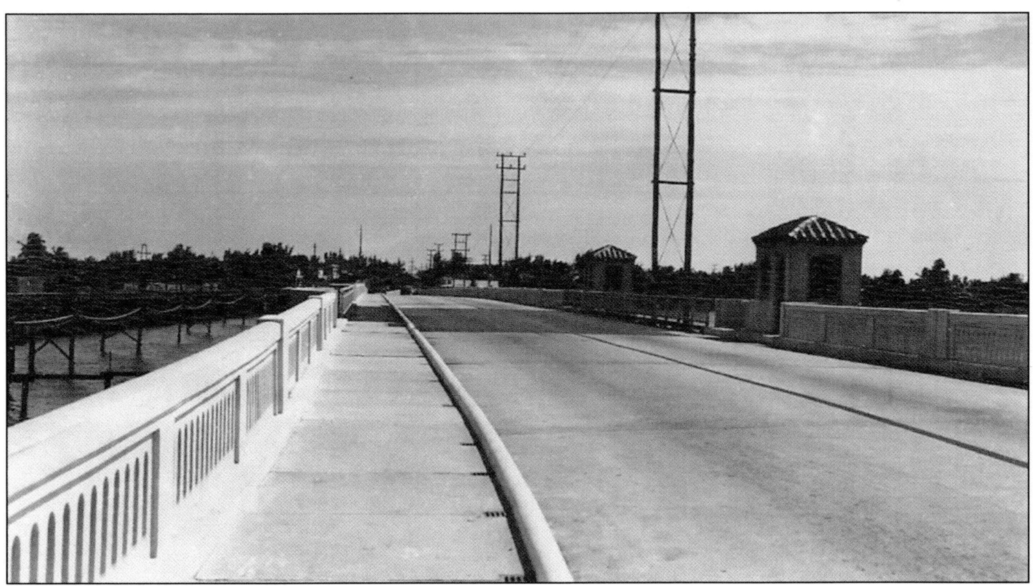

An indispensable motoring link across the St. Lucie River was the $384,000 government-funded, two-lane Roosevelt Bridge, which was dedicated on Tuesday, January 9, 1934. The 1918 auto bridge needed replacing, and the federal monies made that possible. The new bridge featured a five-foot sidewalk. A bridge tender was always present to raise the drawbridge for passing boats.

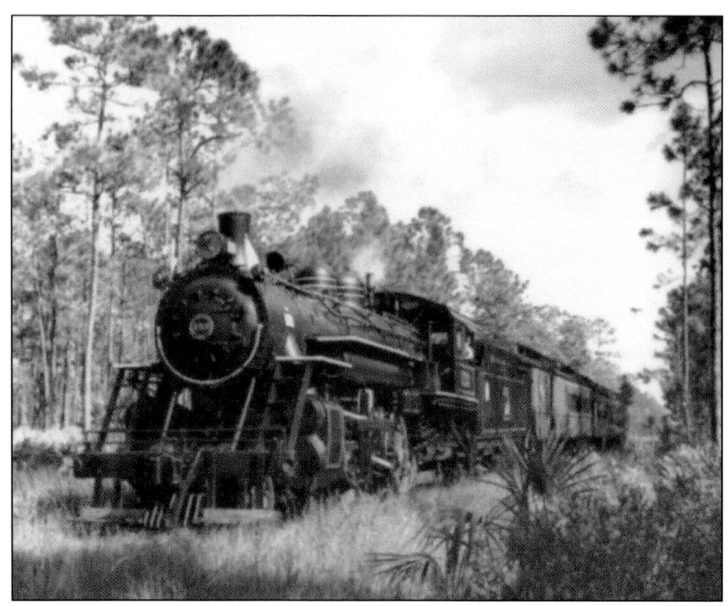

Since 1894, Stuart life had been dependent on the daily arrivals and departures of the train, and this fact was even more true by the 1940s, as the United States entered World War II. People, supplies, and cargo had to be moved efficiently as the supply of gasoline for autos and trucks was limited. In 1944, the Florida East Coast Railway had served as the critical connection for Stuart with the outside world for 50 years. (Courtesy of Florida Memory Project.)

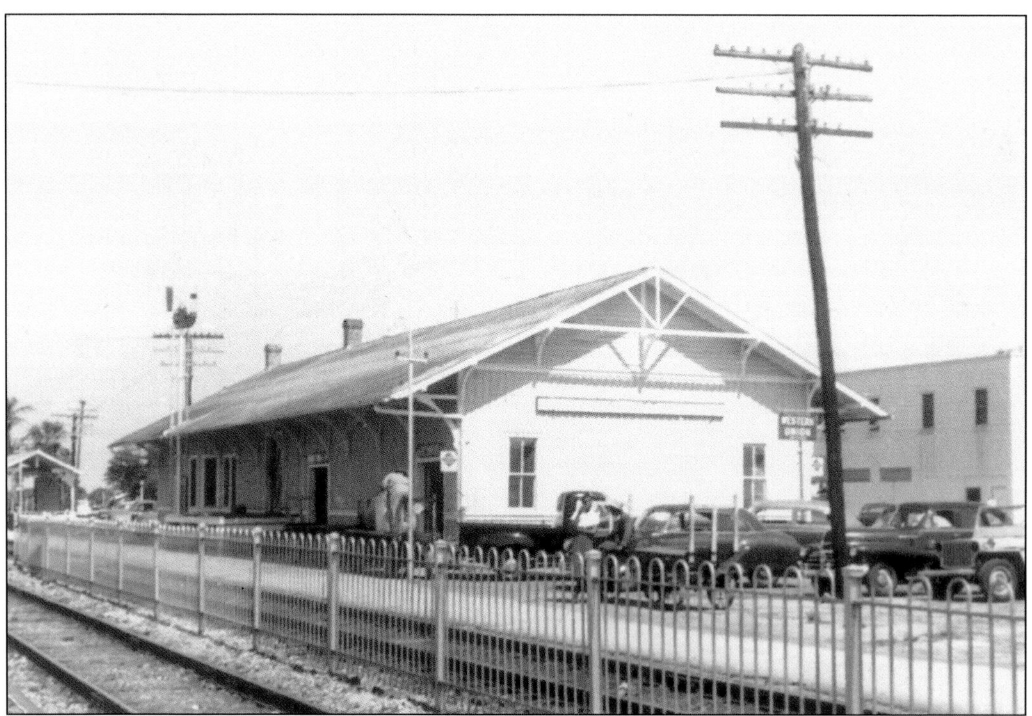

Another important element to train travel was the Stuart train depot, located right along Flagler Avenue. It had been in existence since 1913 and remained an important meeting place. The station agent in the early 1940s, when this photograph was taken, was Robert Boyce McPherson, a longtime resident who eventually served 32 years as the station agent. (Courtesy of MCHS, Elliott Museum.)

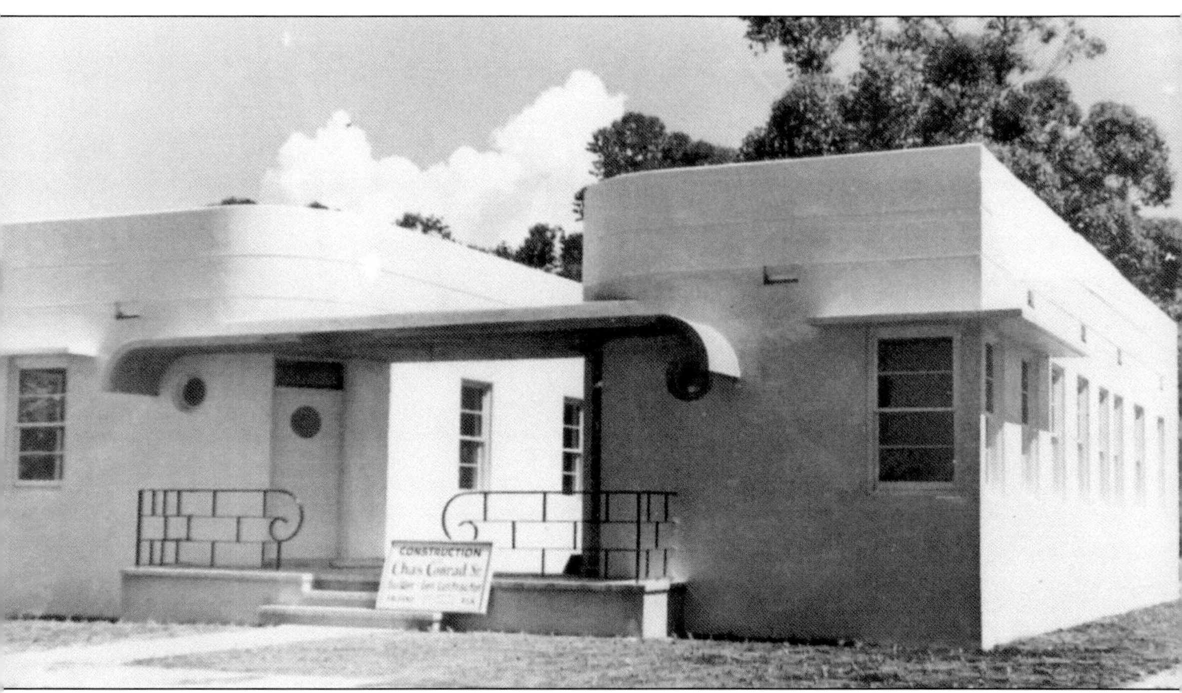

With construction of new buildings starting up again in the late 1930s, one of the most unique was the $10,000 Hipson Dental-Medical Building on Osceola Avenue constructed in June 1941 with a design inspired by the 1939 New York World's Fair exposition buildings. Dr. Harry H. Hipson, a dentist in Stuart since 1923, had his office on the right side, and Dr. John Higgins had his medical office on the left with a sunken garden containing shrubs and flowers in between. (Courtesy of the Hipson Collection, Sandra and Tom Thurlow.)

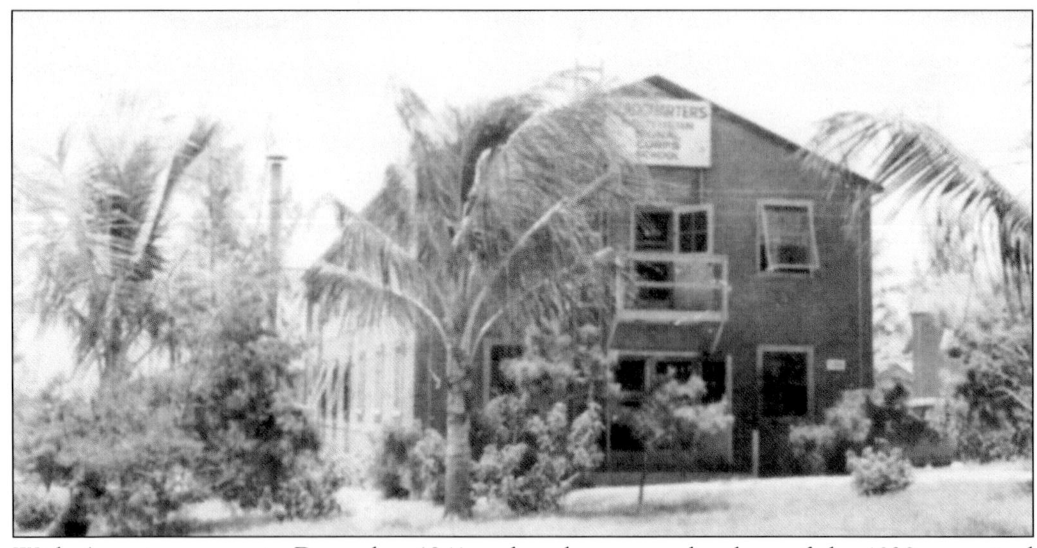

With America at war in December 1941, radar, the new technology of the 1930s, required additional training bases in a year-round warm climate. The Southern Signal Corps School, at the newly created Camp Murphy, south of Stuart near Hobe Sound, was in full operation instructing soldiers how to use radar by mid-1942. The military camp was a complete city unto itself, but with Stuart just 15 miles north, there were numerous activities between both locations. (Courtesy of the Luckhardt Collection.)

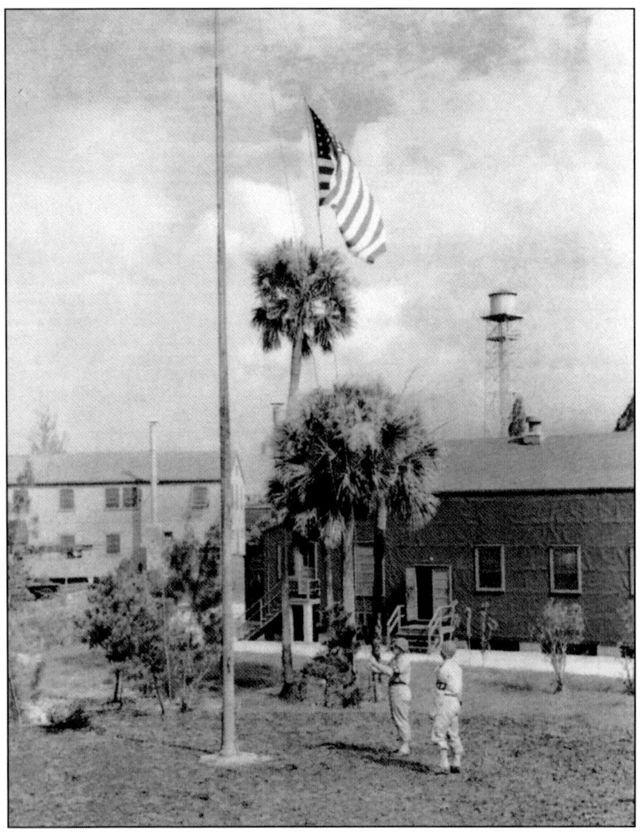

The people of Martin County welcomed Camp Murphy and its inhabitants, offering housing, transportation, hospitality, recreation, or even a home-cooked meal for the soldiers while on leave. The Stuart Service Men's Club was established in June 1942 at the Victory (Peacock Arcade Hotel) on Flagler Avenue; it offered a recreational and entertainment center for the soldiers. The Camp Murphy headquarters buildings are pictured here. (Courtesy of the Luckhardt Collection.)

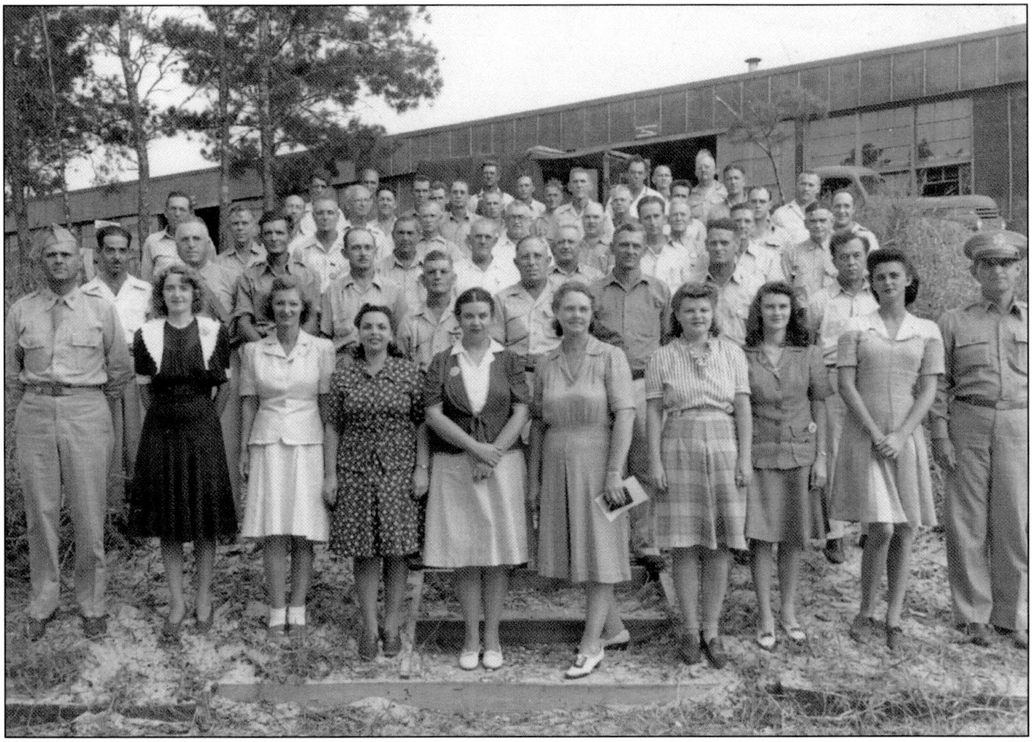

Many Stuart and Martin County citizens worked at Camp Murphy. For transportation, Florida Motor Lines provided the Red Bus Line service beginning in May 1942 between Stuart and Camp Murphy, operating from 3:00 a.m. to 8:30 p.m. An estimated one million passengers, soldiers, and civilians used the bus line to and from Stuart during the camp's 31 months of operation.

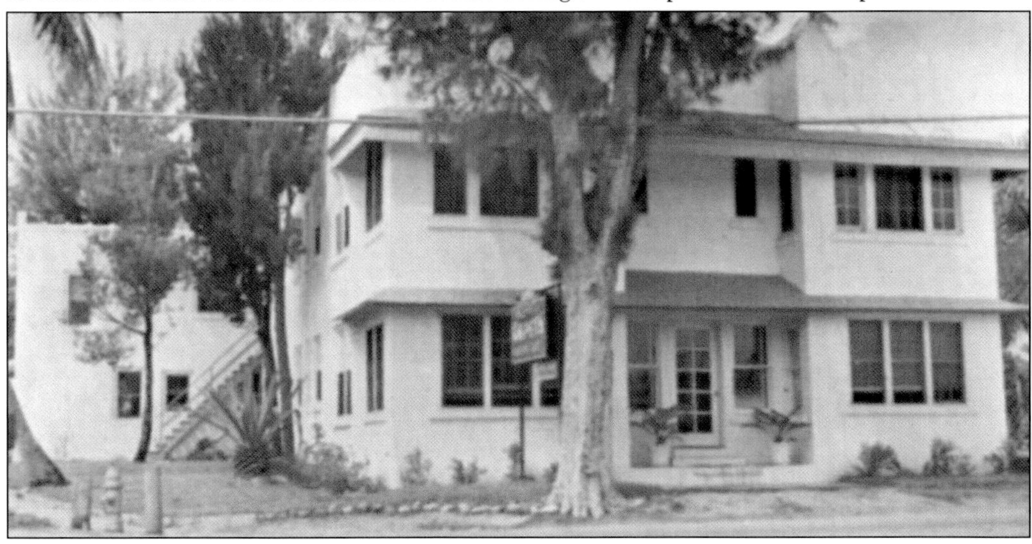

Housing was at a premium due to the influx of soldiers to Camp Murphy. During their radar training period, many of the soldiers brought their families to Stuart. One of the popular rental residences was the Virginia Apartments, built by Robert Roebuck in the 1920s; the apartments were located on US Highway 1 close to the Red Bus Line station. (Courtesy of the Rue-Luckhardt Collection.)

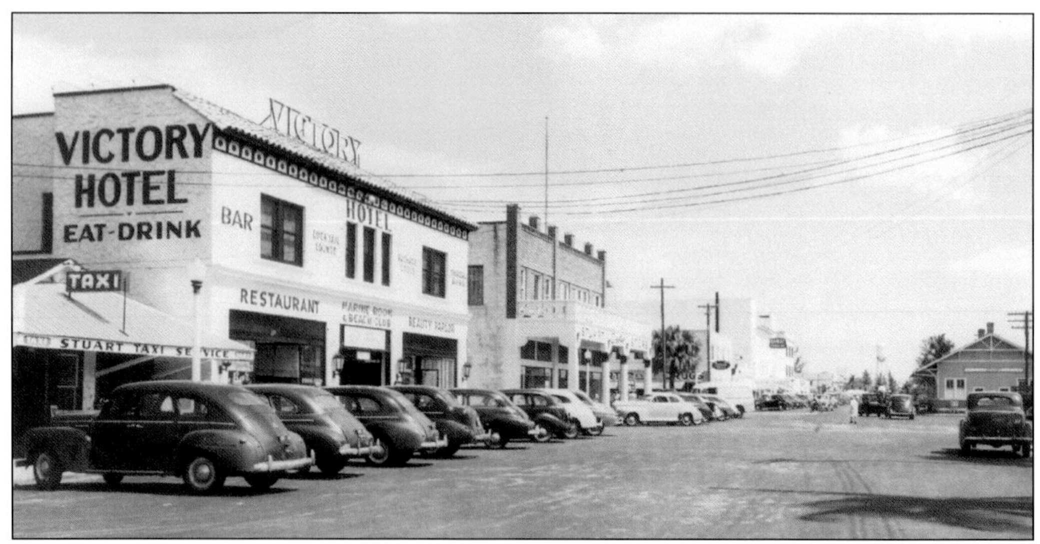

Flagler Avenue businesses flourished during the war years due to military personnel stationed at Camp Murphy and Coast Guardsmen patrolling the shoreline. On the left, the original 1925 Peacock Arcade was renamed the Victory Hotel in support of the war effort. The next store in line was the Stuart Department Store, and across St. Lucie Avenue were the Stuart Rexall Drugstore and the Lyric Theatre. On the opposite side of Flagler Avenue was the train depot. (Courtesy of Martha Penhale Cuthbert.)

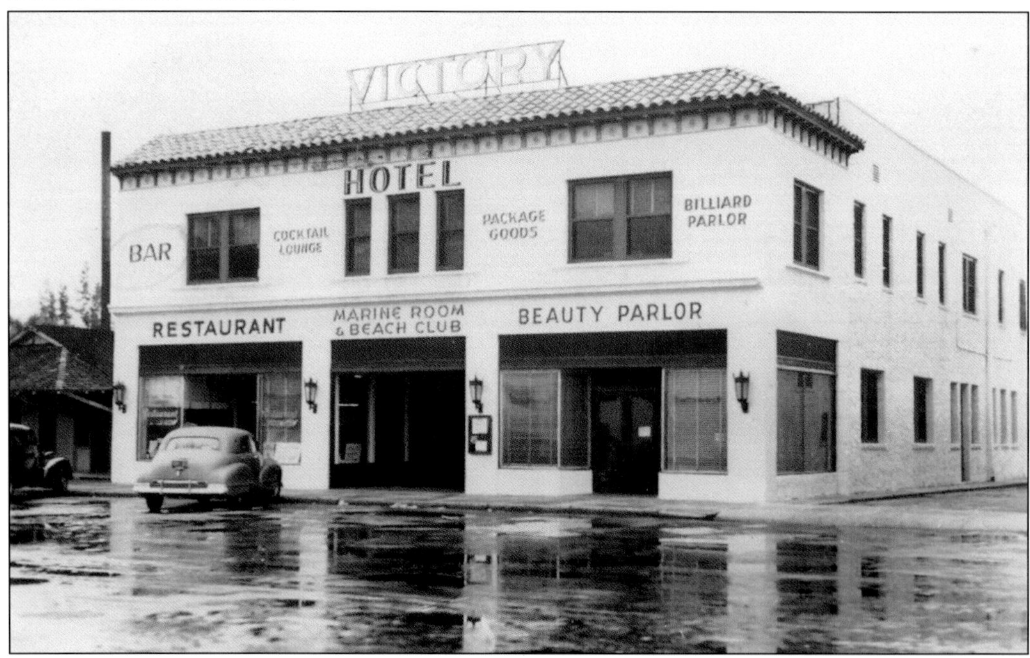

The Victory Hotel offered a variety of services to the public during the 1940s. Everything from a hotel room, a restaurant, bar, a band, and dance floor to a beauty parlor was at this central Stuart location along the St. Lucie River. The building's owner, Carl L. Bess, opened the Marine Room and Beach Club in 1944 as an evening nightclub. The new venue was equipped with billiard tables and other recreational activities during the day and was managed by Kingsley E. Smith. (Courtesy of Sandra and Tom Thurlow.)

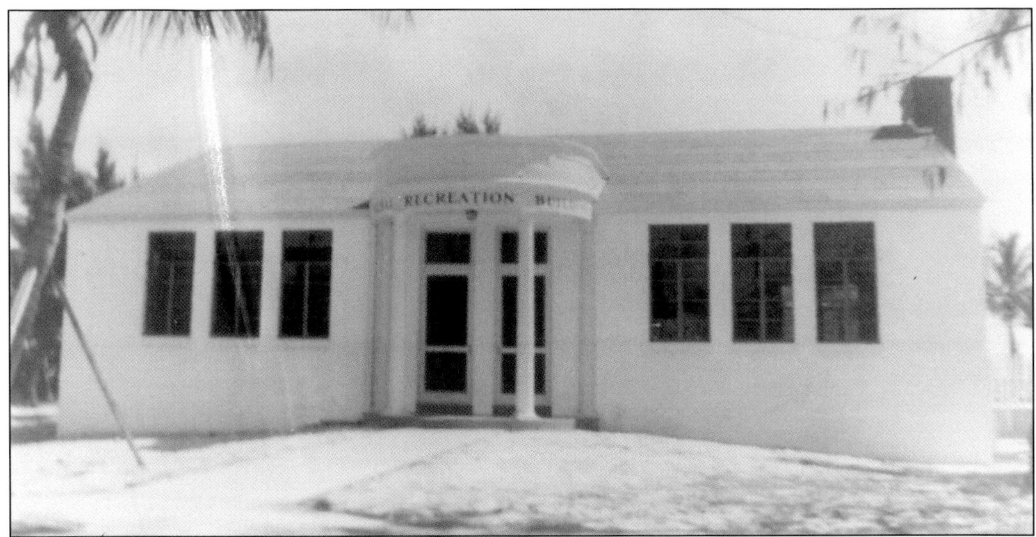

A separate recreational facility was needed, so the Stuart Service Men's Club opened October 10, 1943, on Flagler Avenue, close to where the St. Lucie Yacht Club once existed. It was designed by architect Bert Keck in a colonial cottage style and was built and paid for by the US government at a cost of $35,000. It was a recreation center for troops stationed at Camp Murphy, the Jensen Coast Guard Station, and the Fort Pierce Port. (Courtesy of Sandra and Tom Thurlow.)

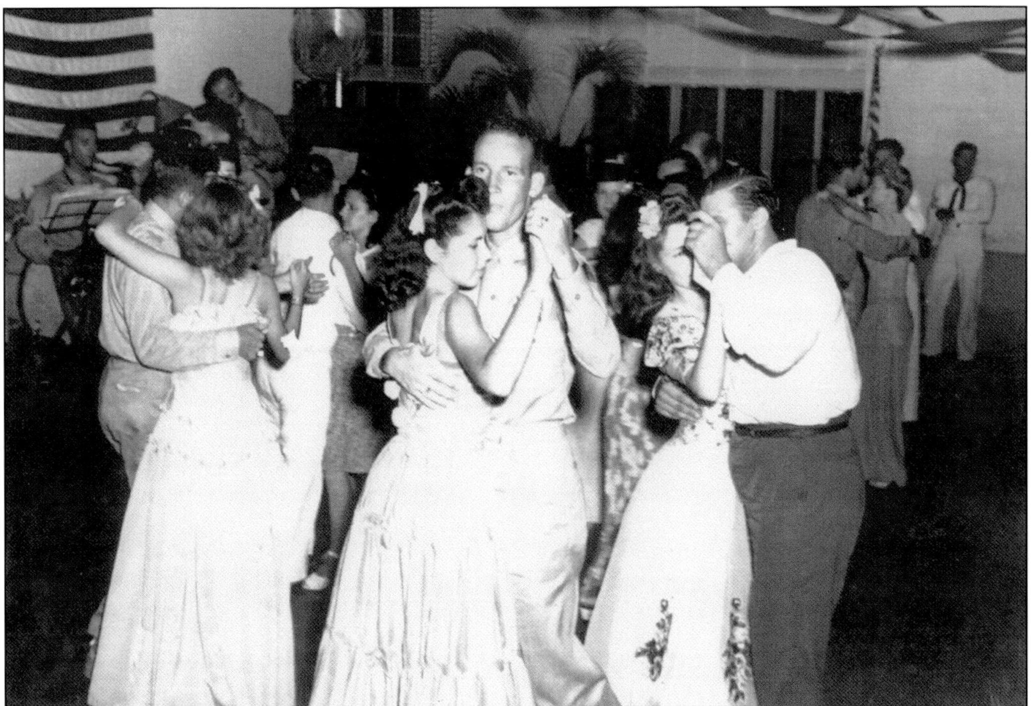

Inside the Service Men's Club there was dancing, ping-pong and card games, and reading. The enlisted men were not only able to mingle with each other but also with locals, which included the many young, single ladies in town. Having a wonderful time dancing are, at center, from left to right, Florence Kanarek, Paul Thomas, unidentified, and George Magos. In May 1946, the building was purchased by the city and made the Stuart Civic Center.

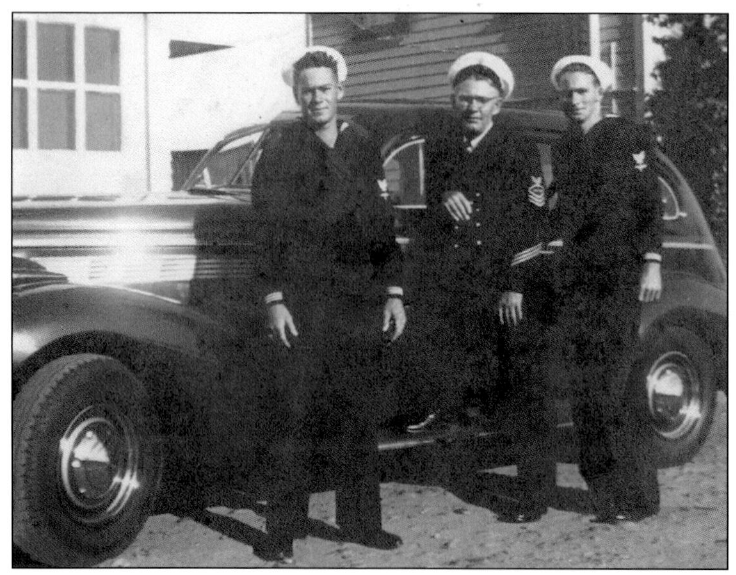

Witham family members who served during World War II included, from left to right, son Paul Homer Witham, a Navy fighter pilot who was shot down and killed in the Aleutian Islands on August 8, 1942; his father, Paul Witham, who was a Navy chief warrant officer for 30 years; and son Phillip Ross Witham, a Navy flier who was a survivor of the attack on Pearl Harbor on December 7, 1941. (Courtesy of the Witham family.)

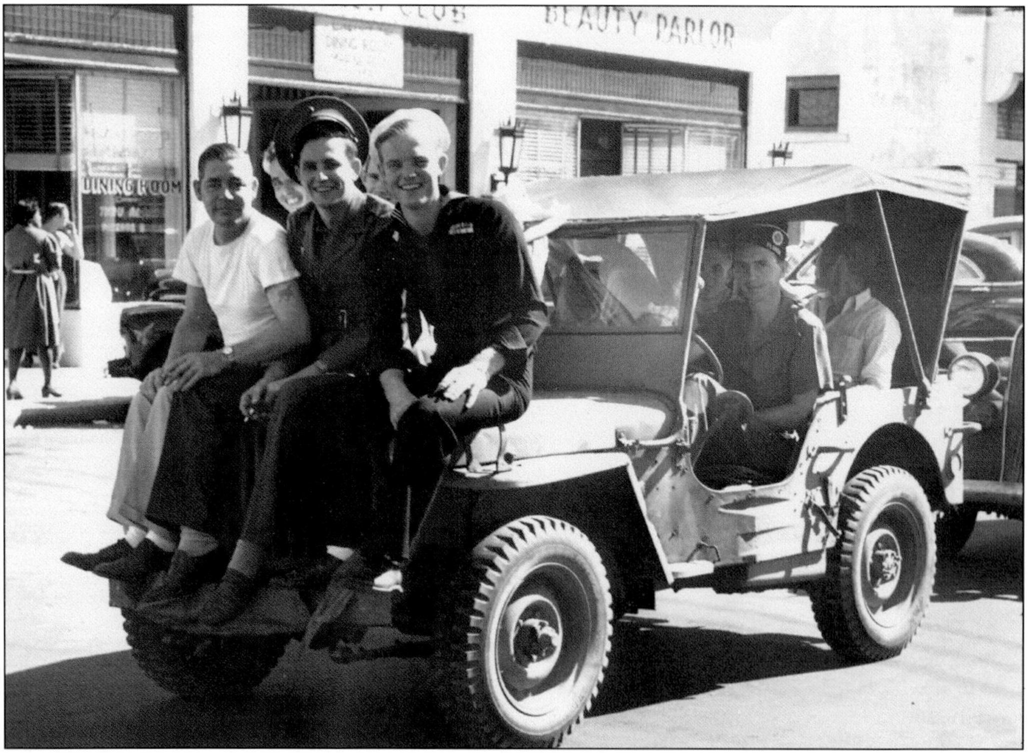

A parade through the streets of Stuart in celebration of returning military veterans after the end of World War II brought a smile to everyone's face. This photograph was taken in front of the Victory Hotel along Flagler Avenue. (Courtesy of Clyde Coutant, Sandra and Tom Thurlow Collection.)

Ten

Poised to Enter the 1950s

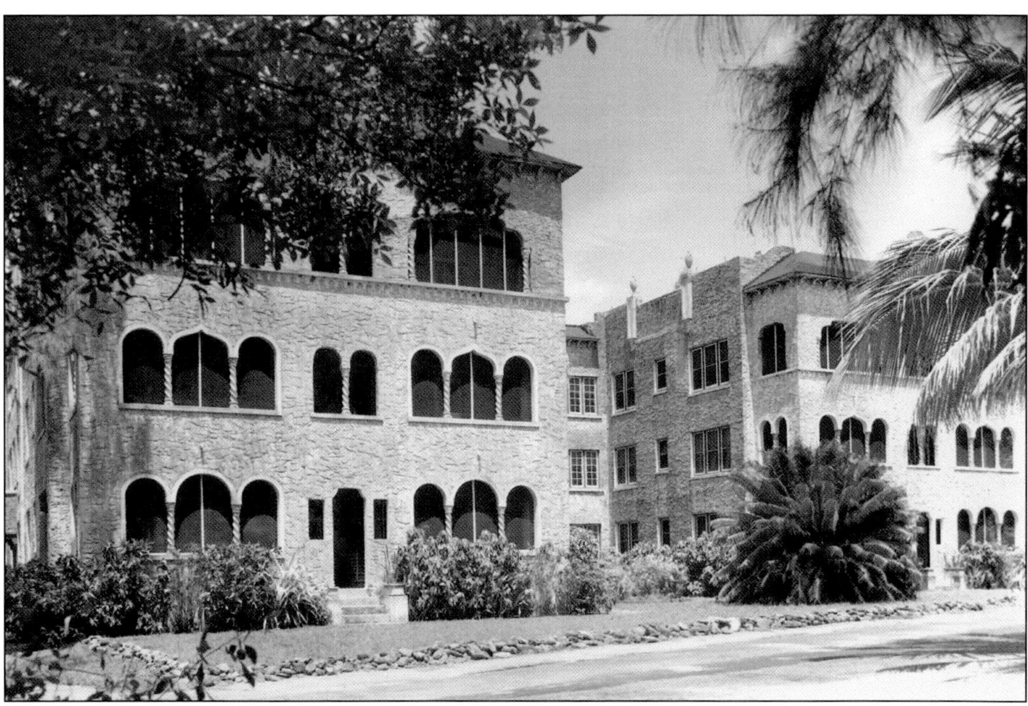

The France Apartments, built by Adam France in 1927 in the St. Lucie Crescent neighborhood, remained a popular apartment building. In 1932, it was sold to William Shepard, who continued the elegance of the France into the 1940s. After Shepard's death, the building was sold three times between 1946 and 1948. William Snow and family purchased it in 1948, did major renovations, and operated it for years. In 1949, a partially furnished apartment rented for about $62.50 a month. (Courtesy of Clyde Coutant, Thurlow Collection.)

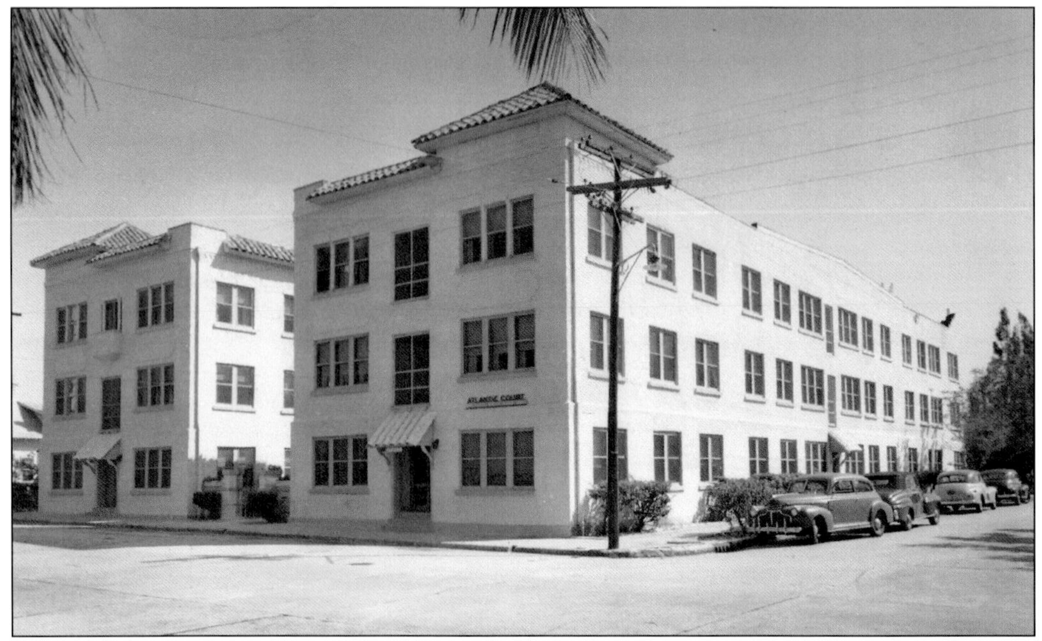

What had started as the El Bit-Lor Apartments in 1926 was purchased and renamed the Atlantic Court Apartments in 1936. Over the next 10 years, it would be sold and purchased by six different owners. In 1948, it had major renovations done, including the installation of air conditioning. Located on Fourth Street, next to the Stuart High School, it remained a favorite residence for teachers and staff at the school. (Courtesy of Clyde Coutant, Thurlow Collection.)

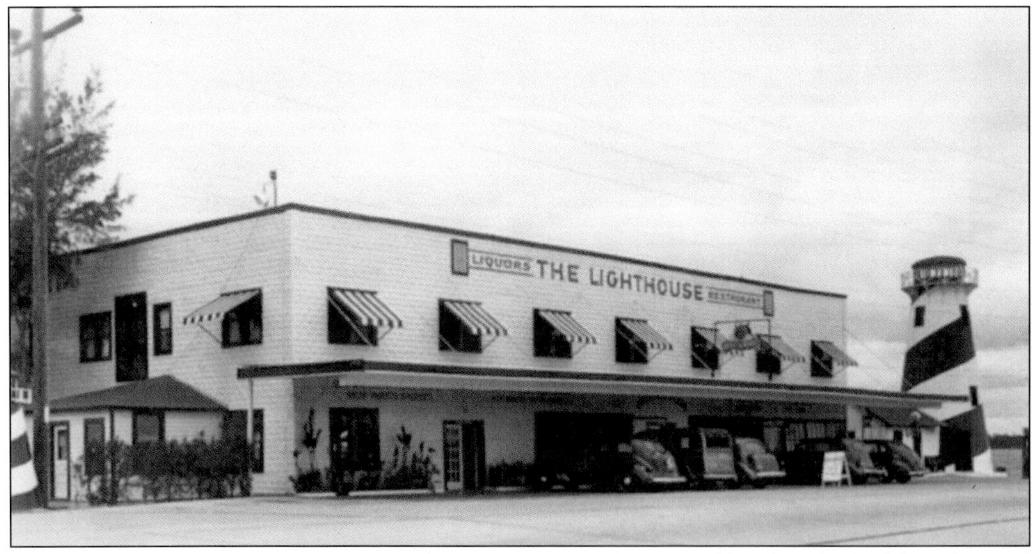

In 1923, Harry Speedy had a garage with apartments on the second level of the building, located near the shore of the St. Lucie River at the north end of the concrete bridge. Speedy's property also included a marina. A model of a lighthouse, with a beacon, was constructed to draw attention to the establishment. It was remodeled in 1934 as Speedy's Inn, and a restaurant, bar, and dance hall were added at that time. After two years and new owners, the popular establishment was renamed the Lighthouse Restaurant and served locals and tourists for years. This photograph was taken in 1948.

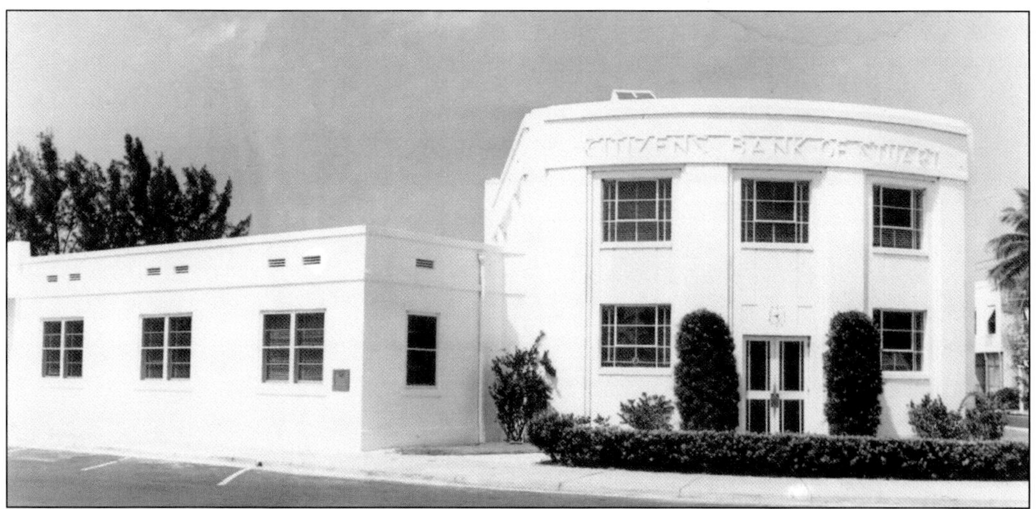

After World War II, many former soldiers returned to Stuart to settle down. With increased population, the late 1940s brought expansion of businesses such as the Citizens Bank of Stuart at the corner of Colorado and Osceola Avenues. In 1946, the hometown bank became a member of the Federal Reserve System. A wing to the left was added in 1949 after repairs were necessary following the 1949 hurricane. (Courtesy of Clyde Coutant, Thurlow Collection.)

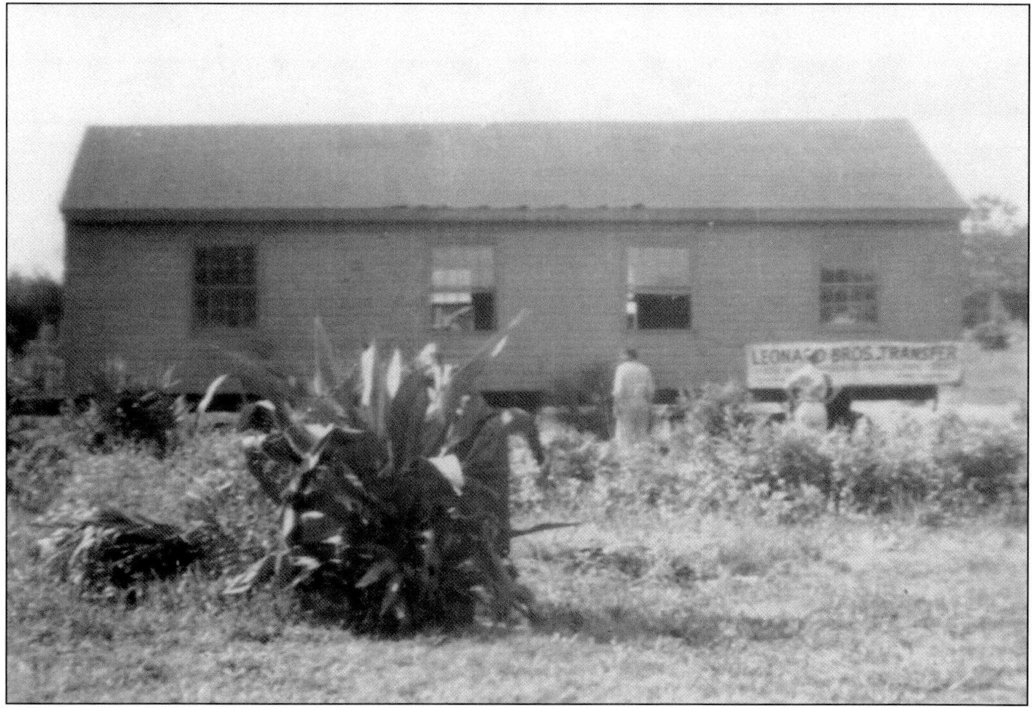

With the closing of Camp Murphy by the US War Department in November 1944, many of the former barracks and other military buildings were auctioned off in mid-1946, and others, in 1947, were transported to new locations and converted into homes, cottages, and new headquarters for the Red Cross and American Legion. The Luckhardt family purchased a large, sturdy, carpenters' workshop and had it transported by Leonard Brothers to Casa Terrace neighborhood in Stuart, where the building was remodeled and made into a family home. (Courtesy of Luckhardt family.)

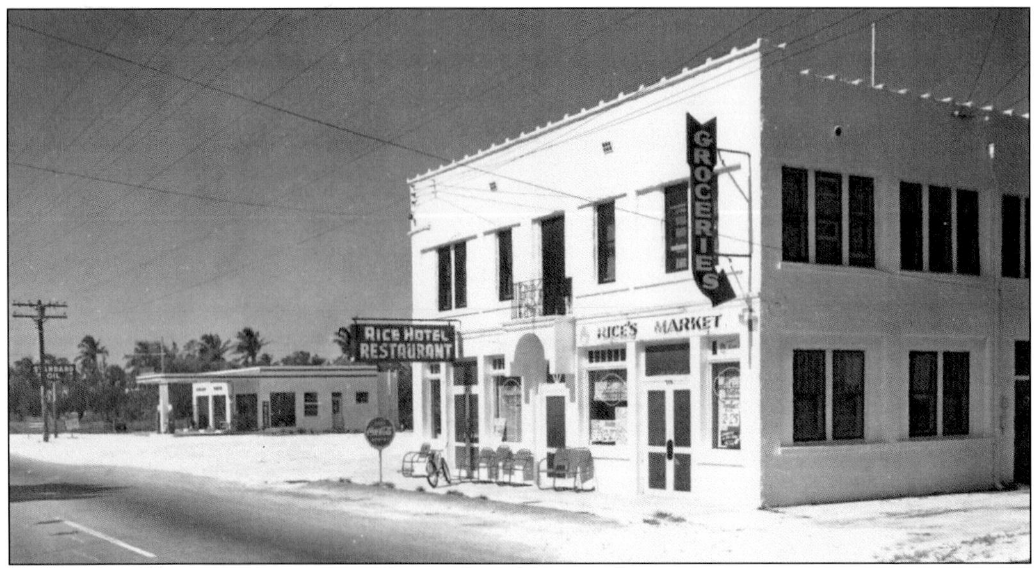

The Rob Roy Hotel, built by Robert Roebuck in 1927, was sold by the family in 1945. New owner William H. Rice immediately remodeled and renamed it Rice's Hotel-Restaurant, with the slogan "It's Never Too Late for Breakfast." At Rice's Restaurant, a cup of good coffee cost a nickel. A hotel was operated upstairs, and Rice added a grocery store named Rice's Market. In November 1949, he constructed a Standard service station nearby. (Courtesy of Sandra and Tom Thurlow.)

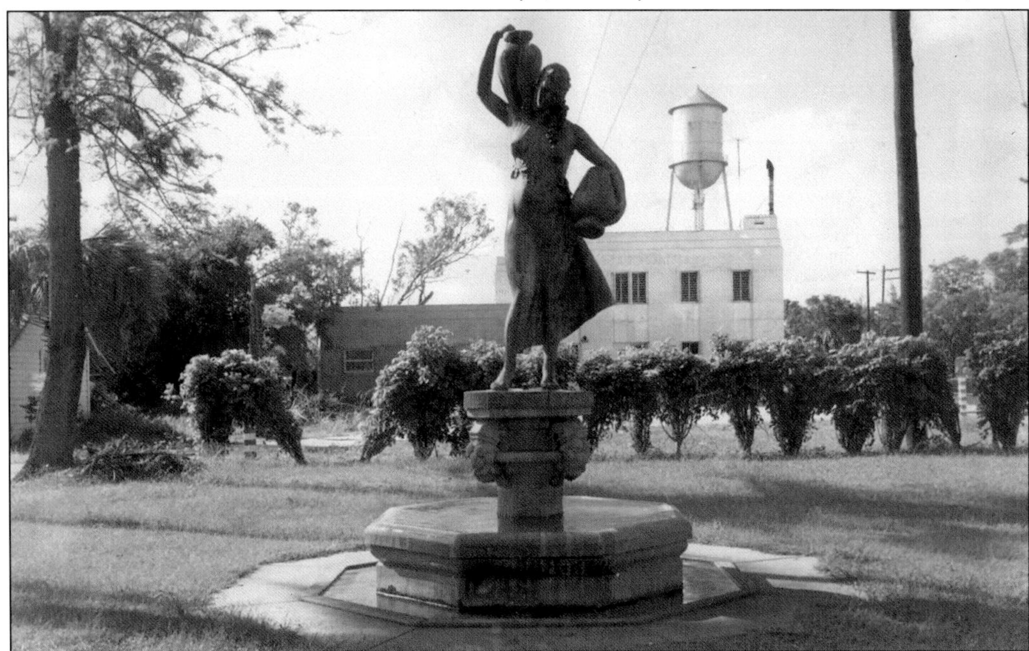

To honor Stuart pioneer Cynthia Haney, the Stuart Woman's Club decided to purchase a statue to be placed in the Haney Circle Park at Colorado and Osceola Avenues. The *Goddess of Abundance* by Manya Konolei was purchased sight unseen for $1,800 in 1949. Upon its arrival, the club felt its scanty attire combined with the grapes (associated with wine) was inappropriate to represent Haney, a longtime prohibitionist. So the 10-foot bronze statue, along with a fountain, was placed on the courthouse lawn. (Courtesy of the Stuart Woman's Club.)

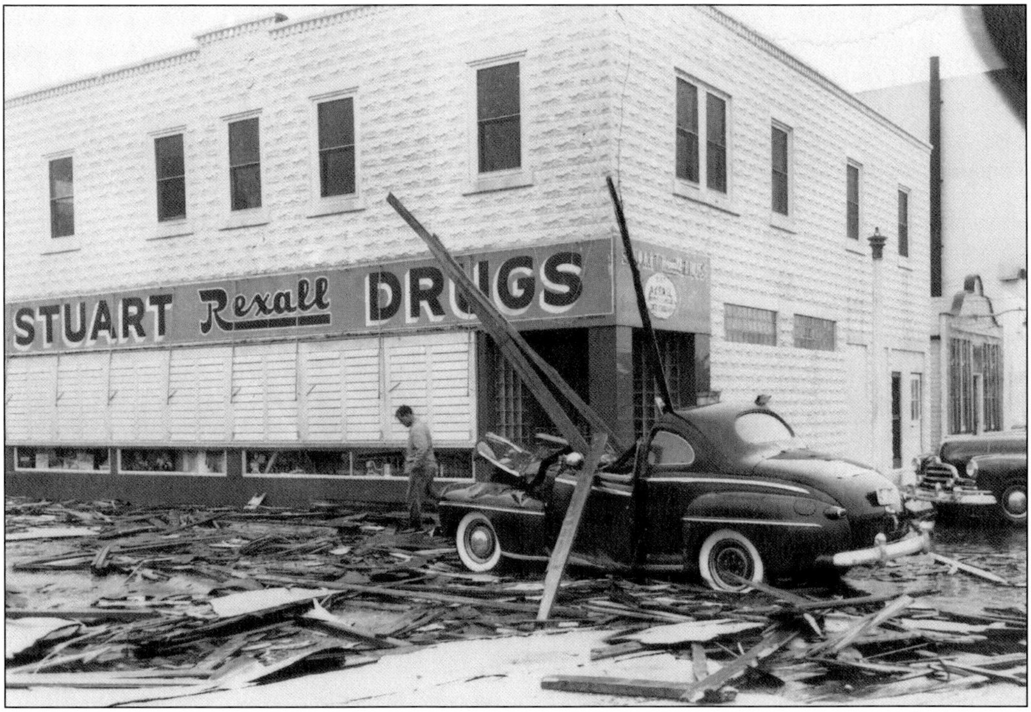

One of the major disasters for Stuart occurred in August 1949 when a hurricane struck the town with 160-mile-per-hour winds and torrential rain. Very few homes, shops, or buildings escaped major damage. Roofs were blown off, windows shattered, and many structures left in rubble. This was just after many new businesses had just opened and renovations to older buildings had been completed between 1948 and 1949. This photograph is of the 1913 concrete-block Feroe Building, which had housed the Stuart Rexall Drugstore for years. (Courtesy of the Lockwood Collection, SHM.)

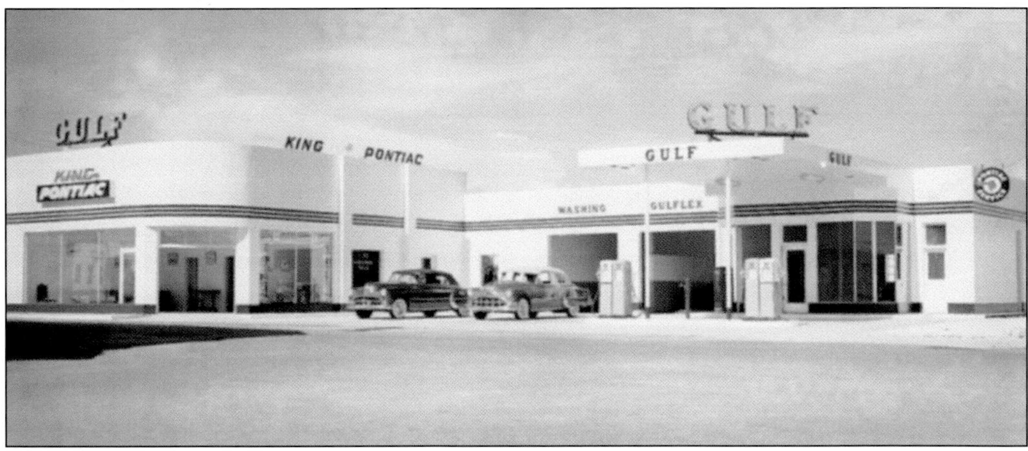

In 1950, Grover C. King and George W. Parks Jr. partnered to build a modern new Pontiac auto and GMC truck dealership, garage, and service station at the intersection of Colorado and Flagler Avenues. The white reinforced-concrete block structure was accented with blue trim and had all the newest auto equipment. The Gulf service station was operated by George Parks Jr. because he was Gulf Oil dealer for the county just like his father had been years prior. (Courtesy of E.D. Ricou, Thurlow Collection.)

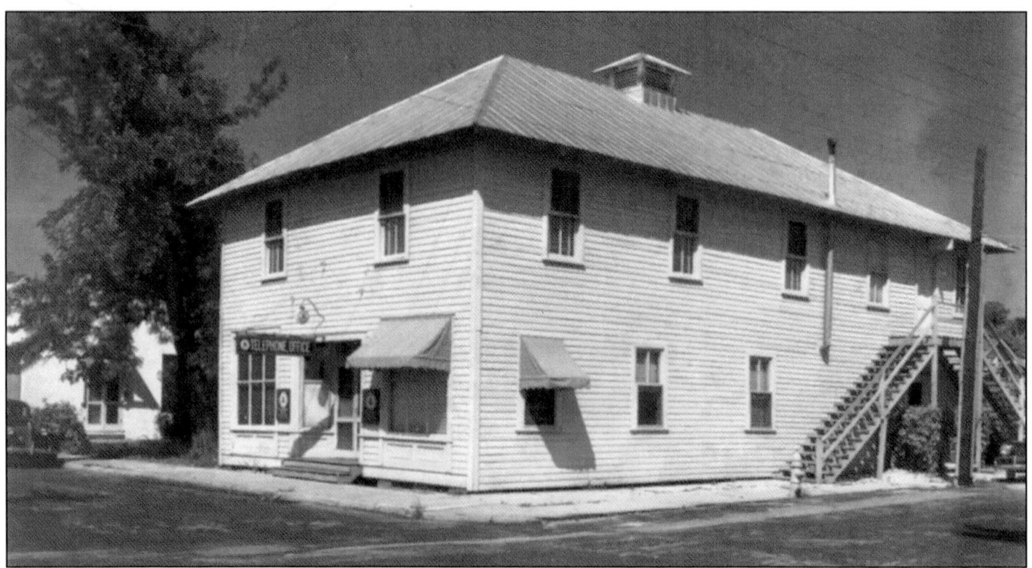

The 1914 Woodmen of the World hall on Third Street remained an important element of daily life in Stuart as it entered the 1950s. Beginning in 1924, Stuart's telephone company was located on the first floor of this structure. The switchboard operators had emergency batteries and switching mechanisms to always provide phone service. Individuals just picked up their phone receiver and were connected to the operators. The upper floor was used by civic groups, including numerous local, political, and fraternal organizations. (Courtesy Sandra and Tom Thurlow.)

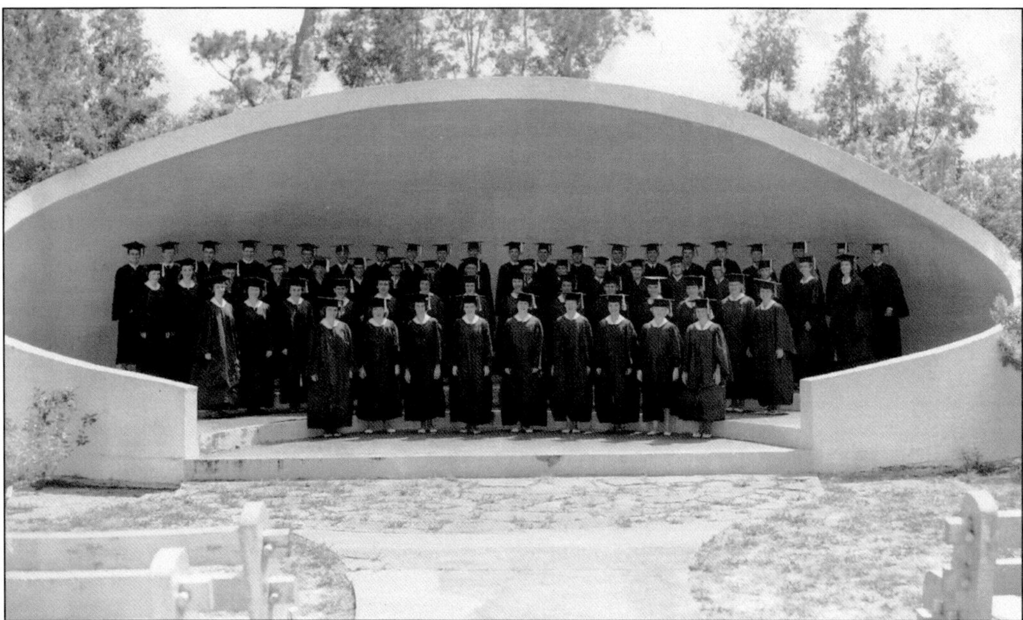

Stuart had bandstands for decades, but by 1939, a new one was necessary. The city financed the construction of a concrete band shell to be located in the City Park (Memorial Park). This unique concave, semi-dome, open-air structure was designed for good acoustics by James Crowley, director of the Stuart High School Band, at a cost of $600. The formal dedication was held April 2, 1940. It was used for speakers, concerts, military celebrations, and even high school graduations. Pictured here is the Stuart High School class of 1950.

There were no chain stores in Stuart, but rather family-owned-and-operated stores. An excellent example was Harry Dyer's Dry Goods store, which started in March 1913 at the corner of Dixie Highway and Gaines Avenue (Colorado Avenue). They stocked clothing and footwear for the family along with a variety of cloth and sewing notions. In 1937, the wood-framed building was modernized, with chromium-edged black Carrara marble and new display windows to highlight the building's facade. Their slogan was "as modern as tomorrow." (Courtesy of Sandra and Tom Thurlow.)

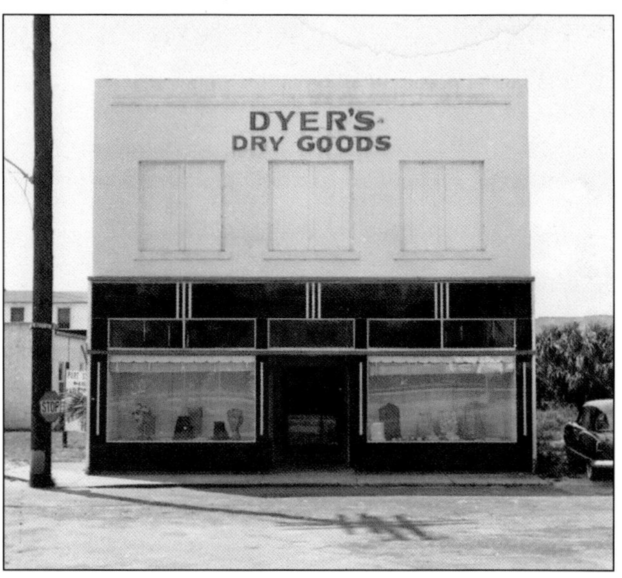

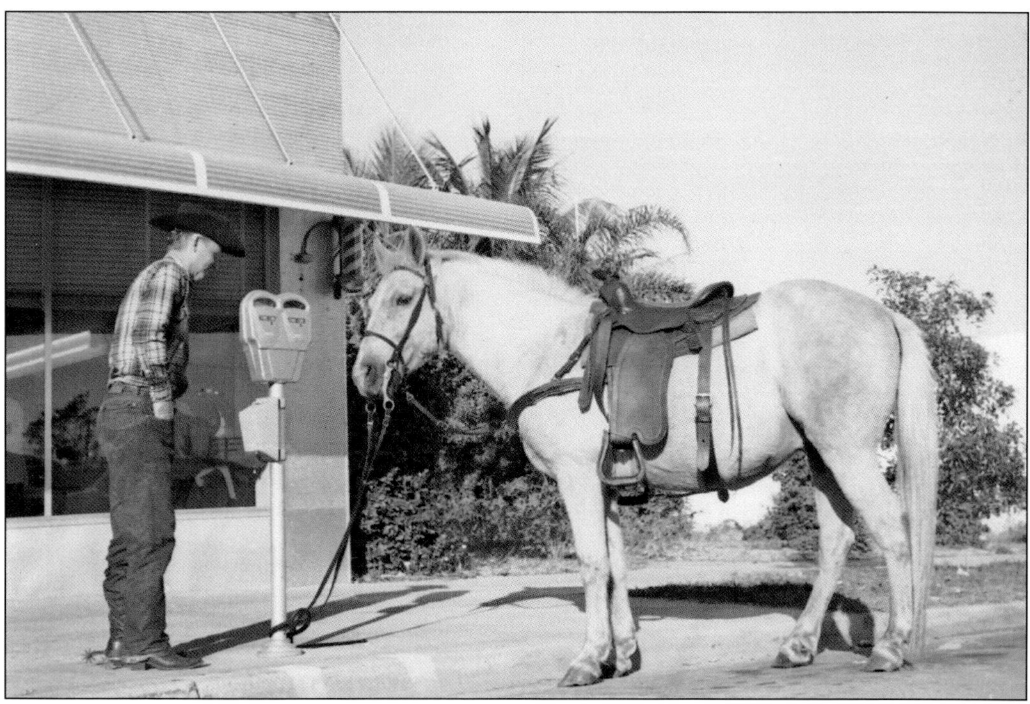

Life had changed in Stuart since the 1880s as it approached the 1950s. However, that hometown atmosphere and friendliness still existed. One of the area's newer, more colorful citizens was Jack James, a pilot, rancher, contractor, and journalist with the folksy humor column *Tail Twisting*. This photograph shows James and his Palomino in town—he was puzzled as to how much was charged to park a horse using the first parking meter in the 1950s near Longbottom's Barbershop. (Courtesy of Frank Clark.)

Consistent with our mission to preserve history on a local level, this book was printed in South Carolina on American-made paper and manufactured entirely in the United States. Products carrying the accredited Forest Stewardship Council (FSC) label are printed on 100 percent FSC-certified paper.

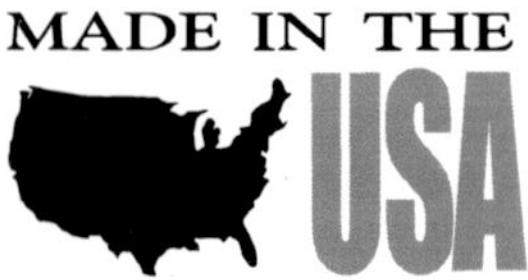